RURAL DEVELOPMENT
AND
RURAL WORKERS

RURAL DEVELOPMENT AND RURAL WORKERS

(A Study in Retrospect and Prospect)

M.M. Rehman

COMMONWEALTH

Rural Development and Rural Workers

First Published : 2006

ISBN 81-311-0105-3

Published by :

COMMONWEALTH PUBLISHERS
4831/24, Prahlad Street,
Ansari Road, Darya Ganj,
New Delhi - 110002
Ph. : 23272541, 23257835
Fax : 91- 011- 23257835
e-mail : campusbooks@hotmail.com

Typesetting by :

Arjun Computers
Delhi - 110051

Printed at :
Roshan Offset Printers
Delhi

Dedicated

to

Professor Moinuddin

Preface

The issue of rural development has been receiving attention of both administrators and academicians over several decades.

It has assumed importance because still an overwhelming number of population of the country reside in rural areas. The issue has also become important because the area identified as rural lacks development of infrastructural facilities, incidence of high level of unemployment, shrinking employment opportunities, increasing environmental problems, decline in investment in agriculture, etc. All these factors have contributed to the present crisis in rural economy and society and also have aggravated the present agrarian situation.

In order to address these issues and problems the Government has been, since independence, launching and implementing a plathora of development programmes and schemes. The main purpose has been to create infrastructural facilities and enhance capabilities of rural people, particularly the deprived sanctions. The main aim is to eradicate poverty by ameliorating their socio-economic conditions.

The present book is an attempt to highlight the perspectives and problems of rural development in India. The volume also discusses ways and means to accelerate rural development process thereby enhancing living standards of rural workers. The book consists of nine chapters.

Chapter one examines the setting against which rural development programmes and schemes have been initiated in the country.

Chapter two discusses the process of implementation of different programmes and schemes launched by the Government during the last five and half decades.

Chapter three briefly narrates the trend and pattern of performance of development programmes and schemes of rural development during the Ninth Five Year Plan period.

Chapter four focuses on the problems and issues with respect to land reforms in India. By analysing the performance of land reform measures, attempt is made to raise the gender question in land reform issues.

Chapter five deals with agriculture and rural development in India and looks into the situation existing today in the country.

Chapter six presents the profile and conditions of rural labourers including agricultural laboures in different states of the country.

Chapter seven suggests the areas in which employment potential for rural labour could be explored.

Chapter eight outlines a framework for micro level rural development strategy which can be used for eliciting participation of rural workers.

Chapter nine provides an example of creating awareness among rural labourers and also narrates the process of organising them for their development.

Lastly the volumes consists of several documents and policy statements on rural development. These have been presented several appendices.

It is hoped that the book will be useful to policy makers, administrators, academicians and students who are interested in rural development in general and development of rural workers in particular.

The author expresses his gratitude to Mr. Ajay Verma, Publisher, Commonwealth Publishers.

M.M. Rehman

Contents

1
The Setting

> *"It is the villages we have to turn to. We have to disabuse them of their prejudices, their superstitions, their narrow outlook and we can do so in no other manner than that of staying amongst them and sharing their joys and sorrows and spreading education and intelligent information among them".*
>
> *—Mahatma Gandhi*

From time immemorial poverty, unemployment and exploitation have been the three most dreaded scourges in rural India. Drought, disease, famines, pestilence, invasions, death and devastation were the tales of this part of the globe ever since the history began to be written. In many of the writings of the past we find the unbearable and poigment description of pitiable conditions of the socially and economically disadvantaged and displaced people. Slavery, the worst form of human exploitation and degradation, was widely prevalent in India as anywhere else in the world (Rehman, 2000). Parents stricken by hunger, selling their children to rich landlords and well-placed people of the then society was not an uncommon sight. The situation has not dramatically changed. In fact, it is existing in some forms or other despite many efforts. The hierarchical social structure, which was often brutal, has not changed much in nature and character. It still remains an overwhelming phenomenon. In the hierarchical social structure the downtrodden has been cleverly and systematically kept divided into various groups. As a result, there was hardly any struggle by the exploited against the exploiting classes in the past. The society was so construed that relations of submission and dependence pervaded the entire social system. Davy observes: "Within the village itself relations of dependence, mediated through the caste division of society, defined the relations between the cultivating peasant castes and the artisans and the those untouchables who performed menial and unclean tasks for the village as a whole (demiurgic system) or for certain leading families in the village community (jaajmani system). The untouchables were at the bottom of the ladder in a society in which successive rights and power were established by conquest and subordination over centuries.

While Hindu religions and ritual as well as social status served to confirm and ideologically justify these social and productive divisions the whole structure was, in the caste analysis, based on force and was always potentially subject to redefinition by the force of arms" (Davy, 1975:17).

The situation had been existing for several millennia i.e. from ancient period to the medieval period; and has been handed down by the history to the present. During the medieval period, under the Mughal especially, the socio-economic system was equally exploitative (Habib, 19).

The so-called self-sufficient villages, the bedrock of economic system was an unit in which unequal system was perpetuated for centuries. Sarup and Brahme observe: "The rural areas consisted largely of self-sufficient] villages. Everything needed for consumption and production was, as far as possible, produced locally. Rural artisans were enmeshed in an inflexible 'Jajmani System' under which they had to provide goods and services to farmers against the receipt of fixed share of agricultural produce. They functioned in a stagnant environment without any opportunity for interaction with outside world. They neither own any capital nor any inputs for innovation or improvement of techniques. In addition to the customary payments to artisans, the farmers had to pay one third or more of their produce to the State by way of land revenue and other charges. This resulted in their living at the subsistence level: they too were left with hardly any means to improve the techniques of production" (Sarup and Brahme, 1990:25).

Under the colonial regime the socio-economic system remained almost the same. Means of production was in the hands of the socially and economically powerful sections of the society. The vast masses of working people who were living in rural areas and were producing surplus for the landed aristocracy had remained perpetually exploited and oppressed. Apart from these, the society was also divided into various communal categories based on different religions. In sum, the socio-economic structure was highly inequitable and pock-marked by antagonism and innumerable differentials. Against this backdrop the country won political independence; and replaced the British rule by the indigenous rulers. Under the new rulers of the independent India the state of the governed did not achieve any dramatic change. Instead of kingship, a democratically elected government came to occupy power who again kept private ownership of property constitutionally safe and existing socio-economic structure mostly the same as it was before the pre-independence period. In addition, India also faced several new problems which exerted a number of disastrous impacts on the country's society, economy and polity. The problems were the partition of the country, the accompanied communal holocaust and dislocation of the economy. On this disturbing backdrop India began to made efforts to transform its economy, society and its people. Writing in the '80s, Desai notes:

"During the last three decades, India has experienced crucial transformations in various domains of its social existence. The post-war partition, the communal holocaust, the unparalleled migrations of Hindus and Muslims, the elimination of princely states, the formation of the Indian Union, the framing of the Constitution of India, and the active participation of the State in the task of overcoming backwardness through the implementation of Industrial Policy Resolutions and series of Five year Plan based on the postulates of mixed-economy indicative capitalist planning, have brought about significant changes in Indian society, economy, polity, education, culture and class and caste configurations" (Desai, 1984:1).

In fact the task that India envisaged was symbolished in ending of poverty and ignorance and disease and inequality of opportunity' (Nehru, 1947). The effort to accomplish this task was made in a scenario where mode of production was semi-feudal and distribution of land was highly skewed. Caste and communal conflicts were at its heights. Independent India even could not get rid of the obnoxious caste ridden system. It, on the other hand, perpetuates the caste system in a more sophisticated form. The new government, perhaps as a political expediency, kept the caste system thriving by making discriminatory protective policy for the alleviation of the poverty of the under-classes instead accepting class identity as a criterion for ending poverty, ignorance and disease and inequality of opportunity. This has helped eventually contain the conflicts which other-wise would have changed the political scenario, though for a shortwhile. In fact, it was concessional measures to contain vocal groups who have been articulate enough to air their grievances. The labourers have been sliding regularly into the dispossessed group and while on the one side the rulers accumulated everything and on the other side the rest have been deprived even their basic necessities. The main effort of the ruling elite was, and remains so today, to 'help the poor' to help themselves the rulers. The process of accumulation or exploitation has been illustrated by Haq in the following paragraph:

> It is well to recognize that economic growth is a brutal, sordid process. There are no short cuts to it. The essence of it lies in making the labourers produce more than he is allowed to consume for his immediate needs, and to invest and to reinvest the surplus thus obtained. It is immaterial what one chooses to call this surplus - whether "surplus value," as Marx usually did; or' "savings" or capital formation," in the terminology of modern economic analysis; or "comrades' voluntary contribution to national growth", as it may perhaps be described by some apologists for the communist technique of exacting this surplus. It is equally immaterial who owns this surplus whether "the capitalists" as in free enterprise economy, or "the State", as in the communist economy. What is important and intellectually honest is to admit frankly that the heart of the growth problem lies in maximising the creation of this surplus (Haq, 1976:3).

The above myopic perspective of the government of any denomination has put untold pressure on the working people of, particularly in the newly independent countries of the third world. As a consequence, human beings have been relegated to the background. They, instead becoming the centre-stage, remained in the periphery and went on and go on now, suffering in the name of growth and development. Haq notes again: "One particular sin of development planning which has persisted, despite some efforts in a few development plans to attend to it, is the general neglect of human resources. Notwithstanding any protest to the contrary, very little investment seems to have gone into the development of human resources in most developing countries, particularly in South Asia" (Haq, 1972: 22).

The whole development process of all the developing countries maintained for a long period that if a bucket of a filled than something will percolate down or trickle down from A's bountiful bucket to B's empty bucket (with a hole below). The staggering level of poverty in India, on one side, and the growing affluence of the rich and richer sections of the society on another side, clearly demonstrates this fact that someone down the line has been brutalised for someone else's benefit. The result, the inexcusably skewed distribution of land, property and other forms of wealth. Raising the implications of these issues and the rule of the Indian Constitution Desai observes:

> To appreciate the significance of the measures adopted by the Government of the Indian Union, it is necessary to grasp the nature of the major aspects of the normative-legal framework provided by the Constitution of the Indian Union which became the matrix within which the measures adopted to reshape rural society were conceived and implemented and the spirit in which they were articulated.
>
> Shorn of its massive verbiage, the central normative-core of the Constitution can be summed up in five major points:
>
> (1) The constitution in spite of all amendments and verbal nuances, accepts the norms of bourgeois society as the permeating principle underlying all its measures. It treats the right to property as fundamental - head core right - (emphasis added) as the bedstrock of the entire endeavor to reconstruct Indian economy:
>
> (2) It recognises and validates legal norms and legislation based on the right to income through ownership, viz., profit, rent and interest. This has been accepted not merely as proper and just, but as a guiding principle to induce economic development.

(3) It does not accept the right to work as fundamental. It has, in fact, accepted the view that labour-power is a commodity, to be used and paid for at rates determined basically by market forces and considerations of profit for employers who produce for market ('supply and demand', ability to pay').

(4) Compensation to the proprietor for acquisition of his property for public purposes, however qualified, is laid down as a basic norm, but not the principle of compensating those whose labour power is not utilised, and not permitted to be utilised, even if the seller of the labour power wants to place it at the disposal of society for augmenting production. There is no assurance of work, minimum wages for work, continuity of work, or compensation for loss of source of livelihood even when society can supply no alternative source. In short, profit, production for the market, and the treatment of labour power as a commodity permeates the normative value system of the Indian Constitution.

(5) By accepting the major economic, social and legal codes (civil, criminal and other) and by accepting the basic bureaucratic administrative structure and principles of the bourgeois British administration as the corner-stone of its socio-economic, politico administrative and legal norms, the Indian Constitution has clearly accepted the norm and legal premises of capitalist society as the underlying guiding objective of reconstruction and development of Indian Society (Desai, 1984: 177-78).

India attained independence in 1947. As we have noted earlier, the country inherited a turbulent social, political and economic scenario characterised by inequality of highest order, skewed pattern of land-ownership, and a population, by and large, dependent on agriculture. Moreover, majority of its population lived in its villages, where illiteracy was very high, and socio-economic exploitation of half of the population was at its height.

The extent of inequalities in rural areas would be clear from the information about the distribution of rural assets. The Reserve Bank of India reported that in 1971 all the assets, including land, houses and moveable property of 10 per cent of the poorest households accounted for 0.10 per cent or one tenth of one per cent of the total assets in the rural areas. The total assets of 30 per cent of all households from the bottom represented only 2.1 per cent or one fifth of rural assets. On the other hand, the top ten per cent owned more than half or 25 times the assets owned by the 30 per cent of the population (Sarup and Brahme, 1990: 103).

What these figures indicate is the most disturbing fact that more than half of the population of the country was grovelling in the darkness of poverty and was in the octopus grip of exploitation by the vested interest whose interests were safeguarded somehow or other, as noted earlier, by the Constitution of Indian Union.

The figures in Table 1.1 show how the poverty level and the number of people in the grip of poverty has remained same or stagnant almost over the last 20 years. It could be seen that in 1973-74 the total number of people below the poverty in rural and urban areas was 2612.90 and 600.47 lakhs respectively. The figures for rural and urban areas were 2642.47 and 646.48 lakhs respectively in 1977-78. The combined figure was 3288.95 lakh and accounted for an increase of 2.30 per cent in 1977-78 over 1973-74.

In 1983 the total number of person in poverty in rural and urban areas were 26519.56 and 109.39 lakhs respectively. The combined figure was 3228.95 lakh. In 1987-99 again the total number of persons in poverty was 3070.5 lakhs out of which 2318.84 and 751.67 lakhs were in rural and urban areas of the country respectively.

In 1993-94 poverty estimate, it may be noted in the table that the number of persons in poverty was 3203.64 lakhs out of which 2440.28 and 763.36 lakh were in rural and urban areas (for state-wise details see Appendix I).

The figures clearly indicate the fact that poverty has remained a chronic problem and so has illiteracy problem. Both have travelled the same path i.e., the pattern of growth remaining stagnant over the years. This phenomenon further demonstrates that the volume of investment was not made according to the need of the people i.e., to satisfy the basic necessitites of the people thereby helping them tide over poverty and attain a basic minimum standard of life.

Table 1.1 : Number and Percentage of Population Below Poverty Line in India

Year	Rural		Urban		Combined	
	No. of Persons (lakhs)	*% of Persons*	*No. of Persons*	*% of Persons*	*No. of Persons*	*% of Persons*
1973-74	2612.90	56.44	600.47	49.01	3213.37	54.88
1977-78	2642.47	53.07	646.48	42.24	3288.95	51.32
1983	2519.56	45.65	709.39	40.79	3228.95	44.48
1987-88	2318	39.09	751.65	38.20	3070.51	38.86
1993-94	2440.28	37.27	763.36	32.36	3203.64	36.97

Source : Planning Commission, Government of India.

It is obvious from the table that the planned attempt by the government to eradicate such a massive poverty was absolutely inadequate. Hasim, writing about the poverty alleviation programmes, notes:

> Over the 20 year period 1973-74, it can be seen that the poverty ratios (i.e., percentage of poor in the total population) has declined from 55 to 36 per cent. However, due to increase in population, number of poor in the country remain more or less the same. There were 321 million poor persons in 1973-74 and a million less even two decades later. One test of adequacy in the rate of decline of the percentage of the poor should be that it should result in a decline in the absolute number of poor persistently. In this regard the effectiveness of our efforts appears to be not adequate, even though poverty alleviation programmes have been strengthened and expanded one plan after the other (Hasim, 1998: xxvi). "The main objective and aim of the five-years plans was to build a socialistic pattern of society". Through gradual growth of productive infrastructure of the nation and distribution of national wealth in the 'most' equitable manner. It was thought that increasing wealth generation would percolate and trickle down to the masses who were the real creators of the wealth. The irony is that, in spite of exhortations and speculation the gain has not been achieved to desired extent and a sizeable proportion of the working masses of the rural are have been continuously sliding into the bottomless pit of poverty.

The Ministry of Rural Development notes this in the year 2001-02 as well :

> India has travelled a long distance on the road to development since Independence and has made significant progress in various sectors. However, the development in rural areas has not kept pace with the overall progress in other facets of national life. Even today, nearly 27 percent of the rural poor subsist in poverty and there remains an acute shortage of basic facilities such as housing, drinking water and roads in rural areas.
>
> The sustainable development of Rural Bharat is essential for the country to realize its potential and unleash the processes of all round growth, based on the latent genius of rural masses (MRD, 2002 : 1).

This clearly shows that despite efforts, sometimes massive efforts, the benefits of growth and development have not reached a significantly large section of the country's population. In Chapter Two an attempt will be made to examine various rural development programmes from the pre-independence period and after post-independence period, emphasising particularly on the programmes launched after the later period.

2

The Process

> *"Our aim must be to restore to the villages the power to meet their own requirement."*
>
> *Rabindra Nath Tagore*

Rural Development Before Independence

The attempt at rural development in India goes back to pre-independence period. The colonial regime, after following a number of disastrous policies that virtually destroyed India's village economy, made certain location specific experiments with rural development. The experiment did not somehow percolate down to the people as they were perceived. In most of the programme design and implementation process the participation of people was virtually conspicuous by its absence. In fact, rural development was not an agenda of the British administration. Maheswari (1994) observes:

> It was famine in India which forced the British Indian Government's involvement in a sphere which, even in great Britain, was thought to lie outside the rightful jurisdiction of the State at that time. The dominant philosophy of the State was Lassez-faire, and the best government was described as one which ruled the least.
>
> The rural development functions in India were assumed by the Government in the context of recurrent famines, but in the beginning, they did not have any legal sanctions behind them. In the first few decades after 1858, some district officers seized (in the midst of famine) the foodgrain stocks and controlled the market to ensure their distribution among the needy. All

this was done without any apparent legal sanction, motivated, as the action purely was, by a determination to control profiteering and alleviate rural suffering. Rural development, thus, began as a humanitarian act, and the practice was not backed by any executive or legal sanction in the beginning. Legality and legitimacy were provided later. Rural development as a function of government initially began as 'search for an alternative to Laissez-faire' (25-26) (see also Misra, 1983).

The following programmes for rural development in post independent period are most important :

- Martandam Rural Reconstruction Experiment (1921): The main objective of the experiment, located in Kerala, was to implement people's own programme. Spirituality and cooperation philosophical perspective.
- The Gurgaon Experiment on self-help, self-respect and Mutual help (1921): In 1920 F.L. Brayne, Deputy Commissioner of Gurgaon, Haryana, moved by the poverty of the people, launched a programme for setting up institutions and made effort to develop agriculture for the improvement of the people's lives of the district.
- Constructive programmes of Mahatma Gandhiji-Antyodya (1925).
- The Baroda Rural Reconstruction Movement (1932).
- The Firka Development Scheme, Madras (1946).
- The Mazdoor Manzil-Nilokheri Attempt (1947).
- The Etawah Pilot Project (1948).
- The Sriniketan Experiment, etc.

The main aim of the experiments was to alleviate the conditions of the poor by improving the village economy. Because the two hundred years spell of British administration virtually destroyed the village economy. The Zamindari and jagirdari system fleeced the peasantry by rack-renting. Moved by their plight, many enlightened individuals made the above localised effort to alleviate the massive poverty of the people. In fact, a close examination of these efforts show that they were philanthropic in nature and more often was patronising in character. For none of the experiment did ever try to change the existing pattern of land-ownership, distribution of wealth and affluence among the working people by structural change.

As we have noted earlier, it was the ever increasing poverty among rural people that attracted the attention of the newly independent government. Because, after the independence, the government embarked upon rural reconstruction activities quite on a kind of war footing so as to thwart the ingress of 'communism'. Because in the fifties alone the total number of poor people in the country were around 200 million and they constituted 47 percent of the total rural population in 1951-52. Since then the situation did not improve till 1993-94 as 37 percent of the total rural population were poor. The fear of discontent was indeed frightening for the ruling apparatus of the country manned by the rising bourgeoisie, who, after the Britishers left, occupied all important rungs of the state machinery by manipulating electoral politics and keeping the old power structure alive in the rural areas. The institutions and ideology were also decadent and privileged-class biased.

The figures in Table 2.1 shows clearly that poverty has remained almost same during last 37 years and the absolute number of people in poverty has increased from 200 million to 300 million in the country. The figures in the table show that poverty ratio was 47.4 per cent in 1951-52 which declined to 37-0 per cent in 1993-94. The ratios do not, however, tell the truth, The absolute number of people living in poverty has increased several times as above i.e. from 200 mls in 1951-52 to 300 mls. in 1993-94.

Table 2.1 : Proportion of the Rural Below the Poverty-Line:

Year	*Poverty Ratio*
1951-52	47.4
1952-53	48.2
1953-54	61.3
1954-55	64.2
1955-56	40.3
1956-57	58.9
1957-58	55.2
1958-59	53.3
1959-60	50.9

Contd....

1960-61	45.4
1961-62	47.2
1963-64	48.5
1964-65	53.7
1965-66	57.6
1966-67	64.3
1967-68	63.7
1968-69	59.0
1969-70	57.6
1970-71	54.8
1972-73	59.4
1973-74	55.7
1977-78	50.6
1983	45.3
1986-87	38.8
1988-89	39.1
1989-90	34.3
1990-91	36.4
1992	43.5
1993-94	37.0

Source : Based on rounds of NSS. Govt. of India.

Rural Development Programmes after 1947

Against this backdrop the government, after Independence, launched the Community Development Programme, under the guidance of Albert Myer, in Etawh, Uttar Pradesh as a pilot project, in 1952. Some details have been provided here on the project.

Community Development Programme (CDP)

It was a multi-programme implemented first in some selected areas of the country, known as Community Development Block (CDOs). Then subsequently, the programme was extended to the entire country by 1963. The main objectives of the programme were:

- To increase agricultural production.
- To increase employment opportunities in rural areas.
- To improve village communication.

- To provide facilities for primary education, public health and recreation in villages.
- To improve housing facilities; and
- To promote indigenous handicrafts and small scale industries.

It was the first experiment in rural upliftment in India after the Independence. And was considered a strategic breakthrough in the development effort for the country. Pandit Jawaharlal Nehru was euphoric on the occasion of the fourth anniversary of the project. He observed:

> A new chapter has begun in this fascinating story of rural India, a new drama is being played in our broad fields and innumerable villages. The actors in this drama are the tens of thousands of our village workers, organisers, etc. Indeed, the actors should include every man and woman and even child. May all of them have this sensation of playing in this great game of building up India, this great adventure that ennoble their lives. It is through great effort that we grow, it is by allying ourselves to great causes that we also develop some touch of that greatness (quoted in Battcharya, 1982: 253:54)

The new programme was viewed as a great break-through. It was thought that the march of India towards a modern state would come forth and its brutal power structure would automatically give way to a new framework for a development paradigm.

The Community Development Programme was considered a landmark effort by the government. In fact, while inaugurating the launch of the programme on 2 October, 1952, India's first President, Rajendra Prasad hailed it as the small seed which will grow into a huge and mighty tree' (HT, 1952). He further observed:

> India lives in villages. Anything done to bring about an all-round improvement of the villages and those inhabit them should not only be welcome but given all encouragement by the State and by the people at large. Mahatma Gandhi used to look upon all work for the common benefit as Yajna and it is in this spirit of Yajna that the work has to be undertaken and accomplished. I can only hope and pray that the government and the people will travel together hand in hand in this mighty effort (*Ibid*)

The Community Development Programme (CDP) was started in 55 Blocks and in the sixties, the programme covered the entire country. The progress of CDP made Pt. Nehru more optimistic and perhaps he saw a kind of hope for India's rural areas liberation from poverty. He exhorted:

> I think nothing has happened in any country in the world during the last few years so big in content and so revolutionary in design as the Community Projects in India. They are changing the face of rural India (quoted in Bhattacharya, 1982: 252).

It may also be noted here that along with CDP another programme was launched in 1953, known as National Extension Service Programme. "The original view underlying these two schemes was that Community Development would mark an intensive phase of rural development lasting for three years, and was thus not permanent whereas the National Extension Service was to be a permanent multifunction extension agency in the block" (Maheshwari, 1955:41).

There is, however, no denying of the fact that CDP was an important watershed in India's effort to develop its rural areas. The programme was launched during the period when *zamindari* and *jagirdari* system were being abolished. Hence it was born during a period when a lot of radical changes were expected and peoples expectation level was very high.

Moreover, the programme also gave the nation an idea about how complex was country's developmental task ahead. Apart from this, it was also first time when administration began to be service oriented - earlier maintenance of law and order was the priority of the administration. While evaluating the CDP, Sharma Observes:

> The biggest achievement of the community development programme was the enthusiasm for development engendered throughout the country. People, for the first time, had the feel of an administration which was committed to serve them through its extension agency and a network of economic institutions, which was in striking contrast to the tradition of the administration established to rule them. There was high expectancy all around. The community development programme itself shared this ethos. It accepted a small frame work of 6 years only for the entire scheme, right from initiating

> the process of development to reaching a stage where the village community could be expected to become self-reliant for development. The first three years were devoted to the establishment of the National Extension Service and the creation of institutional infrastructure, besides making modest beginnings, wherever possible, in the various fields. The following three years comprised a period of intensive development in the area with the participation of people and matching support of the State. This support was to be gradually withdrawn and phased out during the third state of community development by which time the people's initiative would have gathered momentum and become-self-sustaining (Sharma 1989:250-51).

Despite high expectation the CDP could not deliver the goods as it envisaged. The continued food shortage in the country and slowly deadening enthusiasm of the people finally made it to be abandoned. There are several reasons for its unsuccessful demise. First, its administration was rigid. Second, people's participation was marginal. Third, given the skewed ownership pattern of landholding in the rural areas and dominance of the landed classes, the gain of the programme was mostly cornered by rich and powerful (see Maheswari, 1995:50-55). The evaluation of Community Development Programme and National Extension Service by the Planning Commission finally put the death nail on the coffins of both these projects. Maheswari observes: "The single greatest weakness discovered in the programme was its failure to arouse and sustain the people's passionate interest in it" (Maheswari, 1995:53). Similar observations have been made by the Programme Evaluation Organisation of the Planning Commission in 1954 about the indifference of the Committees which were supposed look after the implementation of the CDP :

> There are very few instances indeed in which these committees have worked as they were intended to work. Members of the Committees were expected to be active participants in development work at all stages, from planning to execution. The expectation was that these committees, consisting of district heads of departments and of prominent non-officials including local members of legislatures and representatives of local bodies, would meet regularly, and that they would function in the same corporate manner in which all community

development bodies are expected to function. But unfortunately, several circumstances combined to thwart these expectations. Many of the departmental officers and non-official members tended to avoid them. Some among the latter utilised the occasion to assert their particular points of view. In quite a few cases the first meeting was only one held in the year (Planning Commission, 1956: 26-27).

Apart from such problem the CDP also suffered from other setbacks. For example, it did not provide an integrated approach to development perspective. There was hardly any exercise to understand the problems of the area where the programme was implemented. For example, as Sen observes :

> The C.D. Programme stopped after bringing experts from various fields together. There was no guideline for integrating actual development process in an area. No systematic attempt was made to find out the locational relationships which contribute towards an integration of the entire process of development. Because of the ad hoc location of various economic activities, the expected economic development never materialized (Sen, 1972:10).

The programme implicitly accepted the assumptions that individuals, groups and classes in a village community had common interests, which were sufficiently strong to bind them together. It also assumed that interests were sufficiently common to create general enthusiasm, and that conflicts of interests were sufficiently reconcilable. The assumptions proved to be unrealistic. In fact, the better-off benefited most from the programmes and a growing disparity and inequality became visible in the rural areas.

Similar observations have been made by Berkey:

> It was generally accepted in community development circles that working through the established traditional leaders in the villages, generally the better-off, would automatically benefit the whole community. This did not prove to be the case, and the approach was, therefor, called betting on the strong'. After several consecutive evaluations it became obvious that the better-off, mainly the dominant landowning groups, benefited from the extension work and other projects, rather than the majority of the poor peasants in the community. Huizer concluded that the 'harmony model' of community

development ironically enhanced and sharpened the potential for conflict at the village level (Berkley, 1993:43).

When evaluations of CDP and NESP showed up the seamier sides of the rural development programmes, the authority tried to find the 'sings in implementation' (Maheswari, 1995:57) and it was done by a team headed by Balvantray G. Mehta. The report submitted by the team, subsequently came to be well known as the Balvantray Committee Report. The report suggested that tardy implementation of both projects lied in the fact that grassroots level participation of people was lacking. Hence, the Committee suggested decentralization of democratic institutions and formation of three-tier system of rural local government which would be called Panchayati Raj System. It was thought that revival of Panchayati Raj System would help in the devolution of power to the village level.

This, however, did not take place. On the contrary, in course of time, it was almost non-functional in most of the states, till it was revived again in December 1977. In this year the Government appointed yet another Committee on Panchayati Raj Institutions, under the chairmanship of Ashok Mehta. The main purpose was to create an institutional structure to implement rural/agricultural development project in the rural areas.

The Intensive Agricultural District Programme

The CDP despite its apparent intention could not meet the growing demand for food in the country, and the food scenario was becoming slowly disturbing. In order to save the country from impending food crisis the Intensive Agricultural District, District Development Programme, conceived again by the USA, was launched in 1960. It was, in fact, a comprehensive agricultural development programme covering, use of improved technology, price incentive, soil conservation, etc. in the selected districts.

Despite this programme, the food situation did not improve. Moreover, huge amount was spent in the project area which really did not make much dent in the growing demand for food in the country.

To improve the downslide of the situation the New Agricultural Strategy was lunched in 1966. "This was well synchronized package programme involving action at many levels and sectors of activities" (Maheshwari, 1995:90). In fact, "The essence of the

New Strategy lay in effectively harnessing science and technology to raise farm productivity (Ibid: 91).

The Intensive Agricultural District Programme, however, did not reach benefit to the rural poor. In fact, once again the gain was corned by the rural rich and they not only gained in rich harvest but garnered the rural power as well. As a result, the situation, instead of improving, worsened in many places. Maheswari observes:

> The Intensive Agricultural District Programme accompanied by the introduction of technology in agriculture had the effect... of disrupting the traditional rural socio-economic structure, however unjust it may be, to the obvious disadvantage of the poor. This aroused a concern for the marginal man and, in the process, the Small Farmer's Development Agency was born. Also, land reform acquired an urgency, and measures were initiated to reform the relationship between land and men. No less alarming was a spurt in violence in rural areas as a direct result of the growing discontent among the poor (Ibid: 100).

The IADP created serious regional imbalances and to correct these imbalance the Government created two agencies which were supposed to act as catalyst for the development of small and marginal farmers and agricultural labourers. The two agencies were, namely :

(1) Small Farmers' Development Agency (SFDA).

(2) Marginal Farmers and Agricultural Labourers Agency (MFAL)

The Functions of the SFDA were to:

(a) to identify the eligible small farmers in its area.

(b) to investigate and identify their problems.

(c) to formulate programme incorporating suitable measures to deal with the problems; and

(d) to devise ways and means for implementing the programmes.

To make the small farmers surplus producers was the main purpose of the agency by arranging machines, implements, improved seeds, fertilizers, pesticides, irrigation facilities, credit, marketing facilities, etc. Similarly the important objectives of the MFAL were to:

(*a*) identify eligible marginal farmers and agricultural labourers;

(*b*) investigate their problems;

(*c*) formulate economic programmes for providing gainful employment to them;

(*d*) promote rural industries;

(*e*) evolve adequate institutional, financial and administrative arrangements for implementing various programmes;

(*f*) promote the creation of common facilities for the production, processing, storage and marketing of products; and

(*g*) evaluate the programme from time to time.

Both the agencies were entrusted with the responsibilities of implementing various schemes meant for the small, and marginal farmers and agricultural labourers. Both agencies were registered under Societies Registration Act, 1860 and came into being only in 1972. Though initially the agencies were created independently but in June 1974 they were merged.

Once again the schemes under these agencies failed to make much impact on the small and marginal farmers. In fact, it failed to correct the imbalances created by the Green Revolution in the countryside engineered by IADP and New Agricultural strategy. Since the imbalance was increasing, to the meet this eventuality the Government launched another programme know as Drought-Prone Areas Programme in the seventies. SFDA was merged with Integrated Rural Development Programme in 1980.

Rural Works Programme

The Central Government conceived this programme in the late sixties and launched it in 1970-71. The main purpose was to implement rural work and generate employment in the rural areas. However, the performance of this programme was found not satisfactory in 1972-73. Hence forth the Rural Works Programme was redesigned as Drought Prone Areas Programme.

The Drought-Prone Areas Programme

The programme was launched, as we have noted earlier, to correct the imbalances in the development pattern created by the

Green Revolution, with the objective of generating employment opportunities. The programme's special emphasis was on labour intensive schemes. The programme though extant still was not been without criticism. On many occasion it was found that it did not achieve it objectives which were : (a) reducing the severity of impact of drought; (b) stabilishing the income of people, particularly the weaker sections of the society; and (c) restoring the ecological balance.

Desert Development Programme

A huge tract of India is in the grip of desert. Because of low rainfall and chronic drought situation, employment opportunity of the people of such areas is very marginal. In order to alleviate the conditions of people the central Government launched the Desert Development Programme in 1977-78. Though substantial development has been experienced under the programme still the effort has remained much below the desired level. Not much has been achieved in terms of increasing productivity, income level and employment opportunities. The migration of large number of families every year from various desert-affected areas is an indication of marginal impact of Desert Development Programme. Even in many areas people are least informed about this programme. For example, in Rajasthan, in district like Jodhpur workers in desert areas were found living in precarious conditions. Lack of employment in other economic activities except in stone quarries, turned thousands of families bonded to the money lenders and quarry owners (Rehman & Chauhan, 1998).

The above programme were second generation programmes and they are still extant and is being operated in drought affected districts of various states of the country.

However, the importance of these two programmes to alleviate the conditions of the people cannot be denied. Realising the need of the programme the Government formulated a unified strategy based on the recommendations of the Hanumantha Rao Committee. The main features of the strategy suggested by the committee are :

- Area development programmes to be implemented exclusively on watershed basis.

- Programme activities to be confined to the identified watershed of about 500 hectares and are to be executed on a project basis spanning over a period of four years.
- Watershed project to cover a village as far as possible.
- Elaborate institutional mechanisms at various levels clearly defined for effective participation of local people and Panchayati Raj Institutions in all stages of project management.

DRDA/ZP to be the nodal Government agency at the district level to act as a facilitator and provider of finances and technical assistance to the people's organisations executing the watershed project.

It could be seen in Table 2.2 that till 2002-03 the total number of districts and blocks under the programme was 182 and 972 respectively, and it was covering 7.45 lakh square kilometers.

Table 2.2 : State-wise districts and blocks under Drought Prone Areas Programme

S.No.	*Name of State*	*Districts*	*Blocks*
1.	Andhra Pradesh	11	94
2.	Bihar	6	30
3.	Chattishgarh	8	29
4.	Gujarat	14	67
5.	Himachal Pradesh	3	10
6.	Jammu & Kashmir	2	22
7.	Jharkhand	14	100
8.	Karnataka	14	81
9.	Madhya Pradesh	23	105
10.	Maharashtra	25	149
11.	Orissa	8	47
12.	Rajasthan	11	32
13.	Tamil Nadu	16	80
14.	Uttar Pradesh	15	60
15.	Uttaranchal	7	30
16.	West Bengal	4	36
	Total	**182**	**972**

Source : Ministry of Rural Development, *Annual Report 1998-99*. Govt. of India.

Table 2.3 : Watershed Projects Sanctioned and taken up during the Period between 1995-96, 1997-98.

State	*1st Batch*		*2nd Batch*		*3rd Batch*		*4th Batch*		*Total*	
	Target	*Taken up*	*Target*	*Taken up*	*Target*	*Taken up*	*Target*	*Taken up*	*Target*	*Taken up*
Andhra Pradesh	527	527	60	60	321	321	700	697	1608	1605
Bihar	536	492	0	0	0	0	-	-	536	492
Gujarat	275	270	101	87	19	3	55	0	450	360
Himachal Pradesh	33	33	31	7	0	0	-	-	64	40
Karnataka	453	406	0	0	0		-	-	453	406
Maharashtra	873	794	0	0	0		-	-	873	794
Madhya Pradesh	825	891	0	0	0	-	-	96	891	141
Orissa	222	191	0	0	0		-	-	222	191
Rajasthan	176	176	0	0	0		-	-	176	176
Tamil Nadu	297	297	0	0	0		-	-	339	297
Uttar Pradesh	426	396	124	99	0	0	56	56	606	551
West Bengal	161	153	0	0	0	0	-	-	161	153

Source : Ministry of Rural Development, *Annual Report, 1998-99*, New Delhi, Govt. of India.

The funding of the programme is shared by both the centre and state on 50:50 basis. Since its inception in 1973-74 a large number of projects have been sanctioned. Table 2.3 shows the details of watersheds sanctioned and taken up for implementation during the last four years i.e. after the introduction of new guidelines in 1995-96.

However, the performance of DPAP is not up to the mark. The outlay and expenditure pattern clearly shows this shortcoming. For example, in 1998-99 the target was 6454 watershed projects out of which 5956 were taken up, while 503 watershed projects were left without.

Besides, the unspent balance speaks volume about the tardy and slowness in implementing the project. The unspent balance was Rs. 17189.25 lakh on 1.4.98 and the total fund available was Rs. 25667.16 lakh and expenditure was Rs. 9642.40 thus the total expenditure out of the total funds was 37.57 per cent. No wonder, that despite the existence of this programme for last 24 years it has not made any dramatic impact on the lives of people in the country, especially in the parts of the country where desert is making its progress slowly and steadily and drought is still the important 'natural' phenomenon.

Since the activities under the project have become quite massive, Council for Advancement of People's Action and Rural Technology CAPART) has been involved in the execution of watershed hold development projects in many areas by NGOs.

Table 2.4 : State-wise number of districts and blocks covered under Desert Development Programme.

S. No.	*Name of the State*	*Districts*	*Blocks*
1.	Andhra Pradesh	1	16
2.	Gujarat	6	47
3.	Haryana	6	44
4.	Himachal Pradesh	2	3
5.	Jammu & Kashmir	2	10
6.	Karnataka	3	22
7.	Rajsthan	16	85
	Total	**36**	**227**

Source : Ministry of Rural Development, Annual Report 1998-99, New Delhi, Govt. of India.

But quite often NGOs are not in a position to execute the project in an efficient and effective manner. The result is thus slow progress in the project implementation throughout the country.

Similarly, Desert Development Programme is being implemented both in the hot desert areas of Rajasthan, Gujarat and Haryana and the cold desert areas of Jammu & Kashmir and Himachal Pradesh. The coverage of DDP has been quite impressive. Till 1998-99 the programme covered 227 blocks of 36 districts. The total areas was 457,432 sq. kms. in 7 states (Table 2.4).

The Programme has designed a very elaborate guidelines for watershed development project. The most important feature is its emphasis on the involvement of people through Panchayati Raj. Institutions and other agencies like NGOs, etc. "The guidelines also provide for an elaborate Institutional arrangement at the Centre for monitoring, review and policy making, at the state level for monitoring and review of programmes and district level for selecting watershed projects and project implementation agencies, monitoring and review of implementation of the programme (MRD, 1999:52).

Funding of the programme is essentially done by the Centre depending on the type of eco-system; for example for hot arid (non-sandy) the central share is 75 per cent and for hot arid (sandy) areas and cold arid areas the central share is 100 per cent.

After the introduction of the new guidelines a large number of projects have been sanctioned which are sanctioned for four years for their completion. During 1995-96 and 1998-99 a total of 2147 watershed Projects were sanctioned of which 78.94, 0.74, 1.67 and 18.63 per cent projects were sanctioned in 95-96, 96-97, 97-98 and 98-99 respectively.

> Since inception, till 1994-95 as core sector activities, 1.85 lakha, under land resource development, 0.83 lakh ha. under water resource development and 2.85 lakh ha, under afforestation and pasture development have been developed. Since inception till 31st March, 1998, a total sum of Rs. 845 crores has been spent on the programme.
>
> In 1997-98, a sum of Rs. 70 crores was released to different DRDAS/Z Ps. During 1998-99, a provision of Rs. 90 crores has been made. In the Ninth Five Year Plan (1997-2002) a sum of Rs. 1,430 crores has been proposed (1999:54).

These programme have partially helped generating employment in specific areas of the country. But their impact was more often marginal and short-lived. As a result, there was no strong linkage between growth and employment. The reason behind the slow and more often insignificant impact, was the fact that land reforms measures did not alter the skewed land-ownership pattern. In fact, land still is in the hand of rural rich, and major focus was agricultural development. Mehta observes:

> The underlying presumption of the present government land policy is to reorganise Indian agriculture by relying on the rich farmers in rural area. Other measures, including ceiling on land holding, cooperative farming, cooperative village management, rehabilitation of landless labourers on government reclaimed area, village self-government through democratic decentralisation, security of tenancy under certain defined conditions, show that a precise formulation of tenancy rights are framed and implemented within the matrix of village socio-economic structure based on private proprietorship. The entire structure of land legislation is erected on the foundation of village economy resting on capitalist farmers. Thus, the central thesis of post-independence land policy and land legislation as narrated above is to promote fusion of the right of tenancy and ownership into one entity and thereby to inaugurate an era of a new kulak class.
>
> The present land legislation seeks to resolve the Indian agrarian crisis, inherited from the British rulers, by not only safeguarding but also perpetuating the concept of private property in land in agrarian areas. In other words, the approach of consolidating and strengthening the capitalist base in Indian agriculture instead of resolving any of the basic agrarian problems have intensified the miseries and agonies of the toiling strata in rural India (Mehta, 1975: 78-79).

Similar views were expressed by the Task Force on Agrarian Relations (Planning Commission, 1973: 6-7). The 'trickle down' approach did not work well. The methods used, process involved and instrument applied to rural development in India were more often inadequate, indifferent and ad hoc in nature, evasive in character and anti-poor in action. What emerges from the analysis of various aspects of Indian economy till 1979-80 is the fact that all the resources seemed to have been thrown to a bottomless pit. As a result, poverty, unemployment and corruption lingered as a chronic malignant on the India economy, polity and society as a whole. That land reform was more of an euphemism than the real desire to provide succor to the poor is obvious from the observation here:

> To provide an equitable distribution of land, a ceiling on ownership holding was fixed and the surplus land acquired due to these laws was distributed to the landless. But the progress was very slow. Most of the acquired land was not available for distribution due to litigation and reserved or transferred for public purposes, unfit for cultivation, etc. The total area distributed under the ceiling laws accounted for just 1.5 per cent of the net cultivated area and covered only 3.5 per cent of the people below the poverty line. The main reason for this tardy implementation of land reform measures were lack of political will to enforce legislation effectively, lack of pressure from the poor and the weak who were not organised, the nexus between the lower level functionaries and landlords, a weak administrative structure at the district level and below, legal flows and excessive legal interference, absence of proper updated land records, etc. (Singh, 1998: 12-13).

All this, thus depicts a scenario where it becomes obvious that India's rural economy and its growth did not accompany distributive justice. The ruling elite, in connivance of the bureaucracy, systematically perpetuated the exploitative mechanism of the existing social and political systems and maintained status-quo of the former. Moreover, the package which was designed by the rulers, more often was short changed in the dark alleys of delivery system manned by people who were anti-poor, and quite often, by their upbringing, attitude and opinion, were not favourably inclined to the poor and deprived working people. When the efforts for uplifting the rural working people particularly the agricultural labourers, women labourers and child labourers were found failing, it gave repeated excuses for the planners for new experiments, keeping the old structure intact. As a result, the rural development planners began to experiment with another set of programmes and schemes. The apparent idea was to unleash such activities which would sprinkle down benefits to the poor. By now it was amply evident from the past development experiences that still poverty remained as the most pernicious problem in the development process of rural areas. Against this backdrop IRDP was introduced.

Integrated Rural Development Programme (IRDP)

It was also evident that instead of developing a whole block or a village it would be important to target those sections of society who are most disadvantaged as compared to others. And IRDP had clearly that in mind.

The main purpose of initiating the Integrated Rural Development Programme was to improve the asset base of rural poor and to involve the poor in the production and income generation process. The following observation of the Study Team on Rural Employment is worth quoting here :

> It has been realised that the problem of rural unemployment is essentially a problem of rural development. Further strategy of Integrated Rural development enunciated adopted by the government of India based on decentralised micro-level block planning as full employment as its basic objective. Action plans to implement the new strategy of Integrated Rural Development in 2300 out of 5004 blocks in the country are being drawn with the following objectives:
>
> *(a)* The objective being full employment within a certain time frame the programme must provide gainful employment to persons below the poverty line in the village community such as marginal farmers, landless labourers, artisans, scheduled castes and scheduled tribes and women through productive means.
>
> *(b)* These employment opportunities should be created through making optimum use of the existing local resources-human, animal, plant, soil, water mineral and other resources; science and technology has to be fully harnessed to achieve these objectives.

With this aim in view IRDP was launched in 1978-79 in 2300 blocks out of 5011 blocks, in the country, and from October 2, 1980 the programme was extended to all the blocks of the country. It was assumed that the programme, being comprehensive in nature, would address the problems of 300 million people living below the poverty line in rural areas. This programme also was designed to address all the disadvantaged categories of the rural society such as, agricultural labourers, fishermen, marginal farmers, rural artisans, etc. It also especially addressed the problem of poverty stricken women. IRDP provided beneficiary oriented assistance to increase the production and productivity of the beneficiaries.

Initially IRDP was launched in 2000 blocks in the country where the Small Farmers' Development Agency, Desert Prone Areas Programme and Comprehensive Area Development Programme were in operation. In addition, another 300 blocks were also brought under the IRDP subsequently. These blocks were divided into two categories, i.e., 1000 blocks were selected for intensive employment and another 1000 blocks were selected for intensive development.

> Unlike other development programme emphasis in the IRD programme is on the family as a unit. Households with a total income of Rs. 3,500 per annum are considered eligible for assistance under the programme.
>
> Under it, it has been proposed to provide financial assistance to 600 families in each block per year or 3,000 families in each block during the Sixth Plan Period. At this rate, about 15 million families should be brought above the poverty line by 1985. The identified eligible beneficiaries will be assisted to engage in suitable income generating schemes covering agriculture, animal husbandry, daring, fisheries, khadi, village and cottage industries, small business, and services (Desai, 1988:13).

It was assumed, against this background, that on an average each of the 5011 blocks of the country had 20,000 households out of which about 10,000 were below poverty line, and that under various plans all such households would be brought above poverty line. This, however did not occur despite the fact that under IRDP a huge amount of fund was pumped from 1979-80 to 1988-99. During the sixth Plan Period (1980-85) an aggregated amount of Rs. 1661.17 crores was spent against an outlay of Rs. 1500 crores. In addition, term credit of Rs. 3,101.61 crores was mobilised. The subsidy credit ratio stood at 1:1.87. The Seventh Plan has proposed an outlay of Rs. 3,228.99 crores comprising of Rs. 3,228.99 crores comprising of Rs. 1619.38 in the central sector and Rs. 1609.61 crores of the States (ibid : 13).

The programme was being implemented by an agency registered under Societies Registration Act 1860 and known as District Rural Development Agency (DRDA). Under IRDP there were two subsidiary schemes-one was the Training of Rural Youth for Self-Employment (TRYSEM) and the other one was the Development of Women and Children in Rural Areas (DWCRA).

Achievement and Failure

As we have noted IRDP started with a lot of shenanigans. It was thought that poverty would be banished within a short period of

Table 2.5 : IRDP Performance in the Sixth Plan

Sl. No.	*Items*	*Targets*	*Achievements*	*Percent age of targets*
1.	Total allocation (Rs. Crores)	1500	1767	117.8
2.	Central allocation (Rs. Crores)	750	901	120.1
3.	Central release (Rs. Crores)	750	788	105.1
4.	Total Expenditure (Rs. Crores)	1500	1661	110.7
5.	Total term credit (Rs. Crores)	3000	3102	103.4
6.	Total term credit (Rs. Crores mobilised)	4500	4763	105.8
7.	Total no. of beneficiaries covered (lakh)	150	166	110.7
8.	No. of SC/ST beneficiaries covered (lakh)	50	65	130.0
9.	Per Capita subsidy (Rs.)	1000	1003	100.3
10.	Per Capita credit (Rs.)	2000	1873	93.7
11.	Per capital investment (Rs.)	3000	2876	95.9
12.	Subsidy: Credit ratio	1:2	1:1.87	-
13.	Sectorwise coverage (5%)			
	(a) Primary	66.66@	71.8	10.7.7
	(b) Secondary	16.66@	10.3	61.8
	(c) Tertiary	16.66@	17.3	107.4

Source : Seventh Five Year Plan Vol. II
@ Sixth Five Year Plan.
Seventh Plan Development Outlay on Public Sector (Centre, States & U.Ts)

time. But that did not happen. The nightmare of galloping poverty kept on its pace at an ever increasing rate and continued to haunt the poor; and provided the rich the much needed opportunity to exploit the former in the most ruthless manner.

However, before going into the details of its failure we shall examine here what the IRDP has achieved. During the Sixth Plan i.e. the plan period target', for example, were 150 lakhs beneficiaries and the achievements were 166 lakhs beneficiaries which accounted to be 110.7 per cent achievement (see Table 2.5).

The figures in Table 2.6 show us the distribution of development outlay in public sector during the seventh plan,

Table 2.6 : Seventh Plan Development Outlay in Public Sector Centre States & U.Ts

(Percentage Distribution)

Sl. No.	*Development Heads*	*VI Plan (Actual)*	*VII Plan Outlay 1985-90 target*	*Annual Plan 1985-86*	*Annual Plan 1986-87*	*Annual Plan 1987-88 (Plan outlay)*
1.	Agriculture	6.1	5.9	5.5	5.6	5.3
2.	Rural Development	6.4	5.0	6.7	6.3	6.1
3.	Special Area Programme	1.4	1.7	1.4	1.5	1.6
4.	Irrigation and flood control	10.0	9.4	8.5	8.0	8.4
5.	Village and Small Industries	1.8	1.5	1.6	1.5	1.3
6.	Total (including others)	100.0	100.0	100.0	100.0	100.00
	Total outlays (Rs. Crores)	(109202)*	(180000)	(33060)*	(40261)*	(144698)@

* Exclusive of Expenditure of Works financed by central assistance for relief from natural calamities.

@ Includes Rs. 420.0 crores of surplus carried forward from the previous year.

Source : Economic Survey, 1986-87 and Annual Plan 1987-88.

against the sixth plan outlay. It clearly shows that on different development heads, the percentage shares had declined during the seventh plan. This indicates the growing apathy towards rural development by the Government.

A further examination of the sixth plan pattern of development plan outlays shows that in some cases, for instance, agriculture and rural development, actual achievements had been more than the targets. But in case of other heads like special area programme and inigation and flood control, the actual achievements had been less that the targets.

Table 2.7 : Sixth Plan Pattern of Development Plan Outlays in the Public Sector (Centre, States & U.Ts)

(Percentage Distribution)

S. No.	*Development Heads*	*Target*	*Actual*
1.	Agriculture	5.8	6.1
2.	Rural Development	5.5	6.4
3.	Special Area Programme	1.5	1.4
4.	Irrigation and Flood Control	12.5	10.0
5.	Village and Small Scale Industries	1.8	1.8
6.	Total (including others Total	100.0	100.0
	Outlays (Rs. Crores)	(97500)	(109292)*

* Exclusive of Expenditure on Works financed by central assistance for relief from natural calamities of Rs. 2008.3 crores.

Source : Economic Survey, 1986-87.

During the Seventh Plan similar pattern could be observed with regard to targets and achievements. During the Eighth Plan the achievement was quite high. It could been in chapter three that during the plan more than 108 lakh families were assisted. Because of average level of credit enhancement the average level of per family investment also rose from Rs. 7889(1992-93) to Rs. 14,950 during 1996-97. This figure further increased Rs. 17,771 during 1999.

3

Performance During the Eighth and Ninth Plan

As we have noted earlier, IRDP could not deliver what was expected of it. Today the number of rural labour has remained same as it was during the Sixth Plan period, a staggering 320 million. The business seems to be like pouring water in a bottomless pit. The programme, despite its avowed achievements, had remained steeped in corruption and ineffective implementation. How ridiculous the programme became, could be judged from the following jokes : IRDP *Aiya Rakam Dakaro Piyare* (and about DRDA *(de Yar de)* (the amount has come eat up and yawn and give and just give). Why it failed? The answer was tried to be sought in the lack of participation of people. The Planning Commission observed at length:

> The Plan, whose primary emphasis is on rural development and rural services, will demand a much greater level of organisation and public participation than past plans. It is relatively a simple matter to prepare project for setting up industries or power stations or expanding capacities of ports or airlines or telecommunication systems. A limited number of experts, planners, construction workers managers and cooperatives are needed to implement such schemes. A programme of rural development involve investment decisions by hundreds of thousands of individuals and the ability to evoke the response of millions of potential beneficiaries. Officials at all level can only play a limited role in such an enterprise as effecting the deliveries of certain essential inputs. The efficient management of this countrywide network will,

in the first instance, impose tremendous responsibilities on the Government machinery. But in the final analysis the Plan can only succeed if there is full participation of all the groups who will be affected in one way or another by the massive new rural investment programmes.

"Besides the rural poor, the other groups whose effective participation has to be sought in implementing a radical plan of rural development is the youth of the country. While on the one hand the lack of employment opportunities result in constant pressure for jobs, on the other hand no sustained effort has been made to harness their talent and energy in programmes of national construction. Young people everywhere ask what they can do but we have not been able to provide an answer. The National Service Scheme and the National Cadet Corps could be augmented and reoriented to develop the kind of momentum that is needed. The time has come to organise through these and other agencies, a programme for the involvement of youth on a mass scales for rural development. The scope for such enterprise is wide ranging from schemes of adult literacy and non-formal elementary education to rural sanitation and drives for immunisation and family planning. Rural youth with some degree of technical skill can be organised into groups to implement specific projects in demarcated areas for the development of agriculture, animal husbandry or rural industry. Similarly projects could also be developed for urban slum improvement. The possibility of making a year's national service on rural development and similar projects compulsory for students, which has been mooted in the past, might be re-examined.

"There are four elements needed for the success of any radical plan for restructuring rural life. First there must be a national consensus on the plan itself. Over the years such a consensus has prevailed in respect of every national plan, the strategy set out here is the appropriate one for the next phase of the country's development. The Planning Commission is confident that the objectives, priorities and policies laid down this document will find general acceptance with the Central and State Governments, all political parties and all sections of informed opinion in the country.

Secondly, the plan demands determination of Government as a whole to raise and deploy all necessary resource and to devote all their energies to the fulfillment of its objectives.

"Thirdly, it requires of the community the readiness to accept a degree or restraint on the expansion of its current levels of consumption for the sake of the future.

"Lastly, and most vitally, the plan must evoke the enthusiasm and participation of the vast number of citizens whom it will affect, more particularly the target groups to whom the benefits of the rural employment strategy have to be carried. The poor and the disposed will not come into their own, only by plans and programmes, however well-conceived by declarations of intent for by exhortations to thrift and labour. If the plan is to succeed, they have to be helped to organise themselves to claim as a right the benefits that should flow to them, so that in turn they may make their due contributions to society" (Planning Commission, 1975).

As noted earlier TRYSEM and DWCRA were two important components of the IRDP.

An examination of performance of TRYSEM shows that the achievement level has remained much below the targets. With

Table 3.1 : Financial Performance : TRYSEM

(Rs. In crores) *No. in lakh)*

Year	*Allocation*	*Release*	*Expenditure*	*Target*	*No. of youths*
1992-93	39.87	47.04	47.50	3.00	2.76
1993-94	111.14	89.45	55.02	3.50	3.04
1994-95	89.16	74.03	68.46	3.18	2.82
1995-96	90.25	73.31	94.55	3.54	2.91
1996-97	90.25	70.11	100.27	2.90	3.64
Total	**420.77**	**353.94**	**365.94**	**16.12**	**15.17**
Performance during Ninth Five Year Plan					
1997-98	90.00	68.08	80.74	3.04	2.51
1998-99	89.76	40.61	30.86	2.92	0.66

* Upto November, 98.

Table 3.2 : Physical Performance Under TRYSEM

			No. of trained youths employed			
Year	*No. of Youth to be trained*	*No. of youth trained*	*Self Employed*	*Wage Employed*	*Total*	*% from the total*
1992-93	300000	275993	99334	42058	141392	47.13
1993-94	350000	303821	107919	43004	150923	43.12
1994-95	318436	281874	86466	44965	131431	41.27
1995-96	353980	291450	93665	48450	141115	39.86
1996-97	290079	364377	130812	51725	182537	62.92
1997-98	30412	251387	73358	39384	112742	37.07
1998-99*	292485	66016	12988	11175	31535	10.00

regard to financial allocation it may, however, be noted that whatever fund was released that was spent. In fact the expenditure overshot the fund released. But the gap between number of youth trained and the number employed was considerably high (see Tables 3.1 and 3.2) for example, in 1992-93 out of the total number of trained youth only 47.13 percent were employed either in the self employment sector or in the wage employment sector. These figures show that despite training many rural youth did not get employment. Besides, they also did not get any preference under IRDP assistance (Purushotham, 1998:260-275).

Development of Women and Children in Rural Areas (DWCRA)

DWCRA was initiated in 1982-83 in 50 districts and by 1994-95 it was extended to all the districts in the country. Why DWCRA was launched? The observation by the Ministry of Rural development provides answer to this question:

> The flow of benefits to poor women, in spite of reservation, under various poverty alleviation programmes viz., IRDP and TRYSEM were found to be not making much impact. Therefore, in order to overcome this situation and to involve the rural women more intensely in economic activities and matters that concern the rural community, one of the initiative taken by this Ministry was the introduction of an exclusive programme

for women viz., Development of Women and Children in Rural Areas. Since economic empowerment involves provision of additional channels of funds in the form of working capital and credit, training, employment, management skill etc., DWCRA with exclusive focus on economic empowerment of women provides all these inputs by considering women as critical to development. This intervention aims at only raising the income of rural women of poor households, but also enabling organised participation of groups of women in the programmes of credit, skill training and infrastructure support for self employment, who cannot take up economic activities individually or on their own. DWCRA was introduced for ensuring that the benefits of IRDP programme reach women directly. The programme seeks to improve the access of rural women to health, education, safe drinking water, sanitation, nutrition etc., thereby bringing out an enhancement in the quality of the general well-being of women and children (MRD, 1999-29).

The emphasis of DWCRA was on group formation by women below poverty line.

A performance appraisal shows that during the Sixth Plan period 3, 308 groups were formed against the target of 6,035. In the Seventh and Eighth plans 28,031 and 1,41,514 lakh groups were formed against the target of 35,000 and 91,900 respectively. It may be noted that during the Eighth Plan the achievement was much above the target. Table 3.3 also shows the number of women benefited by the programme were fo women target and performance under DWCRA over the plans. By volume the figures, are impressive indeed.

Table 3.3 : Target and Achievements during Plans : DWCRA

Plan	*Target No. of Groups*	*No. of Groups formed*	*No. of Women benefitted*
Sixth Plan	6,035	3,3308	52,170
Seventh Plan	35,000	28,031	4,69,707
Annual Plan 1990-91	7,500	7,139	1,09,557
Annual Plan 1991-92	7,500	9,378	2,08,012
Eight Plan	91,900	1,41,514	22,68,327
Ninth Plan	91,850	56,093	6,95,803

However the scheme had been criticised on many grounds. It was found quite often that except a few state the scheme did not fare well.

The figures in Table 3.4 show that till 1998-99 a total of 2,45,463 groups against the target of 2,397,85 groups were formed and an amount of Rs. 33251.63 lakh were released. This is indeed a huge amount. However, it may again be noted here that the impact of this programme had been much less than what was expected.

Table 3.4 : Physical and Financial Achievements Under DWCRA since Inception

(Rs. In lakh)

Plan	*Target (No. of Group)*	*Achievement (No. of Groups)*	*Women Benifited*	*Central Assistance Released*
Sixth Plan	6035	3308	52170	298053
Seventh Plan				
1985-86	5000	6008	101056	630.70
1986-87	7500	5545	96132	786.33
1987-88	7500	4959	83589	607.29
1988-89	7500	5968	98636	738.21
1989-90	7500	5551	90294	901.00
Total	**35000**	**28031**	**469707**	**3663.53**
Annual Plan 1990-91	7500	7139	109557	898.00
Annual Plan 1991-92	7500	9378	208012	962.72
Eight Plan				
1992-93	7500	9029	128744	1548.17
1993-94	11000	15483	268525	2365.00
1994-95	13400	37964	592026	3100.00
1995-96	30000	37576	697088	6365.00
1996-97	30000	41462	581944	5696.00
Total	**91900**	**141514**	**226837**	**19074.17**

Ninth Plan 1997-98	30000	36436	460409	4145.43
1998-99	1850 (◆)	19657 (◆)	235394 (◆)	4209.25
Total	**91850**	**56093**	**695803**	**8354.68**
G. Total	**239875**	**245463**	**3803576**	**33251.630**

◆ -Position as on 21.1.99

In many states and districts though a substantial number of groups were formed but hardly a dozen were in operation and actually doing some business despite the fact that under the scheme an impressive array of economic activities were drawn up.

Box. 3.1 : Illustrative List of Economic Activities under DWCRA

1. Tailoring
2. Knitting
3. Embroidery
4. Weaving
5. Readymade Garments
6. Carpet weaving
7. Khadi spinning
8. Fibre making
9. Hand printing
10. Bed making
11. Plam leaf mat making
12. Bamboo basket making
13. Pickles making
14. Food processing
15. Bakery
16. Vegetable growing
17. Fish net making
18. Fishery
19. Poultry
20. Goat rearing
21. Duckery
22. Dairy
23. Piggery
24. Beek Keeping
25. Paddy pounding
26. Brush making
27. Book binding
28 Hand made paper making
29. Candle making
30. Leather works
31. Plastic/Polythene works
32. Agarbati making
33. Match making
34. Stone cutting
35. Pottery
36. Leafplate making
37. Chalk making
38. Paper bag making
39. Envelop making
40. Basket making
41. Soap making
42. Fruit & Vegetable/fish preservation
43. Decoration places/toys etc.
44. Wood works

There were several reasons for the inadequate achievemetns fo the DWCRA. Some of them could be summed up as below from a study (Chouhan and Rehman, 1997 :

Inadequate Training

DWCRA functionaries in the study area expressed that they had not received adequate training for launching the scheme effectively.

Understating

The number of staff required to function properly became an important potential cause for their inefficient function.

Inadequate Transportation

The functionaries stated that they had to travel far and wide and in many interior region of the districts, and non-accessibility of vehicles at time, made their task pretty difficult. Thus, due to non-availability of transportation, the officers did not visit remote places frequently. Hence, the groups and the places were almost forgotten and thus became defunct.

Lack of Motivation

A perpetual hindrance in effective implementation of DWCRA was lack of motivation among the officials with responsibility of the programme implementation. Only a handful of such officials participated in the execution of the scheme with full enthusiasm. Majority of the DWCRA functionaries took it as a routine work.

Target Vs Development Dilemma

Generally, it is perceived that in implementing any scheme for the rural masses, the target approach predominates and development takes a back seat. In the process of target setting and achieving, the real meaning of the scheme gets lost. The launching of the scheme is seen as most important but what goes beyond it is conveniently forgotten. Has it really reached the people in right spirit? Have they followed the operational requirements? When and how they would be trained? These are some of the questions which seem to have been overlooked.

Similarly, DWCRA had not reached to people in meaningful manner. As a result, it had been proved unsuccessful in many places.

Neglect of Women Specific Needs

Some functionaries of DWCRA reported during a interview that normally women specific needs were not taken into account by the male members of the staff. Many a times they had to travel to remote places and when it became dark there was a lot of danger involved. Not much support was provided to them. If the project Director was a concerned person then the resources were provided without difficulty and support extended continuously. But, normally such persons were not many.

Bureaucratic Red Tapism

Many gramsevikas shared with us that they were not paid their TA/DA for two to three years. But there was no response from the higher officials- some of the gram sevikas told us that they belonged to lower economic strata and it was not possible for them to spend very frequently from their own pockets to meet the travel expenses. Many times they were stationed at far off centres from their home places. So maintaining another home setup and travelling on their own expenses became extremely difficult proposition. Some of them were the sole breadwinners and for them it was really hard to meet the family expenses squarely. Besides, the file movement in the department was very slow which delayed many actions and decisions. These unnecessary delays created a lot of frustration in them which in turn killed their motivation to work.

Lack conducive Linkages

During our survey another factor came into view which hindered the successful operation of DWCRA in the area of the study. The linkages between DRDA and BDO office were not always forthcoming. This led to many problems responsible for inadequate functioning. The proper coordination and cooperation among the various units did not take place. This made the process of development operation non-conducive. When APO and gram sevika shared positive and healthy relationship, then they could mobilise support from the BDO's office. These were the problems shared by DWCRA functionaries in Jodhpur that hampered their work efficiency and finally the failure of DWCRA in many panchayats.

Ganga Kalyan Yojna

This was another self-employment scheme under the Integrated Rural development programme launched during 1996-97 with the effect from 1.2.1997 with the purpose of providing irrigation facilities to individuals and beneficiaries belonging to below the poverty line farmers households. This programme has now been sub-sumed under the Swarnajayanti Gram Samiti Yojna since April, 1999.

We have already noted that in order to alleviate poverty and enhance rural development the programme launched several type of programmes and schemes viz.

(1) Self-employment and Entrepreneurship Development Programmes for generating income, employment and asset base.

(2) Wage Employment Programmes to assist families living below poverty line to eke out a living by earning through sponsored project work.

(3) Credit facilities to farmers and entrepreneurs.

(4) Providing infrastructure in rural areas in the form of roads, dams, etc.

(5) Providing foodgrains through the network of public distribution system.

(6) Revamping grassroots level institution- i.e., Panchayat Raj Institution.

(7) Providing assistance to people in rural areas in disadvantaged situation; and

(8) Land Reform Programme

However, among these eight type of programmes, the most important programmes are self-employment and entrepreneurship development and wage employment programme. Here we shall deal briefly with wage employment programmes, such as Jawahar Rozgar Yojna, Employment Assurance Scheme and Million Wells scheme.

Jawahar Rozgar Yojna

Earlier the government launched two programmes for generating wage-based employment programme for the poor employment seeking populace of rural areas, namely, National Rural Employment Programme (NREP) and Rural Landless Employment Guarantee Programme (RLEGP). The programmes were initiated in 1980 and 1983 respectively. Existing for several years, both the programmes were merged into a single rural development programme i.e., Jawahar Rozgar Yojana in April, 1989. The objective of the programme were :

Primary Objective : Generation of additional gainful employment for the unemployed and underemployed person both men and women, in the rural areas.

Secondary Objectives : *(i)* Creation of productive community assets for direct and continuing benefits to the poverty groups and for strengthening rural, economic and social infrastructure, which will lead to rapid growth of rural economy and steady rise in the income levels of the poor. *(ii)* Improvement in the overall quality of life in the rural areas (Ministry of Agriculture, 1989:2)

Performance

Statisticaly the achievements under the programme have been quite impressive. For example, since its inception, the programme has generated 70003.32 lakh mandays employment and the total expenditure during this period i.e., between 1989-90 and 1997-98 was Rs. 27649.00 crores. This is indeed a laudable achievement. Tables 3.5 and 3.6 show utilisation of funds; on an average it has been 78.45 percent and achievement level was 97.64 percent in development project. Under these programme construction of rural link roads had received priority. Besides, whatever assets have been created of which 76.11 percent have been found to be in good conditions. Moreover, during the reference period i.e. from June 1993 to May 1994 "roughtly 11 million mandays were created" (M.R.D., 1999 : 16).

Despite these achievement the programme suffered a number of shortcomings, for example, embazzlement of funds was noticed, panchayat members who were supposed to implement the programme were found not adequately trained, discrepancies in payment of wage between male and female was also observed. Apart from these shortcomings, quite a number of projects could not be completed due to shortage of funds.

Table 3.5 : Funds Available and Utilized

S. No.	*Year*	*Total funds available*	*Funds Utilised*	*Percentage Utilisation*
1.	1989-90 to 1991-92	9576.37	7709.83	80.51
2.	1992-93	3594.63	2709.59	75.38
3.	1993-94	4767.63	3878.71	81.36
4.	1994-95	5418.22	4268.33	78.78
5.	1995-96	5791.90	4466.91	77.12
6.	1996-97	2583.38	2163.98	83.77
7.	1997-98	2872.03	2451.65	82.82
	sub-Total	24604.16	27649.00	79.90
8.	1998-99 (Upto Nov. 1998)	2222.16	1243.71	55.97
	Grand Total	**36826.32**	**28892.71**	**78.45**

Table 3.6 : Achievement Level

S. No.	*Year*	*Target*	*Achievement*	*Percentage Achievement*
1.	1989-90 to 1991-92	25402.64	25481.47	100.31
2.	1992-93	7537.95	7821.02	103.76
3.	1993-94	10383.26	10258.40	98.80
4.	1994-95	9865.45	9517.07	96.47
5.	1995-96	8480.05	8958.25	105.64
6.	1996-97	4141.37	4006.32	93.24
7.	1997-98	3864.90	3960.79	102.48
	sub total	69675.62	70003.32	100.47
8.	1998-99 (upto Nov. 98)	3966.57	1902.80	47.97
	Grand Total	**73642.19**	**71906.12**	**97.64**

Employment Assurance Scheme (EAS)

Introduction : With a view to providing assured purchasing power to the most needy persons in backward areas of the country, the

Prime Minister, in his Independence Day address to the Nation on 15 August, 1993 announced a new Employment Assurance Scheme. This scheme was implemented w.e.f. 2 October, 1993 in rural areas of 1755 identified backward blocks of 257 districts of 23 States and 4 Union Territories (excluding Goa, Punjab, Chandigarh, Delhi and Pondicherry, initially. These blocks were situated mainly in the drought prone areas, desert areas, tribal areas and hill areas in which the Revamped Public Distribution system (RPDS) was in operation.

It was also decided to expand EAS to another 672 blocks in the country. These blocks included the blocks under the DPAP/DDP on the basis of the recommendation of High level committee headed by C.H. Hanumantha Rao, Modified Area Development Approach, pockets and the flood prone areas.

Objectives : The primary objective of the EAS was to provide gainful manual employment during the lean agricultural season to all able bodied adults in rural areas who are in need and who are desirous of work, but cannot find it, either on farm or on other allied operations or on the normal plan/non-plan works during such period. The secondary objective was the creation of economic infrastructure and community assets for sustained employment and development.

Scope : The Scope of the Scheme was as Follows :

- The scheme will provide assured employment for 100 days of unskilled annual works to the rural poor who are in need of employment and seeking it.
- The assurance of 100 days extends to men and women over 18 years and below 60 years of age normally residing in the villages of the blocks covered by EAS.
- A maximum of two adults per family (the generally expected number of adults in a family) would be provided this assurance of 100 days employment under this scheme, if they seek it during the lean agricultural season.
- New works will not be opened under this scheme if employment potential is available through plan and non-plan works already in progress and the assurance could be fulfilled by utilising the same.

- Persons seeking work under EAS should be given employment within the area of the Block of works started from out of the shelf of works prepared for this purpose by the implementation authority.
- It should be ensured that the provision of employment under this scheme results in the creation of durable productive assets in the Block area.

Target Group

The EAS was open to all rural people residing in the area covered by the scheme but targeted to the poor who were needy and wanted work.

Performance

Out of Rs. 600 crores allocated for implementation of Employment Assurance Scheme (EAS) as Central share for the year 1993-94, an amount of Rs. 439.10 crores was released to different States. For the year 1994-95 the Central allocation of Rs. 1200 crore was made for the implementation of EAS against which an amount of Rs. 1128.52 crores was released to states/UTs. For the year 1995-96 the Central allocation of Rs. 1570.00 crores had been made. The details about the performance, as per the reports received from States/UTs for the year 1993-94 and 1994-95 are given Table 3.7

Reasons for Tardy Progress

EAS was launched quite recently, in a massive scale, in different states of the country. It may be stated that since the time required for successful implementation of the project was not enough, but yet the effort to create employment and community assets and resources was commendable.

Two reasons are forwarded for its tardy progress, however: first, Government officials, who were interviewed, reported that in the first year (1993-94) when the scheme was launched, they were not adequately prepared in terms of both information and skill.

It was also reported that it took some time to prepare the 'shelf of project'. Besides, panchayats also took a considerable time to identity bonafide families and their members. The preparation of identity cards thus also consumed substantial time.

Millions Wells Scheme (MWS)

Lack of irrigation facilities has been a major handicap for the small and marginal farms way to increase production and productivity in rural areas. In order to eradicate this problem the Government launched the MWS as a sub-scheme of NREP and RLEGP during 1988-89 and since then it continued as the sub-scheme of Jawahar Rozgar Yojana. But from January 1, 1996 it was being run as an independent scheme.

The main objective of this scheme was to provide open irrigation wells to marginal and other poor farmers belonging to both Scheduled Castes, Scheduled Tribes, released bonded labourers and other non SC/ST farmers below the poverty line.

Operated through DRDA/ZP the fund is shared between the Centre and States on 80:20 basis.

Since its inception in 1988-89 till November 1998, a total of Rs. 6168.28 cores have been allocated to this scheme of which Rs. 4728,17 have been utilised. The total number of wells constructed since its inception is 12,63,090 (See Table 3.7).

Table 3.7 : Achivements under Millions Well Scheme

(Rs. In crores)

S. No.	*Year*	*Allocation*	*Funds Utilised*	*No. of Wells constructed*
1.	1988-89	271.40	132.99	50345
2.	1989-90	0	108.16	87634
3.	1990-91	524.63	279.74	56433
4.	1991-92	524.63	495.19	172328
5.	1992-93	605.33	534.05	180995
6.	1993-94	954.37	639.74	151673
7.	1994-95	1049.61	776.18	158780
8.	1995-96	559.07	538.29	142685
9.	1996-97	559.07	502.33	108897
10.	1997-98	559.07	495.61	103499
11	1998-99 (Upto Nov., 1998)	561.10	225.89	49821
	Grand Total	**6168.28**	**4728.17**	**1263090**

Is the scheme adequate?

Despite the last five decades of endeavour the irrigation facility for small and marginal farmers are still marginal. Besides, simply digging of wells does not help a poor farmer. Other accessories like pumpsets, electric connections etc. matter a lot. Under these scheme there was no funds for such items. As a result, the effect of this scheme has not been fully realised.

Panchayati Raj Institution (PRI)

The need for Panchayat system was felt from the very beginning of the post independent period. However, the increasing poverty and unemployment kept the need at a distance. But when the community Development Programme failed to produce the desired result and it was found that behind the failure there was a serious lack of participation of people especially the poor working masses, the government awakened to the need for the reviving and revitalizing the PRI. However, despite four decades of trial the Panchayati Raj Institution began to breath life afresh only in 1992 the constitutional status by the passage of the Constitution (73th Amendment) Act, 1992. Consequent upon the enactment of the Act, almost all the states/UTs, except J&K, NCT Delhi and Arunachal Pradesh, have enacted their legislation. Except Assam, Arunachal Pradesh, Bihar, NCT Delhi, Pondicherry and Goa (Zilla Parishad), all other States/Uts have held elections. As a result, about 2,27,698 Panchayats at Village level; 5,906 Panchayats at intermediate level and 474 Panchayats at the district level have been constituted in the country. These Panchayats are manned by 34 lakh elected representatives of Panchayats at all levels. Thus, this is the broadest representative base that exists in any country of the world. The feature of the Act are : (i) a 3 tier system of Panchayati Raj for all states having population of over 20 lakhs; (ii) Panchayat elections every 5 years; (iii) reservation of seats for Schedule Castes, Scheduled Tribes and women (30%); (iv) appoint State Finance Commission to make recommendations as regards the financial powers of the Panchayats; and (v) to constitute District Planning committee to prepare draft development plan for the district as a whole (MRD, 1999:57-58).

Revival of Panchayat Raj system has rekindled a new hope among the masses despite some obvious disadvantages. First, today an under-privileged knows that he can make a difference. He also knows that there is a chance for him to exert his influence on the process of development activities undertaken in his/her ward or village. Despite apprehension the Panchayati Raj Institution in its new *avatar* have generated hopes and escalated aspirations of the masses and it has also shown results. For example, in West Bengal Panchayati Raj Institutions have made a great difference in the rural areas through there is still much remained to be done (see Maheswari, 1995 : 84-85). Similar achievements of PRI's could also be found in Karnataka and Gujarat as well.

Today PRIs has also given the villagers a very important power to decide the priority of their development. Apart from this, the PRIs have an important structure to empower women and Scheduled Castes and Scheduled Tribes. Despite skewed distribution of wealth in the villages of India, the Panchayati Raj Institutions have been charting a new path by generating at least hope of the hitherto downtrodden people of rural India.

Indira Awas Yojana

Shortage of housing has been a perennial problem in India. The shortage in fact has been increasing. Today still millions of people live without a roof on their heads. Besides, most of the houses are either semi-pucca or kutcha. In 1991, 30.59 per cent houses were pucca, and 35.65 and 33.76 per cent houses were semi-pucca and kutcha respectively. Together the latter categories formed 69.41 per cent of the total households in 1991. Ministry of Rural Development observes:

> According to the census, the rural housing shortage was 13.72 million consisting of 3.41 million without houses and 10.31 million living in unserviceable kutcha houses. It has also been estimated that another 10.75 million houses would be needed to cover the population growth during 1991-2002, at the rate of an annual growth of 0.89 million houses needed to be constructed or upgraded to achieve the target of providing shelter to all in the rural area by 2002 AD. Of the above 24.47 million houses, 5.7 million houses have been added by various agencies until 31.3.1997. It is anticipated that around 6.17 million houses will be added by different agencies by 2002. Thus the housing shortage to be tackled is 12.60 million houses, of which 10.31 million houses need upgradation and 2.90 million new houses will need to be constructed (MRD, 1999:41).

The above figures were indeed staggering and if not met with challenge the country's sizable number of population will be without a roof on their heads. Once again it is the poor especially those who live below the poverty line, are short of housing facilities.

To eradicate housing shortage the Indira Awas Yojana was launched in 1985-86. Till 1998-99 from its inception an amount of Rs. 7395.19 crores have been spent and a total of 4843178 houses have been constructed (see Table 3.8)

Table 3.8 : Amount spent and number of houses built under IAY

Year	*Expenditure (Rs. in Crore)*	*No. of houses built*
1985-86	57.93	51252
1986-87	149.18	160197
1987-88	235.37	169302
1988-89	149.65	139192
1989-90	188.50	186023
1990-91	213.07	181800
1991-92	263.01	207299
1992-93	238.84	192585
1993-94	481.00	372535
1994-95	500.38	390482
1995-96	1166.36	863889
1996-97	1385.92	806290
1997-98	1596.44	767649
1998-99	769.54	354683
Total	**7395.19**	**4843178**

Source : Same as Table 3.1

It may be mentioned here that the requirement for housing facilities still remains very high, while the provision of facilities provided is very marginal. Hence, housing facilities have not been able to meet the growing need. Even the houses, which have been constituted, in many cases, are unserviceable and away from other facilities like drinking water, sanitary ground, etc. As a result, the scheme has suffered a set back.

Rural Roads

The life line of rural development process is the rural road. Indian villages are not easily accessible. The inaccessibility has also become a hindrance to the development of rural areas of the country. According to census 1991 :

> A large number of villages in the country were still unapproachable through pucca roads. Only little more than one-third villages were connected by 'pucca' roads. More than one per cent villages were connected either by navigable rivers or by navigable canals or other navigable water ways (Registrar General, 1991:14)

As a result of this absence of roads India's rural areas have suffered for a long time. Today one observes that well-off classes with strong political clout, have had benefitted first from the advantage of road. During the 5th Plan special programme has been drawn to connect all villages with population of 1500 with all-weather roads. The figures in Table show the number of villages connected upto 1991-92.

Table 3.9 : Villages connected with roads.

Village category	*Total No. of villages*	*No. of village connected*	*Balance to be connected*
With population 1500 and above	71623	64633	6990
With population between 100-1500	58229	41966	16263
With population	459465	167789	291676

Source : Ministry of Rural Development, (1999) Annual Report 1998-99., Govt. of India.

Road Density

In Table 3.10, it could be seen that in 1996-97 the highest road density, among states, was in Orissa followed by Tamil Nadu and so on.

Table 3.10 : State-Wise road Density in Kms. (Road Length per '000 sq. Kms of area) (Arranged in Rank Order to 1996-97)

Sl No.	States/Union Territorries	1971-72	1981-82	1991-92	1996-97
1.	Delhi	7984	10527	14256	17924
2.	Chandigarh	710*	1250	14000	15377
3.	Pondicherry	3508*	4286	6698	4859
4.	Kerala	3106	2251	3567	3749
5.	Goa	1581*	2141	2005	2245
6.	Orissa	366	772	1260	1687
7.	Tamil Nadu	714	1020	1523	1588
8.	Tripura	386	759	1341	1405
9.	Punjab	594	918	1078	1278
10.	Maharashtra	316	586	730	1176
11.	Nagaland	284	379	901	1107
12.	Dadra & Nagar Haveli	460*	492	643	1086
13.	Assam	383	760	836	872
14.	Uttar Pradesh	382	520	692	868
15.	West Bengal	599	642	700	850
16.	Karnataka	525*	557	701	750
17.	All India	344	466	615	749
18.	Andhra Pradesh	264	468	553	647
19.	Haryana	307	542	601	637
20.	Himachal Pradesh	215	369	459	542
21.	Bihar	670	481	492	508
22.	Manipur	392	239	314	490
23.	Gujarat	221	375	419	463
24.	Madhya Pradesh	162	242	321	451
25.	Rajasthan	146	212	363	379
26.	Meghalaya	303	233	291	378

27.	Sikkim	329*	156	227	258
28.	Mizoram	43*	119	179	229
29.	Arunachal Pradesh	125*	152	131	168
30.	Andaman & Nicobar Islands	82*	83	110	160
31.	Jammu & Kashmir	40	53	56	97
32.	Lakshadweep	n.a.	n.a.	n.a.	31
33.	Daman & Diu	n.a.	n.a.	n.a.	26

Note : *Refers to data for 1975-76
: n.a. (not avialble)

Source : Basic Road Statistics, Ministry of Surface Transport (Various Issues)

Sampoorna Grameen Rozgar Yojana (SGRY)

This is centrally sponsored scheme, is to be implemented with the total outlay of Rs. 10,000 Crores. Under the Ministry of Rural Development basically two types of programs are launched for the development of rural areas i.e.,

1. Employment Assurance Scheme (EAS). The basic objective of this scheme to provide additional employment opportunities during the period of acute shortage of wage employment through manual work to people under BPL. In this programme special emphasis is made on wage employment to women, scheduled castes, scheduled tribes and parents of children withdrawn from hazardous occupations.

2. Jawahar Gram Samridhi Yojana (JGSY). The aim of this Yojana is on one hand to create need based rural infrastructure at the village level, and improve the quality of rural life but also to alleviate poverty by providing employment to rural poors. SGRY was announced by Hon'ble Prime Minister on 15th August 2001. Under this scheme 100 crores Mandays of Wage-employment are generated every year.

- Every worker, working under SGRY will be provided minimum 5 kgs of food grains (in kind) per manday as part of wages.
- The balance of wages will be paid in cash so that they are assured of notified minimum wage.

- The cost of the cash component of the programme is shared by Centre and State in the ratio of 75:25.
- This programme is also in operation in calamity affected rural areas w.e.f. April 2002, with same norms.
- This work can also be undertaken by the Panchayti Raj Institutions as per felt need of the areas.

Implementation Task

Overall supervision of the programme will be done by Zila Parishad. At district level implementation agency is Zila Parishad, at the Samiti level implementation task will be under Panchayat Samiti and at Gram Panchayat level work will carried on by Gram Panchayaṭ. Again in this process, no contractors are permitted to involve in this programme.

Nature of Works Undertaken

The following types of works are undertaken such as : soil and moisture conservation; watershed development; promotion of traditional water resources; afforestation; and construction of village infrastructure and link roads; primary school buildings; dispensaries; veterinary hospitals; marketing infrastructure and Panchayat-Ghars.

Monitoring of the above mentioned task is undertaken by the Deptt. of Rural Development through periodical reports, vigilance and monitoring committees, visits by offices of central and state governments.

Evaluation of the scheme is done by the reputed development institutions and organisations initiated by the central and state governments.

Pradhan Mantri Gram Sadak Yojana (PMGSY)

This yojana was launched on 25th December 2003. It is a totally Centrally Sponsored Scheme.

The aim of this yojana is to provide single all weather road connectivity to over 1.60 lakh eligible unconnected habitats with total investment of Rs. 60,000 crores. This yojana is executed by the state government and monitored by the Ministry of Rural Development.

National Rural Roads Development Agency (NRRDA)

- The Agency was set up under Societies Registration Act to support this programme through advice on technical specifications, project appraisal appointment of part-time quality control monitors, etc.
- All roads under PMGSY are prioritized as per the guidelines in respect of population size and preference to new connectivity. Roads are to be built based on the specifications given in the Rural Roads Manual published by the Indian Road Congress, 2002, which allows for a carriage way of 3.0m where traffic intensity is less than 100 motorized vehicles per day which is not likely to increase in future.
- District monitoring and Vigilance committee, set up by Ministry of Rural Development also monitors the progress under the scheme.
- In order to varify the quality of roads National Quality Monitors (NQM) are engaged and its report is sent to the state government for necessary action.

Review of Performance

It is revealed that 18 states and Union Territory of Pondicherry have by and large completed all road works of 2000-01, which include; Andhra Pradesh, Arunachal Pradesh, Goa, Gujarat, Haryana, Himachal Pradesh, Karnataka, Kerala, Maharashtra, Meghalaya, Mizoram, Nagaland, Punjab, Rajasthan, Sikkim, Tamil Nadu, Tripura and Uttar Pradesh. But the other states like; Bihar, Jharkhand, and Jammu & Kashmir were likely to complete their work soon by the year 2003. UP to December 2003, NQM had also inspected 3378 road works.

Rural Housing

Housing is the most essential need of every human being for its survival as well as to lead a secured and dignified life in the society. According to 1991 census about 3.1 million households are without shelter and 10.13 million households reside in unserviceable kutcha houses. Looking at the magnitude of the problem, the Central Government in 1998 announced a 'National Housing and Habitat Policy' to provide houses to all the facilitated construction of 20 lakh additional housing units (13 lakh in rural and 7 lakh in urban areas).

To implement this scheme, Action Plan for Rural Housing was constituted. It consists of following elements:

- To upgrade unserviceable kutcha houses in the Indira Awaas Yojana in addition to the new construction.
- To set up credit-cum-subsidiary scheme for rural housing.
- To set up innovative stream for rural housing and habit at development.
- To set up Rural Building Centres.
- To set up Samagra Awaas Yojana.
- Enhancement of equity contribution by Ministry of Rural Development of HUDCO.
- National Mission for Rural Husing & Habitat.

Innovative Scheme for Rural Housing and Habitat Development

It is implemented on project basis and assistance is provided to recognized NGOs, Educational Institutions and Corporate bodies. Upto now 125 projects have been approved costing about Rs. 100 crores.

For setting up of Rural Building Centres, so far 77 project proposals have been sanctioned under Samagra Awaas Yojana. Under this Yojana special central assistance of Rs. 25 lakhs is provided for each block for overall habitat development and till now 33 proposals have been approved.

Equity Support to HUDCO

To meet the housing needs of poor households in rural areas, equity support to HUDCO has been raised from Rs. 5 crores in the 8th plan period to Rs. 350 crores in the 9th plan period. However, HUDCO has sanctioned about 12.54 lakh rural dwellings per year in the last 4 years, as against approximately 9-10 lack dwellings to be sanctioned based on the MOU signed with the Ministry and HUDCO was provided for equity support amount of Rs. 50 crore.

Not only this, initiatives has also been taken through workshops, seminars and training to introduce cost-effective techniques for building material, designs and structures for building houses in rural areas.

Table 3.11

	Agricultural Labour Households						*All Rural Labour Households*					
Items	*1st RLE 1964-65*	*2nd RLE 1974-75*	*3rd RLE 1977-78*	*4th RLE 1983*	*5th RLE 1987-88*	*6th RLE 1993-94*	*1st RLE 1964-65*	*2nd RLE 1974-75*	*3rd RLE 1977-78*	*4th RLE 1983*	*5th RLE 1987-88*	*6th RLE 1993-94*
1	2	3	4	5	6	7	8	9	10	11	12	13
Indebtedness												
Percentage of Indebted households	60.6	66.4	52.3	51.1	39.4	35.5	59.2	65.4	50.5	50.4	39.1	35.1
Average Debt per Household (in Rs.)	148	387	345	774	769	1031	148	395	348	806	787	1113
Average Deb per Indebted Household (in Rs.)	244	584	660	1516	1952	2901	251	605	690	1598	2014	3169
Average Debt by source												
Government	-	-	-	44	70	238	-	-	-	65	73	262
Co-operative Societies	12	31	57	119	195	202	14	34	65	163	190	251
Employers	48	59	46	211	254	355	45	58	46	195	246	360
Money Lenders	75	279	246	282	429	652	80	281	253	340	436	875

Table 3.11 : (Contd.)

Shop-keepers	18	39	44	70	151	199	21	44	47	84	186	232
Banks	-	21	40	505	410	600	-	24	45	448	419	598
Relatives & Friends	-	-	-	164	268	373	-	-	-	186	289	395
Others	91	155	227	121	176	82	91	163	234	117	175	195
Average Debt by Purpose												
Household Consumption	130	281	293	461	670	937	130	284	296	512	677	94*
Marriage & other ceremonials	59	110	147	222	270	496	62	117	158	248	311	56*
Productive purpose	29	74	138	628	567	821	30	77	141	610	541	80
Purchase of land & constu. of building	-	-	-	96	166	290	-	-	-	121	223	47
Repayment of debt	-	-	-	-	23	50	-	-	-	-	22	5
Others (more than one purpose	26	118	82	109	256	308	29	127	95	107	240	39

Rural Credit

India's credit markets has been dominated over the century by the professional moneylenders as well as landlord-moneylenders. Marginal and small farmers have always been in the grip of these moneylenders. To lessen this dependence the government has, over the years been trying to lend through institutional financial agencies at a very low rate of interests. Lot of the important steps has been taken up for reviving the cooperative societies. Besides, commercial banks have also been persuaded to extend loan facilities to small and marginal farmers.

Today a varieties of banking facilities are available in rural areas, popularly known as *'gramin banks'*. Though these financial institutions have contributed a great deal to the development process of rural areas, yet a large number of rural poor depend on money lenders. For example, in various Rural Labour Enquiry Reports it is found that the major source of debt had been the money lenders, followed by banks for the rural labour households. The figures in Table 3.11 show that in 1993-94, more than 35 per cent rural labour households were indebted. It can also be observed in the table that the proportion of indebted rural households had declined over the years. For instances while it was 59.2 per cent in 1964-65, the proportion declined to 35 per cent in 1993-94. This indeed a notable phenomenon. Another important point that can be noted in the table is that the amount of average debt per household had however increased from Rs. 251 in 1964-65 to Rs. 3169 in 1993-94.

4

Land Reforms

Earlier we have mentioned that land distribution in the country has been highly skewed. Only a minority of rural households owned the largest share and the majority a smallest share. The size of distribution of ownership holdings in India is characterised by predominance of semi-land less households and marginal holders. The marginal holders and landless constitute about 72 per cent of the rural households but they hardly own 17 per cent of the total area owned. The medium (owing 4 to 10 hectares of land) and large holders (owing more than 10 hectares of land) accounted for only 5.5 per cent of the households but had a combine share of about 40 per cent in the total land owned by all households (NSSO, 1992). This scenario is existing today and is the outcome of a long historical process. In fact, the crux of India's development problems lies hidden here. In an agrarian economy land is the most important factor. A peasant with a piece of land of his own can easily eke out a living of his own and for his family. But if that piece goes away, his heaven falls and he, in the end, becomes destitute and joins the deprived and disposed class. In the post-independence period the dispossession continues unabated. In fact, the land ownership pattern is characterised by marginalisation over the year i.e., marginal and small size classes have been increasing while the concentration of holding has remained more or less the same. The following observation by NSSO clearly brings out the problem :

> During the three decades, the percentage share of area owned by marginal holdes has increased from 8 per cent to 16 per cent, while that of large holders has declined from 28 per cent

to 14 per cent. The progressive downward shift in the distribution of area owned over the periods nevertheless, has hardly caused any change in the prevailing level of inequality in land distribution. The concentration ratio of household ownership holdings for the year 1961-62, 1971-72, 1982 and 1992 are given in Table. It is seen that the concentration ratio of household ownership holdings has remained the same (0.71) in all the last three rounds. Only in the 17th round it was estimated to be 0.73.

Table 4.1 : Concentration ratios (Gini's coefficient) of household ownership holdings:

All India	*Rural*
Years (1)	*Concentration ratio (*)* (2)
1961-62	0.7313
1971-72	0.7087
1982	0.7120
1992	0.7104

* *Note* : Concentration ratio (Gini's Coefficient is given by

$C = 1\text{-}(s(P;\text{-}P;)\ (Q;+Q)/10^4$

Where P and Q are respectively the cumulative percentage of house holds and area owned in the size class of ownership holdings.

Source : NSSO, 1992.

Given this skewed nature of distribution of land among various households it is altogether impossible to reach the gains of various development programmes and schemes to the rural poor who are dependent on the landed households for their survival.

Agriculture is a land-dependent activity. The growth and development of agriculture are entirely dependent upon pattern of distribution of land, productivity and provision of adequate investment. The pattern of ownership and size of holding play a very important role in the overall framework of agricultural development. The emergence of the present pattern is due to two factors : (i) economic compulsion for development, and (ii) political-legislative need for distribution.

The size of holding also plays an important role in decision making in agriculture. It is impossible to formulate any policy measure without taking into consideration various size-classes of holdings. Since agricultural policy generally pertains to provision of institutional credits, supply of fertilisers and other bio-chemical technology, price-regulation, subsidy, etc. the volume of such provision and facilities and its availability and recovery, to a substantial extent, depends on and is guided by the size of holding. The size of holding is basically an amount of 'collateral' for an agricultural household. In fact, it is the size of holding which determines the possibility of availability, allocation, introduction and application of various inputs in different combinations.

Size of Operational Holdings

According to Agricultural Census 1985-86, the number of operational holdings was estimated at 97.16 million. A size-class-wise distribution of the total holdings shows that the marginal holdings size less than 1 hectare of land accounted for 57.8 per cent of the total holdings in 1985-86. The small holdings with 1-2 hectare of land accounted for 18.4 per cent of the total holdings. Similarly, the semi-medium (2-4 ha), medium (4-10 ha) and large holdings (10 ha and above) accounted for 14.0, 13.6 and 2.0 per cent of the total operational holdings respectively.

The interesting point which can be noted here is that the Indian agrarian scenario has been dotted by the 'marginals'. Another important point which emerges from the figures in Table 4.2 that while the first three categories of holdings have registered increases of different dimensions in 1985-86 over 1980-81, the last two categories have registered declines between 1980-81 and 1985-86. The possible reasons which can be attributed to the emergence of this phenomenon are:

(1) Demographic expolusion.

(2) Fragmentation of holdings.

(3) Acquisition of land.

(4) Distribution of surplus land among weaker sections.

Size of Operated Area

The total area operated by all the operational holdings in 198[illegible] 86 was 164.56 million hectares. The area operated remained mo[illegible]

Table 4.2 : Operational Holdings in India

Sl. No.	*Category and Size Size*	*Number of Operational Holding (Million)*				*Area Operated (Million Hectares)*				*Average Size of Holding 1985-86*
		1970-71	*1976-77*	*1980-81*	*1985-86*	*1970-71*	*1976-77*	*1980-81*	*1985-86*	
1.	Marginal (Below 1 ha)	36.20 (51.0)	44.52 (54.6)	50.12 (56.4)	56.14 (57.8)	14.56 (9.0)	17.51 (10.7)	19.74 (12.1)	22.04 (13.4)	0.38
2.	Small (1-2 ha)	13.43 (18.9)	14.73 (18.10)	16.07 (18.1)	17.92 (18.4)	19.28 (11.9)	20.90 (1.8)	23.16 (14.1)	25.70 (15.6)	1.43
3.	Semi-Medium (2-4 ha)	10.68 (15.0)	11.67 (14.3)	12.45 (14.0)	13.25 (13.6)	30.00 (18.5)	32.43 (19.9)	34.65 (21.2)	36.66 (22.3)	2.76
4.	Medium (4-10 ha)	7.93 (11.20)	8.21 (10.0)	8.07 (9.1)	7.92 (8.2)	48.23 (29.7)	49.63 (30.4)	48.54 (29.6)	47.14 (28.6)	5.94
5.	Large (10 ha & above)	2.77 (3.99)	2.44 (3.0)	2.17 (2.4)	1.93 (2.0)	50.06 (30.0)	42.87 (26.2)	37.71 (23.0)	33.00 (20.1)	17.20
	All categories	71.01 (100.0)	81.57 (100.0)	88.88 (100.0)	97.16 (100.0)	162.14 (100.0)	163.34 (100.0)	163.80 (100.0)	164.56 (100.0)	1.68

Note : The figures in brackets are percentage of total in respective columns.

Source : Government of India, Agricultural Census: 1970-71, 1976, 1980-81 and 1985-86 (Provisional), Ministry of Agriculture, Department of Agriculture and Cooperation, New Delhi.

or less at a level of 50 per cent of the geographical area of the country. Table 4.3 shows that the marginal holdings which comprised the overwhelming portion of the total holdings had a share of only 13.4 per cent in the total area operated in 1985-86. The share of small holdings in the total area operated is 15.6 per cent. Thus, the marginal and small holdings together had a share of 28.6 per cent in the total area operated in the country. The semi-medium and large holdings had a share of 22.3, 28.6 and 20.1 per cent respectively in the total operated area. These three categories of holdings together (23.6) had a share of 71.0 per cent of the total operated area. The area operated by relatively smaller holdings such as marginal, small and semi-medium increased between 1980-81 and 1985-86 while it showed decline in the case of medium and

Table 4.3 : Distribution of Number and Area of Operational Holdings in 1980-81 and 1985-86 and Percentage Change in 1985-86 over 1980-81 for all Social Groups

Category of Holdings	*No. of Holdings ('000)*		*Percentage*	*Area Operated ('000 hectares)*		*Percentage*
	1980-81	*1985-86*		*1980-81*	*1985-86*	
Marginal	50122 (56.4)	56147 (57.8)	+12.5	19735 (12.1)	22045 (13.4)	+9.5
Small	16072 (19.1)	17922 (18.4)	+11.5	23169 (14.1)	25708 (22.3)	+10.2
Semi-Medium	12453 (14.0)	13252 (13.6)	+6.4	34645 (21.2)	36666 (22.3)	+5.6
Medium	2068 (9.1)	7916 (8.2)	-1.9	48543 (29.6)	47144 (28.6)	-3.2
Large	2166 (2.4)	1918 (2.0)	-11.4	37755 (23.0)	33001 (20.1)	-12.0
All Categories	88883 (100.0)	97155 (100.0)	+9.3	163797 (100.0)	164562 (100.0)	+0.1

Note : Figures in brackets indicate the percentages of respective columns.

Source : Government of India, *Ministry of Agriculture, All India Bulletin on Agricultural Census 1985-86*

large holdings (See table). The decline was more pronounced in the case of large holdings which may not be of any concern. But, the increase in the number and areas of marginal and small holdings has two aspects: one, the increased area are prone to more fragmentation and as a result, creating more technological and economically non-viable units; two, as a policy measures, the economically and technologically non-viable units have to be pooled together or the technology should be made to suit these units viably.

Average Size of Holdings

An operational holding by itself dos not convey anything clearly. The most important aspect of an operational holding is its size. It can be observed from Table 4.4 that the average size of holding in the marginal category is 0.39 ha., in the small category 1.43 ha., in semi-medium 2.77 ha., medium 5.96 ha., and in large holdings 17.21 ha; in 1985-86. A number of important points arise from the figures of the table. First, the average size of holdings in all categories has declined from 1980-81 to 1985-86. This decline has many implications: one of the important implications is that percapita land-man ratio is becoming adverse. Second, the marginalisation of holdings and its continuous fragmentation accompanied by declining sizes have posed serious constraints on the introduction of modern technology in agriculture. The disadvantage of this decline has been more problematic for households in marginal and small farm categories.

Table 4.4 : Average size of Holding by Major Size-Classes for All Social Groups

Category of Holdings	*Average size of holding (ha)* 1980-81	1985-86	*Percentage Change*
Marginal	0.3937	0.3926	-0.3
Small	1.4416	1.4344	-0.5
Semi-medium	2.79816	2.7668	-0.5
Medium	6.0167	5.9555	-1.0
Large	17.4077	17.2065	-1.2
All categories	1.8428	1.6938	-8.1

Source : Government of India, *Ministry of Agriculture; All India Bulletin on Agricultural Census 1985-86.*

The above facts clearly show that despite the radical slogan "land to the tiller" land did not go to the tiller. The legislative measures were circumvented in all possible manners taking advantage of many the loopholes in the legislative measures. In some cases the whole exercise was an eyewash. Except in West Bengal, where, under the Leftist Front Government, substantial effort was made to implement Land Reforms Act, especially in the case of registration of Bargaders (share-croppers) while in other states no tangible effort was made (see Rehman, 1990).

Present Situation

The figures on (see Table 4.4A) number of operational holdings and area operated by size-groups for all social group provided by Agricultural Census 1995-96, show distribution of holdings under individual, joint and Institutional oepration. It can be noted in the Table that out of the total operational holdings in 1995-96, 87.02 per cent holdings were individual and the rest were joint and institutional.

With regards to the area operated, 83.18 per cent are individual by operated while the 15.95 and 0.87 per cent area are under joint and institutional arrangement respectively.

The figures in Table 4B present the distribution pattern of number of operational holdings and area operated by different size-classes by social groups and gender (also see section : woman and land subsequently). It may be seen that out of the total number of opeational holidays in 1995-96, 12.71 and 0.01 per cent were operated by the Scheduled Castes (S.C.) and scheduled tribes (S.T.). In respect of operational area, of the total area, 8.21 and 10.73 per cent were operated by the S.C. and S.T. social groups respectively.

It has been reported that upto September 1998, under the ceiling laws, a surplus land of 73.74 lakh acres had been declared and 65.11 lakh acres have taken possession of. It has also been reported that 53 lakh acres had been distributed to 53.37 lakh families. Out of the total beneficiaries 50 per cent belonged to Scheduled Castes and Scheduled Tribes i.e. 36 per cent acquired land was given to SC and 14 per cent to ST. (Table 4.5 and 4.6)

Table 4.4A : Number of Operational Holdings and Area Operated by Size Groups-All Social Groups Agricultural Census 1995-96

All India										
Sl. No.	Size of Holding (ha.)	Sex	No. of Operational Holdings (in 000)				Area Operated (in 000 hectare)			
			Individual	*Joint*	*Institutional*	*Total*	*Individual*	*Joint*	*Institutional*	*Total*
1	2		3	4	5	6	7	8	9	10
1.	Below 0.5	M	37300	5278	0	42578	8934	1313	0	10247
		F	5148	310	0	5457	1077	73	0	1151
		T	42447	5588	92	48127	10011	1386	17	11414
2.	0.5-1.0	M	18071	2840	0	20911	13106	2046	0	15152
		F	1953	159	0	2112	1419	114	0	1533
		T	20024	2999	29	23052	14525	2159	22	16707
3.	1.0-2.0	M	17197	2516	0	19713	24422	3569	0	27991
		F	1753	146	0	1900	2479	209	0	2688
		T	18950	2663	30	21643	26901	3778	43	30722
4.	2.0-3.0	M	7652	1221	0	8873	18382	2909	0	21291
		F	667	72	0	739	1585	175	0	1759
		T	8319	1293	16	9628	19967	3084	40	23090
5.	3.0-4.0	M	3621	687	0	4308	12420	2331	0	14751
		F	275	40	0	316	942	139	0	1081
		T	3897	727	9	4633	13362	2470	31	15863

Contd. . . .

1	2		3	4	5	6	7	8	9	10
6.	4.0-5.0	M	2202	425	0	2627	9745	1887	0	11632
		F	150	25	0	176	665	112	0	777
		T	2352	451	7	2809	10410	1999	29	12438
7.	5.0-7.5	M	2372	468	0	2840	14303	2825	0	17129
		F	154	28	0	181	919	167	0	1086
		T	2525	495	8	3028	15223	2992	50	18265
8.	7.5-10.0	M	957	225	0	1182	8152	1915	0	10067
		F	57	12	0	69	486	103	0	586
		T	1013	237	5	1255	8635	2018	43	10695
9.	10.0-20.0	M	842	237	0	1079	11079	3171	0	14251
		F	45	10	0	55	589	135	0	724
		T	887	247	8	1142	11668	3306	114	15089
10.	20.2 & above	M	160	84	0	244	4902	2808	0	7709
		F	7	2	0	9	277	55	0	331
		T	167	86	10	262	5178	2863	1033	9074
All Sizes		M	90373	13981	0	104354	125445	24775	0	150219
		F	10209	803	0	11012	10435	1280	0	11715
		T	100581	14785	214	115580	135880	26055	1422	163357
1.	Marginal	M	55370	8119	0	63489	22040	3359	0	25398
		F	7101	468	0	7569	2497	187	0	2684
		T	62471	8587	121	71179	24536	3546	39	28121
		%	87.02	12.79	0.19	100.00	83.18	15.95	0.87	100.00

Contd. . . .

1	2		3	4	5	6	7	8	9	10
2.	Small	M	17197	2516	0	19713	24422	3569	0	27991
		F	1753	146	0	1900	2479	209	0	2688
		T	18950	2663	30	21643	26901	3778	43	30722
3.	Semi-Medium	M	11273	1908	0	13181	30802	5341	0	36042
		F	942	112	0	1055	2527	313	0	2840
		T	12215	2020	25	14261	33328	5554	71	38953
4.	Medium	M	5530	1118	0	6649	32200	6627	0	38828
		F	361	65	0	425	2068	381	0	2449
		T	5890	1183	20	709234268	7008	121	41398	
5.	Large	M	1002	320	0	1323	15981	5979	0	21960
		F	52	12	0	64	866	190	0	1055
		T	1054	332	18	1404	16847	6169	1148	24163
6.	All sizes	M	90373	13981	0	104354	125445	24775	0	150219
		F	10209	803	0	11012	10435	1280	0	11715
		T	100581	15785	214	115580	135880	26055	1422	163357
		%	87.02	12.79	0.19	100.00	83.18	15.95	0.87	100.00

Source : Gocvernment of India, Agricultural Census 1995-96.

Table 4.4B : Distribution of Number and Area of Operational Holdings by Social Groups and Gender-Agricultural Census 1995-96

All India

Number in '000, Area in '000 hectare,
Average size in hectare

Sl. No.	Size of holding (ha.)	Sex	All Social Groups # Number	All Social Groups # Area	All Social Groups # Average Area per holdings	Scheduled Castes Number	Scheduled Castes Area	Scheduled Castes Average Area Per holdings	Scheduled Tribes Number	Scheduled Tribes Area	Scheduled Tribes Average Area Per holdings
1	2	3	4	5	6	7	8	9	10	11	12
1.	Below 0.5	M	42578	10247	0.24	7062	1541	0.22	2144	597	0.28
		F	5457	1151	0.21	785	151	0.19	202	50	0.25
		T	48127	11414	0.24	7847	1692	0.22	2346	647	0.28
2.	0.5-1.0	M	20911	15152	0.72	2743	1965	0.72	1881	1376	0.73
		F	2112	1533	0.73	255	178	0.70	149	107	0.72
		T	23052	16707	0.72	2998	2143	0.72	2030	1483	0.73
3.	1.0-2.0	M	19713	27991	1.42	2099	2932	1.40	2174	3100	1.43
		F	1900	2688	1.41	176	244	1.39	162	232	1.43
		T	21643	30722	1.42	2275	3176	1.40	2336	3332	1.43
4.	2.0-3.0	M	8873	21291	2.40	731	1738	2.38	1124	2653	2.36
		F	739	1759	2.38	55	129	2.36	82	197	2.40
		T	9628	23090	2.40	785	1866	2.38	1206	2850	2.36

Contd....

1	2	3	4	5	6	7	8	9	10	11	12
5.	3.0-4.0	M	4308	14751	3.42	294	1006	3.42	534	1824	3.41
		F	316	1081	3.42	19	67	3.44	38	128	3.40
		T	4633	15863	3.42	314	1073	3.42	572	1951	3.41
6.	4.0-5.0	M	2627	11632	4.43	158	698	4.43	333	1472	4.42
		F	176	777	4.43	10	43	4.41	23	102	4.39
		T	2809	12438	4.43	167	741	4.43	356	1574	4.42
7.	5.0-7.5	M	2840	17129	6.03	162	973	6.01	361	2163	5.98
		F	181	1086	5.99	9	53	6.05	25	144	5.75
		T	3028	18265	6.03	171	1026	6.01	385	2307	5.98
8.	7.5-10.0	M	1182	10067	8.52	59	499	8.51	148	1289	8.44
		F	69	586	8.54	3	26	8.52	9	72	8.44
		T	1255	10695	8.52	62	524	8.51	157	1321	8.44
9.	10.0-20.0	M	1079	14251	13.21	55	734	13.30	110	1436	13.04
		F	55	724	13.14	2	31	13.21	6	77	12.97
		T	1142	15089	13.21	57	765	13.30	116	1513	13.03
10.	20.0 & above	M	244	7709	31.60	13	386	30.44	18	527	28.73
		F	0	331	37.49	0	13	30.50	1	19	28.38
		T	262	9074	34.58	13	399	30.44	19	545	28.72
	All Sizes	M	104354	150219	1.44	13375	12471	0.93	8828	16369	1.86
		F	11012	11715	1.06	1314	935	0.71	696	1128	1.62
		T	115580	163357	1.41	14688	13406	0.91	9523	17524	1.84

Contd. . . .

1	2	3	4	5	6	7	8	9	10	11	12
1.	Marginal	M	63489	25398	0.40	9805	3506	0.36	4025	1973	0.49
		F	7569	5684	0.35	1040	329	0.32	351	157	0.45
		T	71179	28121	0.40	10844	3835	0.35	4376	2131	0.49
2.	Small	M	19713	27991	1.42	2099	2932	1.40	2174	3100	1.43
		F	1900	2688	1.41	176	244	1.39	162	232	1.43
		T	21643	30722	1.42	2275	3176	1.40	2336	3332	1.43
3.	Semi-Medium	M	13181	36042	2.73	1025	2744	2.68	1658	4477	2.70
		F	1055	2840	2.69	74	195	2.64	120	325	2.71
		T	14261	38953	2.73	1099	2939	2.67	1778	4802	5.70
4.	Medium	M	6649	38828	5.84	378	2170	5.74	842	4883	5.80
		F	425	2449	5.76	22	122	5.64	57	318	5.60
		T	7092	41398	5.84	400	2291	5.73	898	5202	5.79
5.	Larae	M	1323	21960	16.60	68	1119	16.50	128	1962	15.27
		F	64	1055	16.51	3	44	15.93	7	96	14.51
		T	1404	24163	17.21	71	1164	16.48	135	2058	15.24
6.	All Size	M	104354	150219	1.44	13375	12471	0.93	8828	16396	1.86
		F	11012	11715	1.06	1314	935	0.71	696	1128	1.62
		T	115580	163357	1.41	14688	13406	0.91	9523	17524	1.84
	%					12.7	8.21		0.10	10.73	

include Institutional holdings

Source : Government of India, Agricultural census 1995-96, 2004.

Table 4.5 : Land acquired under ceiling laws

Pre-revised and revised ceiling laws	As on 31.3.80	As on 31.3.85	As on 31.3.90	As on 31.3.95	As on 31.3.98
Areas declared surplus	69.13	72.07	72.25	74.10	73.74
Area taken possession	48.50	56.98	62.12	65.42	65.11
Area distributed	35.53	42.64	46.47	51.46	53.37

Source : Ministry of Rural Development, 1998-99

Table 4.6 : Target and achievement in Land reforms during the period between 1985-86 and 1998-99.

Area in Acres

	Target	*Achievements*
1985-86	125180	109245
1986-87	82278	90517
1987-88	270670	82198
1988-89	226479	134458
1989-90	191928	118112
1990-91	82200	89878
1991-92	119270	154067
1992-93	150720	111024
1993-94	598563	70887
1994-95	563860	75082
1995-96	79616	51886
1996-97	77230	25402
1997-98	52300	37362
1998-99 (Oct. 98)	91530	14990

Source : Ministry of Rural Development, 1998-99.

The Ceiling Surplus

One of the important measures of land reform in India was the distribution of land to landless rural households. This is done by acquiring land from landed section by imposing ceiling on their holding size. Since there was no limitation on one's acquiring land earlier i.e. before independence, individuals had acquired huge amount of land through various means. This eventually created widespread inequalities in society and as a result an overwhelming segment of rural society became landless or semi-landless. To mitigate this process the Congress Agrarian Reforms Committee suggested the following measures:

Optimum Holding : The Committee has also felt that there should be a ceiling to the size of holdings, which any one farmer should own and cultivate. In the first place, the supply of land, in relation to the number of people seeking it, is so limited that not to put a ceiling on individual holdings would be irrational and unjust. Secondly, under the present technique of cultivation, the managerial capacity and financial resources of an average cultivator in India, the optimum size of a holding has to be fairly low. The Committee has, therefore, recommended that the optimum size should be three times the size of the economic holding. Certain exceptions, however, have been allowed in cases of joint families and charitable institutions.

It is argued that the imposition of such ceilings to ownership in one sector of economy will create anomalies. The Committee, however, is competent to make recommendations only with regard to the agrarian economy but has every hope that a similar principle of distributive justice would be applied to other sectors of our economy.

Models of Farming

Family Farms : The Committee has recommended restricted* form of family farming for holdings between the Basic and the Optimum sizes. It is decided to lower the limit of family farming below the Economic size in the hope that the provision of multipurpose co-operative facilities would reduce to a great extent the inefficiency involved in farming on such units.

Co-operative Joint Farming—There is, however, a limit below which family farming even with all the co-operative aids implied in better farming ceases to be economic. The Committee has, therefore, recommended Co-operative Joint Farming for holdings below the basic size.

This, however, does not mean that all the below Basic Holdings in a village would be lumped into a single giant co-operative in which the cultivator may lose his individuality, a Co-operative Joint Farm can be formed, whenever the requisite number of below basic holders come together and constitute a holding of the optimum size.

The Committee is convinced that without these co-operative modules Better Farming for family farms and Joint Farming for holdings below basic, the efficiency of agriculture cannot be substantially increased. It has, therefore, recommended that the State should be empowered to enforce the application of varying degrees of co-operation for different types of farming. Thus, while the family farmer (holder of a farm between the Basic and the Optimum) will have to make use of the multipurpose co-operative society for marketing, credit, etc., the below-basic holder will have to cultivate his farm jointly with such other holders. The organisational and other difficulties involved in the implementation of the proposal, however, would necessitate its spread over a period of time. A beginning may be made in selected areas and its extension may be entrusted to specially trained persons under the planned direction and control of a Provincial Co-operative Farming Board. The gradualness of the programme, intelligent propaganda, liberal state-aid and its judicious implementation by a specially trained cadre would to a very great extent reduce the psychological hesitation of the farmer to take to the co-operative patterns recommended by the Committee. The Committee firmly believes that the agrarian traditions of this country are in favour and not against the Committee's recommendations.

Collective Farming—The Committee has recommended the Collective type of farming on a portion of reclaimed lands where landless agricultural labourers would be settled. This will to a certain extent help in satisfying the land hunger of the landless labourers and give an opportunity of the State to test the economics of mechanised farming. In the initial stages the State will have to provide the necessary resources. The Committee is of the opinion that individual settlements should on no account be allowed on newly reclaimed lands.

With regard to the land above the ceiling to holdings, subject to the rights of the tenants, the same should be used for the purposes of co-operative joint farming whenever such land can be obtained in a big bloc. When such land is available in scattered bits, it may be used for making uneconomic holdings economic.

State Farming—The Committee has also recommended the creation of state farms for the purpose of research and experimentation

Rights in Land

On the question of rights in land, the Committee is of the opinion that these should be shared between the community and the tiller. The idea of proprietorship in which the owner could use or misuse land as he likes is incongruous with the economic and social needs of our times. This, however, does not mean that the State should assume all the rights and authority leaving no scope for initiative on the part of the cultivator and for the development of his personality. The cultivator will have permanent, transferable and heritable right of cultivation subject to the following conditions:

(1) that he does not sublet his holding;

(2) that he transfers his holding according to well-defined priorities laid down by the appropriate authority and at a price which is reasonable and not speculative;

(3) that he conforms to the test of good husbandry and the scheme of crop-planning proposed from time to time by the Land Commission.

The rights vested in the community are to be exercised by the Land Commission through agencies at different levels, the basic one being the Village Panchayat elected on adult franchise and proportional representation. The Panchayat will be in charge of all the common assets of the village e.g. the waste land, village sites, tanks, forests, etc. It will also be responsible for the collection of land rates from the cultivators.

These recommendations did not get actualised. Though ceiling laws were passed in states, the loopholes in the implementation process finally did not yield the desired results. A large scale concealment took place through fraudulent transfers. Assessing the impact of ceiling legislation Appu observes :

All in all, the results achieved by the imposition of the ceiling have not been commensurate with the amount of time, money and labour invested in the operation.....the imposition of the ceiling on agricultural holdings in India is a case of inchoate policy, imperfect legislation and inefficient implementation. If only we had been a little more pragmatic and less hypocritical far better results could have been achieved (1996 : 179).

The Present Situation

Surplus Area Declared—The figures in Table 4.7 depict the amount of area declared surplus in different States and Union Territories in 2003. The column 4 in Table 4.7 shows the proportionate shares of each state and Union Territories. It appears from the data that among the States and Union Territories taken together, the proportion of area declared surplus was highest in West Bengal, it was almost one fifth of the total surplus area (18.77).

Table 4.7 : State/UT-wise Distribution of Ceiling Surplus Land as on March 31, 2002

(Area in acres)

Sl. No.	*States/Uts*	*Area Declared surplus*	*%*	*Area Taken possession*	*%*
1	2	3	4	5	6
1.	Andhra Pradesh	799663	10.85	641655	80.29
2.	Assam	613400	8.32	575377	93.48
3.	Bihar	415447	5.63	390752	94.06
4.	Gujarat	227404	3.08	160801	70.71
5.	Haryana	107487	1.46	103017	95.84
6.	Himachal Pradesh	316556	4.29	304895	96.32
7.	Jammu & Kashmir	455575	6.18	450000	98.78
8.	Karnataka	268478	3.64	161834	60.28
9.	Kerala	141427	1.92	96851	68.48
10.	Madhya Pradesh	298763	4.05	260323	87.13

Contd. . . .

1	2	3	4	5	6
11.	Maharashtra	740002	10.04	670449	90.60
12.	Manipur	1830	0.02	1685	92.08
13.	Orissa	179176	2.43	167253	93.35
14.	Punjab	223115	0.30	105834	47.43
15.	Rajasthan	611096	8.29	569211	93.15
16.	Tamil Nadu	200920	2.73	191628	
17.	Tripura	1995	0.03	1944	97.44
18.	Uttar Pradesh	374125	5.07	341464	91.27
19.	West Bengal	1383852	18.77	1294739	93.56
20.	D&N Haveli	9406	0.13	9305	96.93
21.	Delhi	1132	0.02	394	34.81
22.	Pondicherry	2326	0.03	1209	51.98
	Total	7373175	100.00	6500620	88.17

Source : Ministry of Rural Development, Annual Report : 2002-03, New Delhi, Govt. of India, 2003.

Table 4.8 : State/UT-wise Distribution of surplus area distributed to beneficiaries, total number of beneficiaries and per beneficiaries amount of land given.

(Area in acres)

Sl. No.	*States/Uts*	*Area Distributed to indiv. beneficiaric*	*%*	*Total No. of benef.*	*%*
1	2	3	4	5	6
1.	Andhra Pradesh	582319	72.82	540344	1.08
2.	Assam	545870	88.99	445848	1.22
3.	Bihar	306964	73.89	379528	0.81
4.	Gujarat	139853	61.50	32308	4.33
5.	Haryana	102123	95.01	29228	3.49
6.	Himachal Pradesh	6167	1.95	6259	0.99

Contd. . . .

1	2	3	4	5	6
7.	Jammu & Kashmir	450000	98.78	450000	1.00
8.	Karnataka	123204	45.89	33610	3.66
9.	Kerala	68745	48.61	166814	4.12
10.	Madhya Pradesh	186942	62.57	74705	2.50
11.	Maharashtra	642835	86.87	140850	4.56
12.	Manipur	1682	91.19	1258	1.34
13.	Orissa	156948	93.35	139595	1.12
14.	Punjab	104232	46.72	28574	3.65
15.	Rajasthan	461847	75.58	81808	5.65
16.	Tamil Nadu	181295	90.23	143683	1.26
17.	Tripura	1598	80.10	1424	1.12
18.	Uttar Pradesh	258698	69.15	294062	0.88
19.	West Bengal	1064044	76.89	2651619	0.44
20.	D&N Haveli	6851	72.84	3353	2.04
21.	Delhi	394	34.81	654	0.60
22.	Pondicherry	1070	46.00	1464	0.73
	Total	5393681	73.15	5646988	0.96

Source : Same as Table 4.7.

Next to West Bengal was Andhra Pradesh. The proportion of area declared surplus by the state constituted10.85 per cent. This state was followed by Maharashtra (10.04), Assam (8.32), Rajasthan (8.29), Jammu & Kashmir (6.18), Bihar (5.63) and Uttar Pradesh (5.7). The proportion of area declared surplus in other States and Union Territories varied between 4.29 per cent in Himachal Pradesh and 0.02 each in Manipur and Delhi in 2003.

Area Taken Possession : Declaration of surplus area does not resolve the problems of land relations. There are legal hurdles. Many holders of ceiling land go to courts and bring injections. This again leaves sizeable amount of land under litigations. The figures in column 6 in table 4.7 show the percentage of area taken possession by the respective States and Union Territories from the total area declared surplus in each of them. It may be seen that the proportion of area taken possession was highest in Jammu & Kashmir (98.78), followed by Tripura (97.44), Himachal Pradesh (96.32), Haryana (95.84) etc. Among States the lowest proportion of land taken possession of was in Punjab (47.43) and Karnataka

Table 4.9 : States/Uts-wise distribution of beneficiaries of surplus land distributed in the States and Union Territories.

Sl. No.	*Name of State/Uts*	*Percentage*
1.	Andhra Pradesh	9.57
2.	Assam	7.90
3.	Bihar	6.72
4.	Gujarat	0.57
5.	Haryana	0.52
6.	Himachal Pradesh	0.11
7.	Jammu & Kashmir	7.97
8.	Karnataka	0.60
9.	Kerala	2.95
10.	Madhya Pradesh	1.32
11.	Maharashtra	2.49
12.	Manipur	0.02
13.	Orissa	2.47
14.	Punjab	0.51
15.	Rajasthan	1.45
16.	Tamil Nadu	2.54
17.	Tripura	0.03
18.	Uttar Pradesh	5.21
19.	West Bengal	46.95
20.	D&N Haveli	0.06
21.	Pondicherry	0.03
22.	Pondicherry	0.03
	Total	100.00

Source : Same as Table 4.7

(60.28). The details of other States and Union Territories could be found in Table in Col. 6. At All-India level we may find that in 2003, that 88.17 per cent of the area declared surplus were taken possession.

Distribution Area to Beneficiaries : In Table 4.8 it could be noted that in 2003, out of the total area declared surplus, more than seventy three per cent of it were distributed to the individual beneficiaries, and of the area taken possession, the distributed area accounted for 82.97 per cent.

The data of the table also depict State/Union Territory-wise proportion of area distributed to the beneficiaries in the corresponding year. It may be seen that there are five States where the proportion of area distributed from the area taken possession of varied between 90.23 and 98.78. In another five States it varied between 70 and 90 per cent. In rest of the States/Union Territories it ranged from 40 per cent to 69 per cent.

Distribution of Beneficiaries : The data in Table 4.9 show the proportion of beneficiaries of surplus land distributed in the States and Union Territories.

Distribution of Beneficiaries by Castes

As is well known the majority of the disadvantaged rural labourers/agricultural labourers belong to the Scheduled Castes and Scheduled Tribes. They are also the most economically and socially vulnerable. Hence, special attention has been focused on them in terms enabling them by providing access to productive and sustainable means like distribution of land among them.

Table 4.10 : Number of Scheduled castes and scheduled tribes beneficiaries : 2002.

Total no. of Beneficiaries	*No. of SC Beneficiaries*	*No. of ST Beneficiaries*	*Total SC/ST Benefiaries*
5646988	2030221	830386	2860607
	(35.95)	(14.70)	(50.65)

Note : Figure in brackets indicate percentages from total

Source : Same Table 4.7

The figures in Table 4.10 depict the proportion of the Scheduled Castes and Scheduled Tribes to whom suplus land was given in 2003. Out of the total beneficiaries more than 50 per cent were Scheduled Castes and Scheduled Tribes beneficiaries. Of 50.65 per cent, the Scheduled Castes accounted for 35.95 per cent while the share of the Scheduled Tribes accounted for 14.70.

Distribution of Area by Castes

In 2002 out of the total ceiling surplus land distributed, 33.33 and 14.44 per cent were distributed to the scheduled Castes and SCheduled Tribes respectively. However, more than half (52.22) went to other beneficiaries (Table 4.11).

Table 4.11 : Area Distributed to SC/ST beneficiaries : 2002

Total Area	*Area Distributed to SC*	*Area Distributed to ST*	*Others*
5393681	1797859	779347	2816475
(100.00)	(33.33)	(14.44)	(52.22)

Note : Figures in brackets indicate percentage from total

Source : Same as Table 4.7

State-wise Distribution of Ceiling Surplus Land

The figures in Table 4.12 show the pattern of distribution of ceiling surplus land among the three category of beneficiaries like, the Scheduled Castes, the Scheduled Tribes, and others. The table reveals that in 2002 the highest nuimber of beneficiaries of all the categories were concentrated in West Bengal alone. In some other states their preponderances were also substantial.

Tenancy Profile

One of the important aspects of land reform was also tenancy reform. Tefnancy reform had to be undetaken because a large segment of land was cultivated under this agrarian relation. With the introduction of the Permanent Settlement and gradual transformation of economy under the colonial regime, the tenancy system gradually became an important land relation plank.Under this system the tenants were at the mercy of the landowners. With growing land scarcity the terms and conditions of tenancy were always decided by the landlords. The conditions of the tenants became so uncertain that the colonial government had to pass an

Table 4.12 : State-wise Distribution of surplus land among Scheduled Castes and Scheduled Tribes Beneficiaries as on March 2002.

(Area in acres)

SC/ST Beneficiaries				Other Beneficiaries	
SC Beneficiaries		ST Beneficiaries			
No.	Area	No.	Area	No.	Area
1	2	3	4	5	6
225932	231179	83688	121085	230724	230055
43720	86068	42361	58985	359767	400817
234861	182045	43050	39978	101617	84941
14915	84467	13267	29608	4126	25778
12522	43405	NA	NA	16706	58718
3912	2727	329	245	2018	3195
NA	NA	NA	NA	450000	450000
20285	73991	1248	4331	12077	44882
70853	26619	8990	7248	86971	34878
21904	49542	28138	73379	24663	64021
42128	163742	29528	98675	69194	380418
96	128	72	97	1090	1457
48059	49975	51390	65682	40146	41291
11351	44247	NA	NA	17223	59985
29656	144357	11586	49957	40566	267533
64239	68704	204	274	79240	112317
256	217	359	449	809	933
200320	180193	699	1195	93043	77310
983829	365283	512156	221365	1155634	477396
30	53	3321	6795	2	3
495	277	NA	NA	159	117
858	640	NA	NA	606	430
2030221	1797859	830386	779347	2786381	2816475

Source : Same as Table 4.7

act in 1859, known as the Rent Act of 1859. This was followed by the Bengal Tenancy Act 1885.

After independence some efforts have been made to confer some permanent rights to the tenants. In this regard, West Bengal has been in the forefront. The famous "Operation Barga" has indeed been a successful step in the state to detect tenancy and confer to a greater extent some permanent right to the land cultivated by the tenants.

Today still there is a substantial anount of land which is cultivated under tenancy system. It may also be mentioned that yet there remains a large number of tenants who are unrecorded and the area cultivated by them is not available on record.

The figures in Table 4.13 present the scenario of tenancy in the country today. It may be observed in the table that in 2002 a total 124.22 lakh tenants were conferred ownership rights and the area accured to them was 156.30 lack acres. The average area worked out 1.26 acre. The State where highest number of tenant conferred ownership right was Assam, followed by Kerala, West Bengal, Gujarat and Maharashtra.

Table 4.13 : Number of tenants conferred ownership rights (or rights protected) and area accured to them (As on 31.3.2002).

Sl. No.	*States*	*No. of Tenants (In lakhs)*	*Area Accured (lack acres)*
	1	2	3
1.	Andhra Pradesh 1.07	5.95	
2.	Arunachal Pradesh	System not prevalent	
3.	Assam	29.08	31.75
4.	Bihar*	NR	NR
5.	Gujarat	12.76	25.92
6.	Goa	NR	NR
7.	Haryana	Tenancy not prevalent	
8.	Himachal Pradesh	4.01	NR
9.	Jammu & Kashmir	6.10	NR
10.	Karnataka	6.05	26.32
11.	Kerala	28.42	14.50
12.	Madhya Pradesh#	Tenancy not prevalent	

Contd. . . .

1	2	3
13. Maharashtra	14.92	42.90
14. Manipur	NR	NR
15. Meghalaya	Nil	Nil
16. Mizoram	Nil	Nil
17. Nagaland	NR	NR
18. Orissa	1.65	0.98
19. Punjab	NR	NR
20. Rajasthan	0.18	NR
21. Sikkim	NR	NR
22. Tamil Nadu	4.98	6.95
23. Tripura	0.14	0.39
24. Uttar Pradesh@	NR	NR
25. West Bengal	14.60	NR
Union Territories		
26. A.N. Islands	Nil	Nil
27. Chandigarh	NR	NR
28. D&N Haveli	0.26	0.64
29. Delhi	NR	NR
30. Daman & Diu	NR	NR
31. Lakshadweep	Neg	Neg
32. Pondicherry	Neg	Neg
All India	**124.22**	**156.30**

NR Not reported

* Including Jharkhand

Including Chhattisgarh

@ Including Uttaranchal

Source : Same as Table 4.7

Again, as regards the area accrued to tenants is concerned, only four states, namely, Assam, Gujarat, Jammu & Kashmir, Madhya Pradesh and Karnataka, Tenants are accrued land area between

25 lakh acre to 43 lakh acres and in rest of the states they accured below one lakh acre to maximum 15 lakh acre land area.

From the table it can be realised that the not only number of states where this system is prevalent are less than fifty percent but also the states in which this system is prevalent not only the no. of

Table 4.14 : Statement showing the total number of cases and area involved in litigation as on 31st March 2002

(Area in acres)

Sl. No.	State/Uts	Total number of cases and the area involved in litigation			
		No. of cases	% of total	Area involved	%
1.	Andhra Pradesh	2744	17.74	147631	16.35
2.	Assam	112	0.72	38461	4.26
3.	Bihar	1837	11.87	NA	—
4.	Gujarat	1358	8.78	69606	7.71
5.	Haryana	272	1.75	4599	0.50
6.	Himachal Pradesh	5	0.03	8072	0.89
7.	Jammu & Kashmir	NA	—	NA	—
8.	Karnataka	1692	10.94	129244	14.32
9.	Kerala	1020	6.59	25316	2.80
10.	Madhya Pradesh	1154	7.46	79475	8.80
11.	Maharashtra	581	3.75	31384	3.47
12.	Manipur	NA	—	NA	—
13.	Orissa	NA	—	12787	1.41
14.	Punjab	1092	7.06	24591	2.72
15.	Rajasthan	972	6.28	78823	8.73
16.	Tamil Nadu	NA	—	9292	1.02
17.	Tripura	8	0.05	59	0.006
18.	Uttar Pradesh	2563	16.57	50118	5.55
19.	West Bengal	NA	—	191841	21.25
20.	D&N Haveli	NA	—	NA	—
21.	Delhi	13	0.08	183	0.02
22.	Pondicherry	43	0.27	1026	0.11
	Total	15466		902508	

Source : Same as Table 4.7

tenants are very low but also very-very low and fact is that even after implementation of this land ownership protection act implemented in favour of tenants is more dramatic than realistic because such a meagre land area may not help much to provide them at least the survival rights in the rural area.

The Litigation

Table 4.14 relates to the total number of cases and area involved in litigation till March 31, 2002, It shows that of the total 22 States and Union Territories, in 6 States no information is available on litigation cases and in Andhra Pradesh and Uttar Pradesh highest number of (above 2500) cases are found involved in litigation. In Himachal Pradesh, Tripura, Delhi and Pondicherry, the numbers lie between 1 to 1000 and rest of the States the number of cases lie between 500 to 2000.

The table also shows that in states like Andhra Pradesh and West Bengal land area involved is highest i.e. between 1.0 to 2.0 lakh acre and most of the states land area involved is 8 thousand to 80 thousand acres except in Tripura and Delhi where it falls between 59 and 183 acres of land area. It can be observed from the table that where more litigation cases are involved either people are more aware about the land ownership or land is distributed in haphazard manner without following any rules and regulations and made no justification to their basic survival rights.

Distribution of Bhoodan Land

Table 4.15 on Bhoodan land shows that of the 17 States, Himachal Pradesh, Jammu & Kashmir and West Bengal, no land was donated and distributed, only in Bihar an amount of (21.18 lakh acres) of land was donated and rest of the states land area donated falls between 0.01 to 6.39 lakh acre.

However, it is only in the states like, Bihar, Orissa and Uttar Pradesh where between 4 to 7 lakh acres of the land were distribute to their needy inhabitants and in rest of the states land distributed falls between 10 lakh acres to 2.0 lakh acres only. Table 4.15 shows that out of the total land area (39.16 lakh acre), 17.41 lakh acre is still lying idle.

Table 4.15 : Distribution of Bhoodan Land(upto March, 2002)

(Area in lakh acres)

Sl. No.	States	Area Donated	%	Distributed	%	Balance
1.	Andhra Pradesh	2.52	6.43	1.10	43.65	1.42
2.	Assam	0.01	0.02	0.01	100.00	Nil
3.	Bihar*	21.18	54.08	7.23	34.13	13.95
4.	Gujarat	0.34	0.86	0.27	79.41	0.07
5.	Haryana	0.02	0.05	0.02	100.00	Nil
6.	Himachal Pradesh	Neg.	—	Neg.	—	Neg.
7.	Jammu & Kashmir	Neg.	—	Neg.	—	Neg.
8.	Karnataka	0.11	0.28	0.05	45.45	0.06
9.	Kerala	0.02	0.05	0.02	100.00	Nil
10.	Madhya Pradesh#	1.72	4.39	1.41	81.97	0.31
11.	Maharashtra	1.04	2.65	0.27	25.96	0.77
12.	Orissa	6.39	16.31	5.80	90.76	0.59
13.	Punjab	0.05	0.12	0.01	20.00	0.04@
14.	Rajasthan	1.15	2.93	1.14	99.13	0.01
15.	Tamil Nadu	0.24	0.61	0.21	87.50	0.03
16.	Uttar Pradesh%	4.37	11.15	4.21	96.33	0.16
17.	West Bengal	Neg.	—	Neg.	—	Neg.
	Total	39.16		21.75		17.41

@ Area not taken possession

* Including Jharkhand

Including Chhattisgarh

% Including Uttaranchal

Source : Same as Table 4.7

Distribution of Waste Land

Table 4.16 shows that Government has distributed 147.47 lakh acres area of waste land in 21 States and Union Territories. Highest amount of land is distributed in Andhra Pradesh (42.02) and Uttar Pradesh (24.89), Bihar, Gujarat and Maharashtra it is above 10.0 lakh acres and in some states it is 42.0 lakh acre.

Table 4.16 : Distribution of Government Wastelands as on March, 2002.

S.No.	*Name of State/UT*	*Area Distributed in Lakh Acres*	*Percentage from total*
1.	Andhra Pradesh	42.02	28.49
2.	Assam	5.89	3.99
3.	Bihar*	13.21	8.95
4.	Gujarat	13.81	9.36
5.	Haryana	0.00	—
6.	Himachal Pradesh	0.17	0.11
7.	Karnataka	13.72	9.30
8.	Kerala	4.57	3.09
9.	Madhya Pradesh#	0.79	0.53
10.	Maharashtra	10.23	6.93
11.	Manipur	0.32	0.20
12.	Punjab	1.10	0.74
13.	Orissa	7.26	4.92
14.	Tamil Nadu	2.07	1.40
15.	Tripura	1.32	0.89
16.	Uttar Pradesh %	24.89	16.87
17.	West Bengal	4.32	2.92
18.	Goa	0.05	0.03
19.	Mizoram	0.74	0.50
20.	Rajasthan	0.93	0.63
21.	Delhi	0.06	0.04
	Total	147.47	100.00

* Including Jharkhand

\# Including Chattisgarh

@ Including Uttaranchal

Source : Same as Table 4.7

Consolidation of Holdings

Table 4.17 shows that the total area consolidated till March 2002 works out to be 1633.47 lakh acres; and maximum area was consolidated in Madhya Pradesh (526.50), followed by Uttar Pradesh (481.63), Orissa (121.81) and Gujarat (104.38) and rest of the states land consolidated falls below that of the total 32 states and union territories (see Box 4.1).

Table 4.17 : Consolidation of Land Holdings State-wise as on March 2002

(Area in lakh Acres)

S.No.	States/Uts	Area Consolidated	%
1.	Andhra Pradesh	8.18*	0.50
2.	Bihar	96.05*	5.88
3.	Gujarat	69.98*	4.28
4.	Haryana	104.38	6.39
5.	Himachal Pradesh	29.91	1.83
6.	Jammu & Kashmir	1.37*	0.08
7.	Karnataka	26.76#	1.63
8.	Madhya Pradesh	95.53	5.84
9.	Maharashtra	526.50$	32.23
10.	Orissa	26.74	1.63
11.	Punjab	121.81	7.47
12.	Rajasthan	42.30@	2.58
13.	Uttar Pradesh	481.63	29.48
14.	Delhi	2.33	0.14
	Total	1633.47	100.00

* Scheme has been discontinued (in Andhra Pradesh from 1966, in Bihar and Gujarat from 1992).

Consolidation of holding Act, 1966 has been repealed in 1991

@ Scheme discontinued from 1965

$ Implementation of the scheme stopped w.e.f. 1.4.93

Source : Same as Table 4.7

Box 4.1 : Relevance of Agrarian Reform

Agrarian reforms have been a core issue for Rural Reconstruction as a means of ensuring social justice to actual tillers and the landless rural poor, there by creating a sustainable base for the overall growth of the industrial and tertiary sectors of our economy. Generating greater access of landless rural poor to land is considered an important component of poverty alleviation.

The major objective of Land Reforms have been the reordering of agrarian relations in order to achieve an egalitarian social structure, elimination of exploitation in land relations, realising the age old goal of land to the tiller, enlarging the land base of the rural poor, increasing agricultural productivity and infusing an element of equality in local institutions.

Source : Government of India, *Annual Report, 2002-03*. Ministry of Rural Development, p. 10.

Land Reforms and Women

Since one of the obvious purpose of land reforms is social justice, then the question of gender becomes pertinent. So far this issue did not get much attention in the policy of land reforms. From time immemorial women's rights to land has been virtually ignored. No specific policy and conferment measures have yet been adopted to mitigate this injustice committed against women for centuries. As a result of this single most deprivation women have remained in a marginal position in almost all spheres of life. Only recently some states like Karnataka, Tamil Nadu and Andhra Pradesh have amended the Hindu Succession Act 1956 to formalize issues relating to providing right to land and other properties. Some other states have also drawn up plans to give greater access to land and other properties by following respective religious communities personal law. But to what extent these efforts have been succeeded is yet to be ascertained. So far no evaluation has been undertaken to examine the implementation process of there steps. In this respect it is worth quoting here the observation made by the working group on Land Reforms for the Eighth Five Year Plan: 1990-1995 :

The need for ensuring access of women to land and its resources can hardly be over-emphasized. The group has noted that the 6th

Plan recommendation to husband and wife has also not been implemented by all states. Most states have not shown requisite seriousness in dealing with the problem of providing women with access to land. The male dominated social structure still tends to influence government policies in this respect (Ministry of Agriculture, 1989 : 74). Keeping in view the tardy progress in regard to providing women greater access to land the working group made some very important recommendations which are being cited below:

(a) The concept of joint ownership of husband and wife in the matter of allotment of surplus ceiling/Government/ Bhoodan land should be followed in the matter of distribution of other productive assets also

(b) Government of India in consultation with Reserve Bank should evolve a suitable mechanism for ensuring that requisite share of credit from public financial institutions is available to women beneficiaries.

(c) States should review that present arrangement with regard to recording of share of women right-holders in land records and other assets and take necessary steps to see that rights of women are duly recorded in accordance with law.

(d) Wherever rights and interests in regard to sharecropping, collection of minor forest produce, uses of common property resources are recorded in the record of rights, steps should be taken to ensure that the names of both male and female spouse are entered in the concerned records.

(e) In the allotment of Government land/surplus ceiling land and house sites, at least 40 per cent of reservation should be made for eligible women beneficiaries. The remaining pattas should be issued in the joint names of husband and wife. Some states in the South are reportedly issuing all pattas in the name of female member of the household. This could be emulated by other states. Among the eligible women beneficiaries, preference should be give to women head of households, unmarried tribal and Scheduled Castes women who are victims of harassment/rape, etc.

(f) Primacy should be given to women beneficiaries on individual as well as group basis in issue of tree pattas under social forestry schemes on Govt./village/forest land. Even among the women beneficiaries, tribals and Scheduled Caste women should be given priority.

(g) Women beneficiaries should be associated with committees/Groups wherever constituted for looking into policies or assisting in the implementation of land reform programmes.

(h) Wherever in the past, patta in respect of surplus ceiling/Government/Bhoodan land has been issued in the name of male head of the household only, steps may be taken to convert these pattas into joint pattas in a phased manner. If necessary, legal provisions may be made in advance so that no difficulties are experienced while giving effect to this recommendation.

(i) Thorough investigations should be carried out into the methods through which tribal women are deprived of their land through such methods as illegal marriages, concubinage and other fraudulent methods by non-tribal men. Stringent legal provisions should be made to protect the rights of such women and for restoration of alienated land to them.

(j) Where tribal women face harassment in the matter of enjoying their cutomary rights in land, a satisfactory institutional mechanism, if necessary with legal backing, should be devised in consultation with tribal community with a view to protect their interest against such harassment and facilitating enjoyment of their rights.

(k) Women on a group basis should be assigned the responsibility for management of village common lands/forest lands where social forestry programmes are taken up for providing fuelwood, fodder and other facilities.

(l) In north eastern states, where women enjoy much better access to land and its resources than in the rest of the country, recent changes in agrarian relations are eroding this position. Some State Governments are also unwittingly aiding this process by alloting land in the name of the male member of the household on the pattern of the rest of the country and apparently under pressure from men of these areas. It needs to be studied urgently how the position of women's access to land is undergoing changes in areas governed by communal land tenure systems and what effective legal/administrative steps should be taken to protect rights of women therein.

(m) There are some provisions in Agrarian/Reform laws of states which tend to discriminate against women notwithstanding the right of equality enshrined in the Constitution and even conceded under the Personal Law of most communities. Such discriminatory legal provisions should be identified and appropriate measures may be initiated to undo this discrimination.

(n) The bias against women in the administrative machinery deprives women even of the rights which are available to them under law of the benefits they are entitled to under development programmes. Suitable Orientation Programmes should be built into the training syllabi of officers and staff engaged in implementation of land reforms for counteracting this bias.

(o) A massive programme for creating awareness among women should be taken up so that they can form their own organisations and exert requisite pressure on the Administrative machinery and political set up.

Tiny plots.

Under this circumstances, there are two options-either to encourage the beneficiaries to pool their tiny plots together to cultivate on cooperative basis or develop mechanism to help the beneficiaries to cultivate their land on their own through provision of facilities which are required to make their land produce as per the substantial landowners' land.

Without addressing this issues, it would be impossible to achieve equity in distribution of development benefits across gender and other section of society.

The De facto Position

According to Agricultural Census 1995-96, the total number of operational holdings was 115.58 million. Out of these holdings possessed by female was 11.01 million which accounted for 9.53 per cent of the total holdings.

With regards to possessing operational area by female, out of the total area of 163.35 million hectare, they owned only 1.17 million hactare. This worked out to be only 7.17 per cent of the total area (for detailed see Table 4.18).

Table 4.18 : All India Distribution of Number of Operational holdings and Area Operated by Size Group, Social Groups & Gender (in percentage)

(Number in '000, Area in '000 hectare)

Sl. No.	Social Group/ Gender	Marginal		Small		Semi-medium		Medium		Large		Total	
		Number	Area	Number	Area	Number	Area	Number	Area	Number	Area	Number	Area
1.	*Scheduled Caste Holdings*												
	Male	90.41	91.41	92.27	92.32	93.27	93.35	94.60	94.69	96.08	96.21	91.06	93.03
	Female	9.59	8.59	7.73	7.68	6.73	6.65	5.40	5.31	3.92	3.79	8.94	6.97
	Total	100.00	100.00	100.00	100.00	100.00	100.00	100.00	100.00	100.00	100.00	100.00	100.00
2.	*Scheduled Tribe Holdings*												
	Male	91.98	92.62	93.06	93.05	93.26	93.23	93.78	93.88	95.11	95.34	92.70	93.56
	Female	8.02	7.38	6.94	6.95	6.74	6.77	6.33	6.12	4.89	4.66	7.31	6.44
	Total	100.00	100.00	100.00	100.00	100.00	100.00	100.00	100.00	100.00	100.00	100.00	100.00
3.	*Others #*												
	Male	88.74	89.91	90.65	90.69	92.22	92.34	93.68	93.72	93.96	90.15	89.91	91.64
	Femal	11.04	9.92	9.17	9.14	7.56	7.43	5.99	5.92	4.55	4.37	9.85	7.29
	Total	100.00	100.00	100.00	100.00	100.00	100.00	100.00	100.00	100.00	100.00	100.00	100.00
4.	*All Social Groups #*												
	Male	89.20	90.32	91.08	91.11	92.43	92.53	93.74	93.79	94.18	90.88	90.29	91.96
	Female	10.63	9.54	8.78	8.75	7.40	7.29	6.00	5.91	4.55	4.37	9.53	7.17
	Total	100.00	100.00	100.00	100.00	100.00	100.00	100.00	100.00	100.00	100.00	100.00	100.00

#Include Institutional Holdings

Source : Government of India, Agricultural Census 1995-96, 2004.

5

Agriculture and Rural Development

Agriculture and Rural Development

Agricultural development is synonymous with rural development but rural development is not synonymous with the development of rural labourers, particularly the agricultural labourers who constitute the largest segment of rural labour force.

Agricultural development means growth of foodgrains and non-food crops, extension of irrigation facilities, introduction of modern technology, increase in livestock, etc. The overall development of these sectors may lead to increasing volume of production, and consequently rural development. But the fruits of development may not be shared equally by all the stakeholders. For, the stake of different holders are different in many respects. We shall make an attempt here to examine how, despite tremendous development of agriculture during the last five decades of rural development the conditions of a substantial segment of rural laboures, particularly the agricultural labourers have remained abysmally low in terms of equality and standard of life.

Foodgrains

In 1964-65 the total foodgrains production in the country was 89.36 million tones. This increased to 211.32 million tones in 2001-02, which worked out to 57.71 per cent over 1964-65. Table 5.1 shows that during Fourth Five Year Plan (1973-74) 104.67 mil. tons. of foodgrains were produced and since then till the Ninth Plan, the production continued to rise, and it was 211.32 ml. tons. in 2001-02.

Table 5.1 : Foodgrains Production during various Five Year Plans.

(Million tones)

Comm-dity	*IV Plan (1973-74)*	*V Plan (1978-79)*	*VI Plan (1984-85)*	*VII Plan (1989-90)*	*VIII Plan (1996-97)*	*IX Plan (2001-02)*
Rice	44.05	53.77	58.34	73.57	81.74	91.61
Wheat	21.78	35.51	44.07	49.85	69.35	71.47
Coarse Cereals	28.83	30.44	31.17	34.76	34.10	34.72
Pulses	10.01	12.18	11.96	12.86	14.24	13.52
Total Foodgrains	104.67	131.90	145.54	171.04	199.44	211.32

Source : Government of India (2002) Tenth Five Year Plan : 2002-2007 Sectorial Policies and Programmes, Volume II. New Delhi, Planning Commission.

The figures in the table also indicate the pattern of growth of individual foodgrain. For example, the growth of rice more than doubled during the period between 1973-74 and 2001-02.

However the growth rates with regard to coarse cereals and pulses recorded marginal increase as during the years highlighted in the table. Even though wheat and rice production has shown very high rate of growth, the near stagnant production of pulses and coarse cereals demonstrates clearly the declining per capital consumption of pulses over the years in the country.

Several factors have contributed to such an all-round growth in agriculture such as :

> increase in net sown area; expansion of irrigation facilities; land reforms, especially consolidation of holdings; development and introduction of high yielding seeds, fertilizers, improved implements and farm machines, technology for pest management; price policy based on MSP and procurement operations; infrastructure for storage/cold storage; improvements in trade system; increase in investments, etc. (GOI, 2002 : 514).

It may be noted here, however, that despite this success still there remains much more potential than whatever has been realised. For instance, per hectare production of paddy in India is still lower than the production in some countries, for example, China, Japan, USA, etc.

With regard to wheat though per hectare production was close to these countries, yet the gap in yield level is still quite high. The figures in Table 5.2 clearly highlight this picture.

Table 5.2 : Comparative Yield of principal Crops in various Countries (1999).

(Kg. per hect.)

Country	*Paddy*	*Wheat*	*Maize*	*Ground Nut*	*Sugar Cane*
India	2929	2583	1667	913	68012
China	6321	3969	4880	2799	85294
Japan	6414	—	—	2336	—
USA	6622	2872	8398	3038	80787
Indonesia	4261	—	2646	1523	—
Canada	—	2591	7974	—	—
Vietnam	4105	—	—	1435	—
World Average	3845	2711	4313	1336	65689

Source : Same as Table 5.1

Apart from this lower per unit production in agriculture, the country has suffered from the following impediments, such as :

Proportion of outlay in agriculture has been declining since Five Year Plan. In the First Five Year Plan the percentage of plan outlay was 14.9 which declined to 11.3 per cent in Second Five Year Plan. It, however, rose to 16.7 and 16.4 per cent in Annual Plans in 1966-69 and 1979-80. Table 5.3 depicts the pattern of share of plan outlay by Agriculture and Allied Sector from First to Tenth Five Year Plan.

Soil conditions have deteriorated due to excessive use of ground water and imbalance use of fertilisers. "The organic matter content in the soil has gone down because of less use of organic inputs and micro nutrient deficiency has become alarming" (GOI, 2002 : 515).

Highlighting the problem of mismanagement of natural resources the Tenth Plan document observes:

Table 5.3 : Plan Outlay in Agriculture and Allied Sectors

(Rs. Crores)

Plans	*Total Plan Outlay*	*Agriculture and Allied Sectors*	*% of Agriculture & Allied Sectors to Total*
I Plan (1951-56)*	2378	354	14.9
II Plan (1956-61)*	4500	501	11.3
III Plan (1961-66)*	8577	1089	12.7
Annual Plans (1966-69)	6625	1107	16.7
IV Plan (1969-74)**	15779	2320	14.7
V Plan (1974-79)	39426	4865	12.3
Annual Plan 1979-80	12177	1997	16.4
VI Plan (1980-85)	97500	5695	5.8
VII Plan (1985-90)	180000	10525	5.9
Annual Plan (1990-91)	58369	3405	5.8
Annual Plan (1991-92)	64751	3851	6.0
VIII Plan (1992-97)	434100	22467	5.2
IX Plan (1997-2002)	859200	42462	4.9
X Plan (2002-07)	398890	20668	5.2

* Includes Animal Husbandry, Special Area Programme, Rural Development and Forestry and Wildlife.

** Includes buffer stocks of Rs. 140 crores for 1968-69, Rs. 24 crore for 1969-70, Rs. 50 crore for 1971-72 and Rs. 25 crore for 1972-73 and Rs. 24 crore for 1973-74. Thus the figures for V plan work out to Rs. 124 crore against the original plan provision of Rs. 225 crore.

Source : Same as Table 5.1

Natural resources like land and water have not received the attention they deserve. The sustainable development of land and water resources becomes all the more important for the nation like India, which shares about 16 per cent of the global population but has only 2.4 per cent of the total land and 4 per cent of the total water resource. Scarcity of water in rainfed areas causing serious hardships. Ground water resources are dwindling fast due to poor water harvesting leading to excessive run off and poor recharging of ground water. This is accompanied by excessive drawl/exploitation mainly to the household needs of growing population as also irrigation needs of high yielding crops. *The number of dark blocks/mandals where there is over exploitation of ground water (over 85 per cent) is increasing in most of the States with large rainfed areas (Andhra Pradesh, Karnataka, Rajasthan, Madhya Pradesh, Chattisgarh etc.). Between 1984-85 and 1998-99 the number of dark blocks increased from 253 to 428* (emphasis is ours). If this continues, the number of over exploited blocks will double over a period of every twelve year and a half years. The drinking water problem in some of the areas has persisted largely due to the adoption of cropping patterns with high water demanding crops. The hydrological chain has been disrupted and needs to be restored on priority. Effective groundwater recharging measures as also regulations for sustainable exploitation need to be put in place on an urgent basis (GOI, 2002 : 516).

Land Degradation

India has a huge geographical area. And a vast proportion of this area is available for present cultivation purpose. But has also a vast area which has left degraded due to abuse and misuse. For instance :

Out of the geographical area of 328.73 million ha(mha), an area of about 107.4 m.ha is estimated to be degraded. Under the programmes of Department of Agriculture and Cooperation, Department of Land Resources and Ministry of Environment and Forests and other programmes, up to the end of the Eighth Plan, only 17.96 m.ha. had been covered/treated. A sizeable area of degraded/rainfed land needs soil conservation, water harvesting and vegetative cover (GOI, 2002 : 516).

Irrigation Resources

The Development of agriculture is absolutely dependent on irrigation. It is life line of any development effort. Without proper irrigation facility and also its proper use a sustained agricultural development is unimaginable. In this area the country's efforts have remained much to be desired. This is evident from the present irrigation situation in the country :

The availability of inputs and their use in agriculture has remained sub-optimal. Only about 40 per cent of the net sown area of 142.8 m. ha could be brought under irrigation and the remaining is dependent on rains. The larger dependence of crops on monsoon has adversely affected the use of inputs and adoption of improved crop production technologies, because of high risk involved in crop production and low/no profit margin. (Ibid).

Some other problems which have been exerting debilitating impact on agriculture could be summed up as lack of proper seeds, imbalanced application of chemical fertilizers, improper application of pesticides, unsatisfactory farm machinery, outmoded information support system, declining factor productivity, unfavourable terms of trade, etc. The observations by the Planning Commission on the above clearly bring into sharp relief those problems

Seed availability and seed replacement rates (SRRs) for most of the crops remained inadequate and below the desired levels. There is also a mismatch in availability and demand of seeds of different varieties, especially in case of crops varieties specific to the problem areas. The average fertiliser consumption at 92 kg/ha remained low and imbalanced in terms of the use of [Nitrogen, Phosphorous and Potash (NP&K)] (6.69:2.59:1.0) (2001-02). The per hectare fertiliser use remained very low in some States, especially northeastern States, Himachal Pradesh (42 kg), Orissa (47 kg), Rajasthan (35 kg) and undivided Madhya Pradesh (29 kg). Besides, the increasing deficiency of micro nutrients, especially zinc, iron, etc. in the soil has been observed in recent years.

Though the consumption of pesticides seems to have declined, because of the propagation of the integrated Pest Management (IPM) approach and the increasing awareness about the hazards of pesticides, the availability of quality pesticides remained a matter of concern. The infrastructure for enforcing the provisions of the Insecticide Act, 1968, also remained inadequate.

The availability of quality farm machines and implements has remained unsatisfactory. The reservation of the manufacture of agriculture machinery and implements for the small-scale industries (SSIs) seems to have also adversely affected the development of this sector. Although the use of tractors in agriculture has increased rapidly, the availability of the right type of mechines and implements, which could help reduce drudgery, adoption of modern technologies and precision farming has remained grossly inadequate. Because of inefficient farming operations, the cost of production has also remained high as compared to the developed countries.

The agriculture extension machinery and information support in most States seems to have become outmoded. The staff created under the World Bank assisted Training and Visits (T&V) programme do not have much mobility. The need to revamp the extension services in the country by using print and electronic media and information technology along with the involvement of the private sector is being felt increasingly. The private sector, especially the input agencies and traders, are now one of the main sources of information for the farmers. Radio, television and the print media have become powerful means of education and technology dissemination.

Growth in Total Factor Productivity (TFP) seems to has declined suggesting a drop in the force of technology impact. Inadequate storage/cold storage facilities affected post-harvest handling processing and value addition. On top of this, poor marketing support, delay in announcing MSP, non-realisation of MSP/ remunerative prices affected the profitability of the farmers and diversification.

The share of agriculture in GDP has declined from 61 per cent in 1950-51 to 24.2 per cent (TE 2001-02), whereas the dependence of population on agriculture has declined only marginally from 77 per cent to 69 per cent during the period. In all the developed countries, there has been a major shift of population from agriculture as an occupation to other sectors. However, this has not happened in India. Secondly, the average size of holdings has reduced from 2.28 ha in 1970-71 to 1.57 hain 1990-91. So, the pressure on per unit of land has increased by about 2.25 times.

The terms of trade have generally remained unfavourable to agriculture. The Commission for Agricultural Costs and Prices (CACP) in its 'Report for the crops sown during 2000-2001 season' has made following observations :

"....in the period before 1975, the terms of trade fluctuated considerably with declines during 1952-63, a sharp upturn during the mid-sixties, a high average level during 1964-74 and sharp fall again in 1975-76. As compared to this, the trend has been much more stable after 1980, with a slow upward trend. It may be noted that since the terms of trade came into the Commission's terms of reference the stability it has shown is unusual by international standards and exhibits much less volatility than elsewhere. Also, the upward trend is counter to the general trend of international agricultural prices to fall relative to those of manufacture. According to the World Bank, the real international price of agricultural commodities (i.e. relative to manufactures) fell by 45 per cent between 1980 and 1998. Thus, the Indian price policy has ensured a much more stable price environment for farmers and has also protected them so far from the terms of trade losses being suffered by farmers elsewhere." (GOI, 2002 : 16-17).

The Crux : Lack of Investment

Investment by the government in agriculture is most important for its growth and development. Investment in irrigation, electricity, agricultural research, roads, markets and communication finally decides the pace of growth of agriculture and this subsequently leads to rural development and if the development process is based on equity it will eventually lead to development of disadvantaged rural workers by increasing their income and by providing greater access to different opportunities and services. Despite the fact that the number of absolute number of poor has not declined from what it was in 1951 (200 million), the government has slowed down investment in agriculture. For instance, investment in agriculture declined from 1.6 per cent of GDP in 1993-94 to 1.3 per c ent in 1998-99 (Table- 5.1.4) : This decline was due to a fall in public investment from Rs. 4,467 crore in 1993-94 to Rs. 3,869 crore in 1998-99. There has, in fact, been a continuous decline in public investment in agriculture from 1995-96 till 1998-99. Although, the declining trend in public investment was halted in 1992-2000, with the public sector capital formation rising to Rs. 4,122 crore from Rs. 3,869 crore in the preceding year, there has not been any improvement in the share of investment in agriculture GDP from the preceding year's level of 1.3 per cent. This calls for a review of policies which led to the diversion of scarce resources away from the creation of productive assets to subsidies for fertilisers, rural electricity, irrigation, credit and other agricultural inputs.

The declining trend in public sector investment will need to be reversed by better targeting of subsidies, increasing investment in productive assets such as irrigation, power, credit and developing rural infrastructure. The trend of percentage share of agriculture in total GCF is given in Table 5.4.

Table 5. 4 : Gross Capital Formation Agriculture (At 1993-94 Prices).

(Rs. crores)

Year	*Gross Capital Formation*				*Percentage Share of*			*Investment*
	agri-culture	*Total economy*	*Public Sector in agri.*	*Private Sector in agri-culture*	*Public Sector in agri-culture*	*Private Sector in agri-culture*	*Agri. to total*	*in Agri-culture as per-centage of GDP*
1993-94	13,523	181,133	4,467	9,056	33.0	67.0	7.47	1.6
1994-95	14,969	229,879	4,947	10,022	33.0	67.0	6.51	1.6
1995-96	15,690	284,557	4,849	10,841	30.9	69.1	5.51	1.6
1996-97	16,176	248,631	4,668	11,508	28.9	71.1	6.51	1.5
1997-98	15,942	256,551	3,979	11,963	25.0	75.0	4.77	1.4
1998-99	14,895	243,697	3,869	11,026	26.0	74.0	6.11	1.3
1999-00	16,582	268,374	4,112	12,470	24.8	75.2	6.18	1.3
2000-01*	16,545	274,917	4,007	12,538	24.2	75.8	6.02	1.3

* Quick Estimates

Source : Same as Table 5.1

Table 5.5 : Share of Agriculture & Allied Sector in Total GCF(%)

Year	*Public Sector*	*Private Sector*	*Total*
1970-71	13.8	14.6	14.3
1971-72	13.3	15.0	14.3
1972-73	13.7	16.2	15.0
1973-74	13.0	15.2	14.3
1974-75	12.8	12.8	12.7
1975-76	12.2	15.1	13.9
1976-77	14.5	20.4	17.6
1977-78	17.1	14.6	15.7
1978-79	16.3	18.9	17.8
1979-80	16.1	19.0	17.7
1980-81	17.7	13.6	15.4
1981-82	14.1	9.2	11.2
1982-83	13.1	12.3	12.7
1983-84	13.5	14.4	13.9
1984-85	11.8	11.5	11.7
1985-86	10.2	9.5	9.8
1986-87	8.9	10.1	9.6
1987-88	10.1	13.2	11.7
1988-89	8.8	9.7	9.3
1989-90	7.5	9.1	8.4
1990-91	7.1	11.9	9.9
1991-92	6.6	9.9	8.7
1992-93	6.7	10.5	9.1
1993-94	6.9	9.4	8.4
1994-95	6.7	7.7	7.3
1995-96	7.1	5.9	6.2
1996-97	7.0	7.5	7.4
1997-98	6.2	7.5	7.1
1998-99	5.7	7.8	7.2
1999-2000	5.1	8.2	7.2
2000-01	4.9	8.2	7.1

* Quick Estimates.

Source : Central Statistical Organisation, New Delhi.

The percentage of Plan outlay in agriculture and allied sectors to total outlay varied in between 11.3 per cent to 14.9 per cent from the First Plan to the Fifth Plan. This sector includes animal husbandry, special area programme, rural development and foresty and wildlife. From the Sixth to the Ninth Plans, the share of agriculture and allied sectors to total varies between 4.9 per cent and 5.9 per cent. Here, agriculture and allied sectors include animal husbandry and research and education only. Plan-wise position is given in Table 5.5.

Towards Future

The importance of agriculture cannot be minimised when a substantial segment of the work force of the country is still dependent on agriculture and allied activities for their livelihood and survival. Since the wellbeing of millions of people depend on agriculture, its development should be given a top priority. The National Agriculture Policy highlights the importance of agriculture in its opening paragraph as :

> Agriculture is a way of life, a tradition, which for centuries, has shaped the thought, the outlook, the culture and economic life of the people of India. Agriculture, therefore, is and will continue to be central to all strategies for planned socio-economic development of the country. Rapid growth of agriculture is essential not only to achieve self-reliance at national level but also for household food security and to bring about equity in distribution of income and wealth resulting in rapid reduction of poverty levels.

But agriculture development by itself will not bring about any development for the millions of disadvantaged rural workers. Their development will finally depend on equitable distribution of means of production, proper valuation of their products and due pricing of the products they purchase in the markets. Therefore, at all the stages of production, exchanges, distribution and consumption, a strategy to bring about equity has to be devised so as to reach the benefit of development equitably to all in the society.

Rural Workers : Present Status

India has a total workers numbering more than 402.51 million, according to 2001 census. The figures in Table 5.6 show that out of the total workers 77.17 percent were rural workers. This clearly shows the importance of agriculture and rural development in the country. It could be seen further in the table that out of the total workers, 31.70 and 26.69 per cent were cultivators and agricultural labourers respectively. Together these two categories constituted 58.39 percent of the total workers who are directly engaged in agricultural and allied activities in rural areas. Their livelihood is thus directly dependent on agriculture. Planning Commission rightly observes :

> With a 24.2 per cent contribution (trienniun ending 2001-02) to the gross domestic product (GDP), agriculture still provides livelihood support to about two-thirds of the country's population. The sector provides employment to 56.7 per cent of country's work force and is the single occupation. Agriculture accounts for about 14.7 per cent of the total export earnings and provides raw materials to a large number of industries (textiles, silk, sugar, rice, flourmills, milk products). Besides, the rural area are the biggest market for low-priced and middle priced consumer goods, including consumer durables and rural domestic savings are an important source of resource mobilisation (GOI, 2002 : 513).

Thus the development of this vast segment of rural labourers depends on development of agriculture and overall rural development. But rural development on its own cannot bring about any development among the rural labourers as is evident in the experience of last five decades in the country.

Development of rural labourers, particularly those who are most disadvantaged, like agricultural labourers, can only take place if it is especially focused on them. If the programmes and schemes are in commensurate with their numerical magnitude, the volume of their needs are clearly delineated and innovatively designed on the principles of participatory implementation strategy, then the benefits of development will reach them.

Here we shall make an attempt to bring into relief the state-wise profile of rural workers in the country. This will help us to underline the needs of rural workers, specific to its magnitude. It can be observed that out of the total workers in the country, the largest segment of rural workers is concentrated in eleven States, namely, Rajasthan, Uttar Pradesh, Bihar, West Bengal, Madhya

Pradesh, Gujarat, Maharashtra, Andhra Pradesh, Karnataka and Tamil Nadu. More than 66 percent (66.44) percent rural workers are concentrated in these States alone.

Among the States, the highest proportion of concentration could be found in Uttar Pradesh (14.44), followed by Andhra Pradesh (9.06), Maharashtra (9.04), Bihar (8.32), West Bengal (7.04) and Madhya Pradesh (6.71) and so on.

The level of concentration of rural workers also indicates the need for specific plan and programmes in specific areas, keeping in view geographical situation, topographical make and environmental conditions. A blanket programme cannot be the answer to any effort at uplifting the disadvantaged rural workers in the country.

The figures in the table also show the proportion of rural workers in each State/Union territory from its total workers in 2001. In the country as a whole out of the total workers, 74.94 per cent workers are consituted by rural workers alone.

In three states, such as, Himachal Pradesh, Bihar and Sikkim the proportion rural workers to each of states total workers were 92.66, 92.08 and 90.77 per cent respectively. These proportions were highest amongest all other states and union territories.

There are thirteen states and U.Ts namely, Rajasthan (83.59), U.P. (82.81), Arunachal Pradesh (84.20), Nagaland (86.75), Tripura (84.84), Meghalaya (86.40), Assam (88.66), Jharkhand (84.82), Orissa (88.19), Chattishgarh (86.57), Madhya Pradesh (81.01), Dadra Nagar Haveli (80.22) and Andhra Pradesh (80.77) the proportion of rural workers to total workers varied between 80.00 and 89.00 per cent according to census of 2001.

In the category between 70.00 and 779.00 but less than 80.00 per cent there are a member of states like Jammu & Kashmir (77.78), Haryana (77.01), Manipur (79.15), West Bengal (74.22), Gujarat (70.41), Daman and Diu (72.14), Karnataka (72.82) and Kerala (74.58). In the rest of the States and Union Territories the proportion of rural workers was below 70.00 per cent, the lowest proportion being observed of course in two Union Territories, namely Chandigarh (11.80) and Delhi (6.82). Among the major.states the lowest proportion of rural workers could be observed in Tamil Nadu (63.18) in 2001.

Table 5.6 : Whole Out of the Total Workekrs, 74.94 per cent Workers are Constituted by rural Workers Alone

S.No	*Country/ State*	*Total Workers*	*Total Rural Worker*	*Percentage of rural workers from Total Rural Workers*
0	India	402,512,190	301,655,339 (74.94)	100.00
1	J&K	3,688,875	2,869,319 (77.78)	0.92
2.	H.P.	2,991,448	2,771,978 (92.66)	0.89
3.	Punjab	9,141,760	6,382,662 (69.82)	2.05
4.	Chandigarh	339,021	39,993 (11.80)	0.01
5.	Uttaranchal	3,133,281	2,501,791 (79.85)	0.80
6.	Haryana	8,382,890	6,455,946 (7.01)	2.07
7.	Delhi	4,526,737	308,766 (6.82)	0.09
8	Rajasthan	23,781,257	19,877,709 (83.59)	6.39
9.	Uttar Pradesh	54,180,232	44,865,277 (82.81)	14.44
10.	Bihar	25,080,004	25,856,125 (92.08)	8.32
11.	Sikkim	263,320	239,025 (90.77)	0.07
12.	Arunachal	482,206	405,998 (84.20)	0.13
13.	Nagaland	849,982	737,386 (86.75)	0.23

S.No	Country/ State	Total Workers	Total Rural Worker	Percentage of rural workers from Total Rural Workers
14.	Manipur	1,069,578	846,595 (79.15)	0.27
15.	Mizoram	469,597	257,488 (54.83)	0.08
16.	Tripura	1,158,190	982,635 (84.84)	0.31
17.	Meghalya	956,425	826,334 (86.40)	0.26
18.	Assam	9,557,064	8,473,127 (88.66)	2.72
19.	West Bengal	29,503,278	21,897,521 (74.22)	7.04
20.	Jharkhand	10,127,733	8,590,029 (84.82)	2.76
21.	Orissa	14,272,764	12,587,554 (88.19)	4.05
22.	Chhatisgarh	9,685,260	8,384,439 (86.57)	2.69
23.	Madhya Pradesh	25,756,485	20,865,600 (81.01)	6.71
24.	Gujarat	20,368,799	14,341,413 (70.41)	4.61
25.	Daman & Diu	72,654	52,413 (72.14)	0.01
26.	Dadra & Nagar Haveli	114,121	91,545 ((80.22)	0.02
27.	Maharashtra	42,053,330	28,106,602 (66.84)	9.04

S.No	*Country/ State*	*Total Workers*	*Total Rural Worker*	*Percentage of rural workers from Total Rural Workers*
28.	Andhra Pradesh	34,865,117	28,159,160 (80.77)	9.06
29.	Karnataka	23,521,117	17,129,318 (72.82)	5.51
30.	Goa	522,565	274,744 (52.28)	0.08
31.	Lakshadweep	15,349	7,998 (52.11)	Neg.
32.	Kerala	10,291,258	7,675,096 (74.58)	2.47
33.	Tamil Nadu	27,811,647	17,572,083 (63.18)	5.67
34.	Pondicherry	342,101	127,635 (37.31)	0.04
35.	Andaman & Nicobar Islands	136,331	94,035 (68.98)	0.03

Source : Govt. of India, *Census of India, 2001*. Census Commission, New Delhi.

6

Overview of Rural Labour

RURAL LABOUR IN INDIA

Introduction

Rural labourers constitute the largest segment of the labour force in the country. They are also the most vulnerable group in the rural society, for they lack virtually all-productive assets, such as land, capital, skills, etc. In most of the cases they are absolutely dependent on the landed classes in rural areas. Being unorganised, their barganing capability is very marginal; and this leads to their ruthless exploitation by moneylenders, rich and capitalist farmers. Besides, rural labourers are constituted largely by people belonging to socially and economically oppressed classes like Scheduled Castes, Scheduled Tribes and Other Backward Classes. They are not a homogenous group. Some of them are free, some are attached and still many of them are bonded. However, they have one thing in common., they are deprived even of basic minimum needs for their existence and have been made dependent on others. The progress of the country since 1947 has bypassed them largely. Thus leaving them to grovel in the darkness of poverty and utter deprivation.

The number of rural labourers is very large. Accordingly to "National Commission on Rural Labour's (NCRL) definition, the estimated number of rural labour in 1987-88 is around 150 million. This would include about 97 million rural labour as defined in Rural Labour Enquiry (RLE) [self-employed, regular and casual workers in rural labour household], about 9 million casual workers in self-employed household and other households besides 44 million workers deserving to be categorised as rural labour in the self-employed households belonging to landless, marginal and small categories. The above estimate includes unemployed excluding graduate and above in the rural labour force. The 'rural labour' as per NCRL definition accounts for above 60 per cent of the total rural labour force in the country" (Govt., 1991).

Structure and Trend of Rural Labour Households

The first Rural Labour Enquiry was conducted in 1964-65 when the total number of rural households was estimated to be 70.4 million. Since then six more enquiries have been conducted, the last and the seventh being conducted in 1999-2000. In the seventh enquiry the total estimated number of rural households reached an estimated number of 137.1 million, an increase of 66.70. million households in 1999-2000 over 1964-65. In the case of rural labour households in general and agricultural labourers in particular, it could be seen in the table that in the case of former it constituted 25.4 and 40.2 per cent in 1964-65 and 1999-2000 respectively, while in the case of the latter it was 21.8 per cent in the first enquiry period and 32.2 per cent in the sixth enquiry period.

The household size in both the cases remained almost the same over the years. With regard to average earning strength for both agricultural and rural labour households it may be seen that the number has registered a slight decline over the years. For instance, the average earning strength per household was 2.1 in 1964-65 which declined to 1.8 in 1999-2000. In the case of average number of wage-earners it may be found that for both the household types, the number has recorded a decline. This may be due to the fact that children are being sent to school or female labourers are being withdrawn from economic activities because of economic restructuring and consequently change in production processes.

It could be seen in Table 6.1 that the extent of wage employment (in days) in agricultural employment for both male and female has remained erratic over the years. For instance, for male agricultural and rural labourers the number of days of employment was 217 and 219 respectively in 1964-65 which came down to 193 and 192 in 1977-78 but rose marginally in 1993-94. During the corresponding years similar trends could be observed in the case of female agricultural and rural labourers.

Table 6.1 : Structure of Rural Labour/Agriculture Labour Households in the RLEs.

Items	*1st Rural Labour Enquiry 1964-65*	*2nd Rural Labour Enquiry 1974-75*	*3rd Rural Labour Enquiry 1977-78*	*4th Rural Labour Enquiry 1983*	*5th Rural Labour Enquiry 1987-88*	*6th Rural Labour Enquiry 1993-94*	*7th Rural Labour Enquiry 1999-2000*
1	2	3	4	5	6	7	8
1. Estimated number of Rural Households (in Million)	70.4	82.1	95.7	100.5	108.4	119.5	137.1
2. Percentage of Rural Labour House-holds to Rural Households	25.4	30.3	36.8	37.3	39.7	38.3	40.2
3. Percentage of Agricultural Labour House-holds to Rural Households	21.8	25.3	29.9	30.7	30.7	30.3	32.2
4. Average size of the Households							
A	4.5	4.8	4.7	4.6	4.6	4.4	4.6
B	4.5	4.8	4.7	4.6	4.6	4.6	4.7

Contd. . . .

1	2	3	4	5	6	7	8
5. Average earning Strength							
A	2.1	2.3	2.1	2.1	2.0	2	2.0
R	2.1	2.3	2.1	2.0	2.0	2	2.0
6. Average number of wage-earners							
A	2.0	2.2	1.8	1.9	1.4	1.7	1.8
R	2.0	2.2	1.7	1.8	1.3	1.6	1.7
7. Extent of wage employment (in days) in Agricultural employment Male							
A	217	193	229	227	231	247P	—
R	219	192	229	227	230	237P	—
Female							
A	149	138	186	190	157	220P	—
R	161	136	186	189	157	215P	—

A = Agricultural Labour Households, R = Rural Labour Households, P = Provisional

Source : Various Rural Labour Enquiry Reports

The Question of Landlessness

The most disquieting and ominous result of under-development of rural economy coupled with the swelling number of rural labour households, particularly agricultural labour households, is the growing landlessness and shirnking per capita land-man ratio. It could be seen in Table 6.2 that the number of rural households without cultivated land has increased from 29.3 million in 1977-78 to 38.2 million in 1987-88. The NCRL notes, "even in agricultural labour category, the households without cultivated land increased from 14.7 million to 17.5 million to 17.5 million or by 19 per cent. In other households comprising self-employed and other rural households, the increase in landlessness is of higher magnitude (36 per cent). This indicates that the land base of agricultural labour household has been gradually eroded. Further, such deprivation is of higher order in households in self-employed category, thereby swelling the ranks of labouring class" [*Ibid.*, p.10.]

Table 6.2 : Rural Labour Households with & without Cultivable Land

(Figures in million)

Household	With Land			Without Land			Total		
category	*77-78*	*1983*	*87-88*	*77-78*	*1983*	*87-88*	*77-78*	*1983*	*87-88*
1. Ag. Lab.	13.9	13.6	15.8	14.7	17.3	17.5	28.6	30.9	33.3
2. Non-Ag. Lab	3.2	2.6	4.3	3.4	4.0	5.5	6.6	6.6	9.8
3. Rural Labour	17.1	16.2	20.1	18.1	21.3	23.0	35.2	37.5	43.1
4 Other	49.3	48.9	50.1	11.2	14.1	15.2	60.5	63.0	65.3
Total	66.4	65.1	70.2	29.3	35.4	28.2	95.7	100.5	108.4

Source : Rural Labour Enquiry Reports of various years.

Division by Sex and Employment

It could be seen in Table 6.3 that casualisation of rural labourers, both male and female, has increaed; the proportion of casual labour has increased from 22.2 per cent in 1972-73 to 31.4 per cent in 1987-88 for males and from 31.4 per cent to 35.5 per cent for females for corresponding period. The proportion of self-employed and regular employee has declined by 7.3 per cent and 2.1 per cent for males respectively in 1987-88 over 1972-73. Similarly, the declines for females were 3.7 per cent and 0.4 per cent respectively.

Table 6.3 : Percentage Distribution of rural Workdrs by Employement and Sex

	Male				Female			
	72-73	77-78	1983	87-88	72-73	77-78	1983	87-88
Self employed	65.9	62.8	60.5	58.6	64.5	62.1	61.9	60.8
Regular employed	12.1	10.6	10.3	10.0	4.1	2.8	2.8	3.7
Casual Labour	20.0	26.6	29.2	31.4	31.4	35.1	35.3	35.5

Source : Sarvekshana : Special Number Sept. 1990 NSS 43rd Round.

AGRICULTURAL LABOURERS IN INDIA

Introduction

Agricultural labours constitute a distinct section in the peasantry. However, their total strength, community allegiance, comparative socio-economic status and political position in agrarian society, have been overlooked and undifferentiated. This is happening because the agricultural labourers have been an extremely exploited and brutally oppressed class in the rural society. In all possible cases, agricultural labourers work on others land in various capacities without owning any means of production. They possess only their physical strength and mental power. Since they belong to the lowest economic strata in agrarian social hierarchy and 'absolutely dependent upon the land-owners, they are unable to organise themselves despite being a 'class in itself'.

Tracing Agricultural Labourers in History

In every period of a particular society there have been two distinct classes-the powerful and the powerless. Historically, socio-economic power was concentrated in the hands of powerful chieftains in slave holding age in the hands of feudal lords in feudal period and in the hands of capitalists in the age of capitalism. Mencher quotes N. Sastri to race the origin and development of agricultural labourers : "From casual references in the inscriptions, we can dimly perceive the existence of a class of hired day-labourers who assisted in agricultural operations on the estates of other people and received a daily wage, usually in grain. There was no clear line of division between the absolutely landless agrarian labourers and the small peasant hiring himself out in his spare time..... In several instances a gift of land for same public purpose..... is found to include some proportion set part for the residences of the families of labourers engaged in its cultivation. Such labourers were not peasant proprietors by any means, and were nearer the class of hired labourers than tenants; they were entitled to the use of house site near enough to the place of their work and to get wages fixed in advance, the proceeds of their labour on land being altogether the property of the institution that owned the land on which they worked" (Mencher, 1983 : 569-70).

The 'Varna' system of earlier times was a mechanism of social differentiation among the masses. The socio-economically advantaged and subjugated groups also denote primitive process of class-differentiation. In many places, the working people have been identified by various names. For example, as Raj mention : "At the bottom of the hierarchy were communities at the periphery of hindu caste structure such as Pulayas, who generally supplied labour for the more arduous operations involved in cultivation (like ploughing, weeding and harvesting of land under paddy) and were in effect agrestic slaves." (Raj & Tharakan, 1980 : 32).

K. Saradamoni has also talked about the slave pulayas : "Pulayas in the beginning of the 19th century did not have a life of their own. They never worked or earned a living for themselves. Their entire life was dependent on the master. They did not even own their children. They begetted Children so that the master could have a continuous supply of workers. Naturally they did not make decisions or plans either for themselves or for their children. Their time was wholly their master's and they had no particular house, which they could call their own. Not a day in a week was granted them either for rest or for prayer." (Saradamoni, 1980 : 53).

In India and other parts of the world the social origin of agricultural workers as a proletariat class is an outcome of the process of property differentiation which had its roots in the class domination by the ruling class. Thus, the social origin is an economic issue which could be seen in various socio-economic structure. This point is highlighted in the following quote of Mencher." There were those who were absolutely indigent in the fullest sense, the landless labourers. Members of the depressed castes not only undertook work considered abhorrent by the caste peasants, such as tannery, scavenging, etc. but were also in a large measure agricultural worker..... Thus *chamars* and *Dhanuks* who had their own prescribed occupations, worked as agricultural labourers. The caste system seems to have worked in its inexorable way to create a fixed labour reserve force for agricultural production. Members of low castes, assigned to the most menial and contemptible occupations, could never aspire to the status of peasants holding or cultivating land on their own." (Mencher, 1983 : 120-21).

The above evidence clearly indicates the origin of agricultural workers.

Agricultural Labour : Magnitude

Agricultural labourers constitute the largest segment of rural labour. The number of agricultural labourers is growing over the years. According to 1951 census, it was 27.50 million. The 2001 census has put them to a staggering figure of 107.45 million. In fact, the growth of agricultural labourers during the past decade (between 1999-2001 and 1991) has been 5.3 per cent per annum.

Of the 107.45 million agricultural labourers in 2001, 57.35 (53.38%) million were male and 50.09 (46.62%) million were female (for details see Table 6.4).

Another important aspect of agricultural labourers is their social composition. According to 1981 census, the percentage of Scheduled Castes and Scheduled Tribes agricultural labourers among the total number of agricultural labourers were 32.88 and 12.93 per cent respectively which together accounted for about 46 per cent of the total agricultural labourers in the country.

Table 6.4 : Total Population, Total Workers and Agricultural Labourers and Cultivator for the Census years from 1901 to 2001.

Year	*Total Population*	*Total Workers (All occupations)*	*Agricultural Labourers*	*Cultivators*
1	2	3	4	5
1901	236.28	110.71	17.26	51.95
1911#	252.12	121.30	24.06	58.47
1921	251.35	117.75	19.65	61.60
1931#	279.02	120.67	22.11	57.67
1951@	356.86	139.42	27.50	69.74

Contd. . .

1	2	3	4	5
1961@	439.24	188.68	31.52	99.62
1971	548.16	180.48	47.49	78.27
1981	665.29	244.61	64.41	102.85
1991	838.60	314.13	74.60	110.70
2001	1,025.25	402.51	107.45	127.62

Source : (1) Ministry of Home Affairs, Office of Registrar General of India, Govt. of India.

(2) (a) Indian Labour Statistics, 1977 (b) Census of India 1981.

Note : (i) Figures are not available for the 1941 Census since detailed analysis was not made.

Exclusive of figures for Dadra and Nagar Haveli, Goa, Daman & Diu, Aruanchal Pradesh and Pondicherry.

@ Exclusive of figures for Jammu and Kashmir also as no Census was available.

Increasing Landlessness

In 1983, about 44 per cent of agricultural labour households possessed some land while the rest 56 per cent did not possess any. However, the average size of land cultivated by agricultural labourers was quite insignificant : it was 0.70 hectares in 1983 which declined to 0.3 hectares in 1987-88.

One alarming feature of the rural economy is the growing marginalisation of operational holding. Over the years, it has been found that the number of marginal holding is increasing either because of fragmentation of holding which is due to devolution of family or alienation of land from small and semi-medium farmers. This results in the increasing number of agricultural labourers and a decline in the employed farmers. The distribution of holdings over the major size-classes shows that in 1985-86 the highest increase was noticed in the case of marginal holdings followed by small holdings. Another important feature is that average size of holding is declining thus registering declining per capita landholding. (see Table 6.5).

The figures in the table also show that continuously increasing. For example, in 1985-86, the proportion of marginal holdings from

Table 6.5 : Distribution of Number and Area of Operational Holdings in India by Major Size Class of Holdings for all Social Groups in 1980-81 and 1985-86 and area per size.

S. No.	Major Size	Number of Holding (Thousand)		Percentage Change	Area Operated (Thou. Hect)		Percentage Change	No. of Operational	Area Operational
		1980-81	1985-86		1980-81	1985-86		1995	1996
1.	Marginal	50122 (56.4)	56147 (57.8)	(+) 12.0	19735 (12.1)	22042 (13.4)	(+) 11.7	71179 (61.58)	28121 (17.21)
2.	Small	16072 (18.1)	17955 (18.4)	(+) 11.5	23169 (14.1)	25708 (15.6)	(+) 11.0	21643 (18.73)	30722 (18.81)
3.	Semi-Medium	12455 (14.0)	13252 (13.6)	(+) 6.4	34645 (21.2)	36666 (22.3)	(+) 5.8	14261 (12.34)	38953 (23.85)
4.	Medium	8086 (9.1)	7916 (8.2)	(–) 1.9	48543 (29.6)	47144 (28.6)	(–) 2.9	7092 (6.14)	41398 (25.34)
5.	Large	2166 (2.4)	1918 (2.0)	(–) 11.4	37705 (23.0)	33002 (20.1)	(–) 12.5	1404 (1.21)	24163 (14.79)
	All size Classes	88883 (1000.0)	97155 (100.0)	(+) 9.3	163796 (100.0)	164562 (100.0)	(+) 0.47	115580 (100.00)	163357 (100.00)

Note : Figures in brackets indicate the percentage of respective columns.

Source : Government of India, *Agricultural Census of* Various Years, Ministry of Agriculture.

the total holdings was 57.8 per cent which rose to 61.58 per cent in 1995-96. Of the total area operated, the area under marginal holding was 17.21 per cent. This thus clearly indicate the precarious landholding size under the over-whelming marginal farmers of the country.

THE PROBLEMS AND ISSUES

Poverty

All this indicates increasing poverty, exploitation, dependence, malnutrition, ignorance and illiteracy for a large number of country's population, particularly for the asset-less rural/agricultural labourers who are unorganised and acutely vulnerable. In 1988 about 360 million people lived in poverty which accounted for 43 per cent of the total population. About 80 per cent of this poor people lived in rural areas and invariably all of them were agricultural labourers and marginal farmers. The poor live in households which have few assets other than labour resources and poverty arises fundamentally because these labour resources cannot find adequate and adequately remunerative employment and underemployment is the basic cause of poverty. This is obvious from the fact that households with members in regular wage employment are rarely poor. The poor generally belong to either casual labour households or self-employed households in both rural and urban areas. In rural areas, the majority belongs to casual labour households: in urban areas, a majority belongs to self-employed households.

Though a large number of poverty alleviation programmes have been launched, the capacity of these programme to alleviate poverty has not been very high. Consequently a large number of people are still living below the poverty line. Table 6.6 shows the distribution population below poverty line in 1999-2000 (see also Table 6.7).

Problems

Problems faced by the rural labourers in the country are many and all of them are complex and interconnected. They may, however, be classified into six broad categories :

(i) Social Problems.

(ii) Economic Problems.

Table 6.6 : Number and Percentage of Population below Poverty line for States, Union Territories and India during 1999-2000

State/Union Territory	*Rural*		*Urban*		*Total*	
	No. of Persons (Figures in lakhs)	*Percentage of persons*	*No. of Persons (Figures in lakhs)*	*Percentage of persons*	*No. of Persons (Figures in lakhs)*	*Percentage of persons*
Andhra Pradesh	58.13	11.05	60.88	26.63	119.01	15.77
Arunachal Pradesh	3.80	40.04	0.18	7.47	3.98	33.47
Assam	92.17	40.04	2.38	7.47	94.55	36.09
Bihar[1]	376.51	44.30	49.13	32.91	425.64	42.60
Goa	0.11	1.35	0.59	7.52	0.70	4.40
Gujarat	39.80	13.17	28.09	15.59	67.89	14.07
Haryana	11.94	8.27	5.39	9.99	17.34	8.74
Himachal Pradesh	4.84	7.94	0.29	4.63	5.12	7.63
Jammu & Kashmir	2.97	3.97	0.49	1.98	3.46	3.48
Karnataka	59.91	17.38	44.49	25.25	104.40	20.04
Kerala	20.97	9.38	20.07	20.27	41.04	12.72
Mahya Pradesh[1]	217.32	37.06	81.22	38.44	298.54	37.43
Maharashtra	125.12	23.72	102.87	26.81	227.99	25.03

(Contd.) Table 6.6 : **Number and Percentage of Population below Poverty line for States, Union Territories and India during 1999-2000**

State/Union Territory	Rural		Urban		Total	
	No. of Persons (Figures in lakhs)	Percentage of persons	No. of Persons (Figures in lakhs)	Percentage of persons	No. of Persons (Figures in lakhs)	Percentage of persons
Manipur	6.53	40.04	0.66	7.47	7.19	28.54
Meghalaya	7.89	40.04	0.34	7.47	8.23	33.87
Mizoram	1.40	40.04	0.45	7.47	1.85	19.47
Nagaland	5.21	40.04	0.28	7.47	5.49	32.67
Orissa	143.69	48.01	25.40	42.83	169.09	47.15
Punjab	10.20	6.35	4.29	5.75	14.49	6.16
Rajasthan	55.06	13.74	26.78	19.85	81.83	15.28
Sikkim	2.00	40.04	0.04	7.47	2.05	36.55
Tamil Nadu	80.51	20.55	49.97	22.11	130.48	21.12
Tripura	12.53	40.04	0.49	7.47	13.02	34.44
Uttar Pradesh[1]	412.01	31.22	117.88	30.89	529.89	31.15
West Bengal	180.11	31.85	33.38	14.86	213.49	27.02
Andaman & Nicobar Islands	0.58	20.55	0.24	22.11	0.82	20.99

(Contd.) *Table 6.6* : Number and Percentage of Population below Poverty line for States, Union Territories and India during 1999-2000

State/Union Territory	*Rural*		*Urban*		*Total*	
	No. of Persons (Figures in lakhs)	*Percentage of persons*	*No. of Persons (Figures in lakhs)*	*Percentage of persons*	*No. of Persons (Figures in lakhs)*	*Percentage of persons*
Chandigarh	0.06	5.75	0.45	5.75	0.51	5.75
Dadra & Nagar Haveli	0.30	17.57	0.03	13.52	0.33	17.14
Daman & Diu	0.01	1.35	0.05	7.52	0.06	4.44
Delhi	0.07	0.40	11.42	9.42	11.49	8.23
Lakshadweep	0.03	9.38	0.08	20.27	0.11	15.60
Pondicherry	0.64	20.55	1.77	22.11	2.41	21.67
India	1932.43	27.09	670.07	23.62	2602.50	26.10

Source : Planning Commission estimates.

1. Due to creation of new states after 1991, the data for the years prior to 2001 for the states of Bihar, Madhya Pradesh and Uttar Pradesh include the data of newly created states namely Jharkhand, Chattishgarh and Uttarachal, respectively.

Note : Reference period used : 30 days recall period.

Table 6.7 : Age specific unemployment rates[1] by sex for India

Year	Male						Female					
	Age-group (in years)						Age-group (in years)					
	5-14	15-29	30-44	45-59	60 & above	Total	5-14	15-29	30-44	45-59	60 & above	Total
Rural												
1977-78	2.0	4.9	0.6	0.4	0.3	2.2	4.7	8.5	4.1	3.0	2.0	5.5
1983	2.8	4.7	0.5	0.2	0.2	2.1	1.2	2.8	0.5	0.4	0.6	1.4
1987-88	3.2	6.2	0.9	0.5	0.5	2.8	2.9	5.4	2.4	1.9	1.8	3.5
1989-90	1.9	3.6	0.5	0.0	0.6	1.6	1.4	1.5	0.4	0.6	NA	0.8
1990-91	0.6	3.2	0.3	0.3	0.2	1.3	NA	1.0	0.3	NA	NA	0.4
July-Dec 91	3.7	4.3	0.4	0.2	0.2	1.8	2.7	2.0	0.6	0.5	0.6	1.2
1992	1.3	3.8	0.3	0.2	0.3	1.6	1.6	2.1	0.3	0.3	NA	1.2
Jan-June 93	3.7	3.7	0.2	0.2	0.1	1.6	2.1	2.0	0.3	0.2	0.5	1.0
1993-94	1.6	4.9	0.4	0.1	NA	2.0	0.8	3.2	0.4	0.2	NA	1.4
1994-95	0.8	3.1	0.3	0.0	0.0	1.3	0.0	1.5	0.0	0.1	0.0	0.4
July95-June 96[a]	1.6	3.6	0.6	0.2	0.1	1.4	0.0	1.6	0.3	0.1	0.0	0.8
Jan-Dec 97[a]	3.3	3.8	0.3	0.0	0.0	1.6	1.2	2.1	0.3	0.0	0.0	0.9
Jan-June 1998[a]	2.1	5.0	1.1	0.8	0.6	2.4	4.4	4.1	1.0	0.7	0.6	1.9
July 99-June 2000	2.2	5.1	0.6	0.1	0.2	2.1	1.2	3.7	0.4	0.2	0.4	1.7

Table 6.7 : Age specific unemployment rates[1] by sex for India

Year	Male						Female					
	Age-group (in years)						Age-group (in years)					
	5-14	15-29	30-44	45-59	60 & above	Total	5-14	15-29	30-44	45-59	60 & above	Total
Urban												
1977-78	7.7	14.0	1.3	1.0	1.5	6.5	7.8	31.4	10.4	4.8	2.2	17.8
1983	10.6	12.2	1.4	0.7	0.6	5.9	2.3	15.5	2.1	0.7	9.1	6.9
1987-88	9.3	13.6	1.2	0.7	1.1	6.1	4.1	18.8	3.5	1.1	1.1	8.5
1989-90	11.1	9.7	0.9	0.9	1.8	4.4	NA	7.9	1.1	0.5	NA	3.9
1990-91	9.0	11.3	0.8	0.3	0.9	4.5	NA	13.2	1.4	0.4	NA	5.4
July-Dec.91	12.0	9.6	1.0	0.6	0.2	4.5	3.9	11.2	2.5	NA	NA	5.5
1992	14.8	10.2	1.3	0.4	2.1	4.6	17.2	13.8	1.8	0.3	1.0	6.7
Jan-June 93	7.2	9.2	0.8	0.4	0.2	3.8	NA	8.6	2.6	0.5	NA	4.3
1993-94	4.5	10.8	1.1	0.4	0.3	4.5	2.6	19.6	2.8	0.4	NA	8.2
1994-95	6.8	8.5	1.1	0.2	NA	3.7	2.7	10.0	0.3	0.0	NA	4.3
July 95-June 96[a]	7.9	9.9	1.0	0.3	0.2	4.0	0.0	0.8	0.3	0.3	0.0	3.6
Jan-Dec 97[a]	4.3	10.0	0.9	0.3	0.2	3.9	3.1	13.2	1.7	0.0	0.0	5.1
Jan-June 1998[a]	18.8	11.5	1.9	1.2	1.4	5.2	38.8	16.6	2.4	1.7	4.7	8.3
July 99-June 2000	5.7	11.5	1.4	0.4	0.0	4.8	3.3	16.6	2.8	0.5	0.0	7.1

Source : National Sample Survey Organisation.

Note : The figures of different rounds relate to the usual principal status.

0.0 Negligible NA: Not available

1. The percentage of unemployed in labour force.

a. The figures are based on thin sample.

(iii) Political Problems.

(iv) Cultural Problems

(v) Health Problems

(vi) Environmental Problems

Social problems

We have noted earlier that almost half of the rural labourers belong mostly to Scheduled Castes and Scheduled Tribes. In fact the figure may go up to 2/3 if other Backward Classes are included. Traditionally, the social status of these sections in the existing social milieu has remained at the lowest rung of the hierarchical social order. Being economically dependent and assetless, they have been subjugated for centuries. The subjugation has led to their social unacceptability by the socially powerful sections. As a consequence, untouchability and other evil practices have inflicted a heavy moral, psychological and material suffering on these oppressed people, majority of whom eke out a precarious livelihood in rural areas.

Another aspect of social problem is reflected in the gender discrimination. About 40 per cent of the agricultural labourers are constituted by female agricultural labourers. Because of the existing social practice, the female agricultural labourers are paid less than their male counterparts.

Economic Problems

Of economic problems, the most important one is lack of employment opportunity for majority of the agricultural labourers. For good part of the year they remain unemployed or under-employed. Apart from this problem, the wage rates are always very low-it is more often than not less than the prescribed Minimum Wage. Increasing prices of essential consumption items impinges on their precarious living standard.

Rural labourers being too numerous in some regions, all of them do not find employment in their locality. In search of employment they migrate to places and regions where employment is available. The migrant agricultural labourers are more vulnerable, and exploited brutally by their employers.

Box 6.1 : The Crisis Continues

"Perhaps there is no region in India where there is a greater disparity between rural and urban wages and standards of living than Bihar.

"The economic condition of the bulk of agricultural workers approximates to virtual slavery in considerable parts of Bihar and Orissa. Where wages are paid in cash they earn only 9 pies per die together with a *seer* of cereal or only 1 *anna* in the aggregate. In such districts as Muzaffarpur, Darbhanga, Bhagalpoore and Monghyer hereditary boundslaves still exist with a burden of debts usually incurred for marriage going back to five generations; they are often assigned, 1 to 5 *kottahs* of lead land and paid an *anna* or 2&1/2 *seers* of cereal per dime, which they forfeit when there is no work in the field."

Radhakamal Mukerjee (1945), *The Indian Working Class.* Bombay, Hind Kitab.

Indebtedness

It is the chronic problem. Many rural labour households get caught in the vicious cycle of indebtedness. Not having any opportunity and collateral, they borrow from village money-lenders and landlords at exorbitant rate of interest. It results in their bondage to landlords, sometimes for generation. Institutional credit system still is not available to them to an adequate extent

Political Problems

Rural labourers are unorganised. The attitude of organised political parties towards them is still 'ambivalent'. As a result, rural labourers, particularly the agricultural labourers do not have much political influence. Being unorganised they are also politically exploited by vested interests; and consequently their bargaining capacity for determining their wages, taking decision for their development and participating in the planning and implementing process of programmes and schemes is minimal and sometimes insignificant (See Table 6.8 and 6.9).

Table 6.8 : Percentage Distribution of Labour Force by Educational Status by Sex and Sector in India

Educational level	1972-73		1977-78		1983		1987-88		1993-94		1999-2000	
	Male	*Female*	*Male*	*Female*	*Male*	*Female*	*Male*	*Female*	*Male*	*Female*	*Male*	*Female*
Rural												
Illiterate	61.1	91.6	55.0	88.1	52.1	86.2	48.3	82.3	43.2	78.0	39.6	73.9
Literate but upto primary	29.0	7.1	30.8	9.1	29.2	10.2	29.6	12.0	28.2	14.2	27.4	15.7
Middle	6.3	0.8	8.5	1.6	10.8	2.1	11.6	3.2	13.9	4.4	16.0	5.8
Secondary	3.1	0.4	4.7	1.0	6.4	1.2	8.4	2.0	11.3	2.8	13.5	3.6
Graduate & above	0.5	0.1	1.0	0.2	1.5	0.3	2.1	0.4	2.8	0.6	3.4	1.0
Total	100.0	100.0	100.0	100.0	100.0	100.0	100.0	100.0	100.0	100.0	100.0	100.0
Urban												
Illiterate	24.8	67.4	22.1	58.2	21.7	56.5	19.6	51.8	17.8	45.9	15.9	41.2
Literate but upto primary	37.2	16.5	33.6	17.9	30.1	17.5	30.5	19.0	25.3	19.0	21.9	17.0
Middle	15.0	4.0	17.2	6.7	18.1	6.3	16.4	7.3	17.6	8.9	18.8	9.7
Secondary	16.6	8.0	18.4	10.8	19.9	11.6	21.8	12.3	24.7	14.0	26.4	15.7
Graduate & above	6.4	4.1	8.7	6.4	10.1	8.0	11.7	9.6	14.5	12.2	16.9	16.4
Total	100.0	100.0	100.0	100.0	100.0	100.0	100.0	100.0	100.0	100.0	100.0	100.0

Source : National Sample Survey Organisation

Note : Figures relate to usual status of individuals. Figures for the year 1972-73 and 1977-78 relate to the population aged five years and above while figures for the year 1983 and 1987-88 relate to the population aged 15 years and above. Thus the figures relating to 1983, 1987-88, 1993-94 and 1999-2000 would be slightly reduced if the persons in the labour force in the age group of 5-14 are included in the estimation.

Table 6.9 : Labour Force Participation Rates (LFPR) for Educated Persons by Sex and Sector in India

Year	*Educational level*	*Rural*		*Urban*	
		Male	*Female*	*Male*	*Female*
1983	Literate below secondary	84.92	25.85	82.55	12.38
	Secondary & higher secondary	74.24	23.76	71.69	17.38
	Graduates & above	88.78	37.60	87.37	35.29
1987-88	Literate below secondary	83.80	26.35	81.25	12.78
	Secondary & higher secondary	74.20	26.30	70.70	16.20
	Graduates & above	91.10	89.90	86.40	37.70
1993-94	Literate below secondary	85.24	25.80	81.75	13.69
	Secondary & higher secondary	72.08	20.01	68.38	14.47
	Graduates & above	91.30	44.80	86.20	35.50
1999-2000	Literate below secondary	86.38	36.64	81.96	17.85
	Secondary & higher secondary	74.66	19.47	68.23	12.72
	Graduates & above	89.80	41.00	85.40	30.20

Source : National Sample Survey Organisation.

Note : 1. The LFPRs are for person of age 15 years and above.

2. The rates are according to the usual principal status.

3. The rates are based on the results relating to NSS 38th (1983), 43th (1987-88), 50th (1993-94) and 55th (1999-2000) rounds respectively.

Cultural Problem

Agricultural labourers being drawn from the socio-economically and politically disadvantaged sections, are also deprived of life-preparatory opportunities such as education, information, skills, aids, etc. Thus this lack of opportunities helps perpetuate their poverty and ignorance which again act as formaidable road-blocks to their development. The great majority of the agricultural labourers are illiterate. This massive illiteracy accentuated their poverty and by the prevalence of rampant corruption among those who are vested with the power to ameliorate their condition by delivering assistance. More often the illiterate agricultural labourers do not know what is their right. Thus being culturally under-privileged they are deprived of their rightful share to what is their due.

Health Problem

Agricultural labourers, being economically disadvantaged, do not get adequate medical facilities. Malnutrition add to their bad health, and throughout their life they remain susceptible to many diseases and disabilities. Their ignorance and illiteracy also add to their physical suffering. Ill health often forces them to remain without employment and this increases their chance of deprivation and dependence.

Environmental Problem

Wide-spread environmental degradation also adds to the level of unemployment of a sizable section of tribal and non-tribal population who are dependent on forest resources. Today, food, fodder and fuel are in short supply. When forest was abundant, rural labourers used to get a good part of their supply met through free resources which were available in the forest, for rearing their domestic animals, cooking and meeting food requirement, such as vegetables and other edible items. Sadly, the impoverishment of the poor is accompanied by a simultaneous erosion of the basic means of their subsistence, namely, the environment with its life supporting natural resources: land, water, forests, etc. The irrigated area is less than a third of the cropped area. The bulk of the area being at the mercy of the climate with highly uneven rainfall. All this has contributed a great deal towards destruction of environment and ecology. Forest land is being turned into crop land which has further added to the uncertainty of rainfall or draught in many parts of the country. In sum, environmental problem has affected rural agricultural labourers more than any other segment of labour force in the country.

INDEBTEDNESS

Indebtedness among the agricultural labour households is a permanent feature and a chronic problem. For various purposes, the agricultural labourers take loans from money lenders and their employers. For such loan, they pay a very high rate of interest. Many a times they are able to pay only the interest. The money lenders or employers exploit them mercilessly and show them never ending debt against them. Indebtedness leads to bondage, sometimes from one generation to another. Till recent past, the number of bonded labourers was quite high. Even today, several states have bonded labourers, but statistically their number has noticeably decreased as stated by many states.

Table 6.10 : Incidence of Indebtedness among Agricultural/Rural Labourers

Items	*Agirucltural labour Households*						*All Rural Labour Households*					
	1st RLE 1964-65	*2nd RLE 1974-75*	*3rd RLE 1977-78*	*4th RLE 1983*	*5th RLE 1987-88*	*6th RLE 1993-94*	*1st RLE 1964-65*	*2nd RLE 1974-75*	*3rd RLE 1977-78*	*4th RLE 1983*	*5th RLE 1987-88*	*6th RLE 1993-94*
Indebtedness												
Percentage of indebted households	60.6	66.4	52.3	51.1	39.4	35.5	59.2	65.4	50.5	50.4	39.1	35.1
Average Debt per Household (in Rs.)	148	387	345	774	769	1031	148	395	348	806	787	1113
Average Debt per Indebted Household (in Rs.)	244	584	660	1516	1952	2901	251	605	690	1598	2014	3169
Average Debt by Source												
Government	—	—	—	44	70	238	—	—	—	65	73	262
Co-operative Societies	12	31	57	119	195	202	14	34	65	163	190	251.
Employers	48	59	46	211	254	355	45	58	46	195	246	360
Moneyienders	75	279	246	282	429	852	80	281	253	340	436	875
Shopkeepers	18	39	44	70	151	199	21	44	47	84	186	232
Banks	—	21	40	505	410	600	—	24	45	448	419	598
Relatives & Friends	—	—	—	164	268	373	—	—	—	186	289	395
Others	91	155	227	121	176	82	91	163	234	117	175	195
Average Debt by Purpose												
Household Consumption	130	281	293	461	670	937	130	284	512	677	946	
Marriage & Other ceremonials	59	110	147	222	270	496	62	117	158	248	311	564
Productive purposes	29	74	138	628	567	821	30	77	141	610	541	804
Purchase of land & Constr. of building	—	—	—	96	166	290	—	—	—	121	223	476
Repayment of debt.	—	—	—	—	23	50	—	—	—	—	22	58
Other (More than one purpose)	26	118	82	109	256	308	29	127	95	107	240	322

Source : Rural Labour Enquiry Reports of various years.

In Table 6.10, the status of indebtedness among the agricultural households is being presented. The data are given in the Rural Labour Enquiry conducted from 1964 to 1994.

Incidence of Indebtedness

First Rural Labour Enquiry (1964-65) 60.6 per cent families of agricultural labourers were under debt. Their percentage increased in 1974-75 (66.4 per cent), IInd Rural Labour Enquiry). From 1977-78 the percentage shows a decreasing trend. In 1977-78 their proportion was 52.3 per cent. The proportion of indebted agricultural labour households in 1987-88 was 39.4 per cent and 35.5 per cent in 1993-94 as shown by 6th RLE.

Average Debt Per Households (in Rs.)

The table shows that in 1964-65, the debt was Rs. 148. The amount of debt clearly indicates an ascending trend. It can be noted that in 1974-75 the debt amount was Rs. 387, Rs. 345 in 1977-78, Rs. 774 in 1983, Rs. 769 in 1987-88 and Rs. 1031 in 1993-94.

Average Debt Per Indebted Households (In Rs.)

The table highlights that during the first Rural Labour Enquiry in 1964-65, Rs. 244 was taken as loan by indebted agricultural labour households. In 1974-75, it was Rs. 584, Rs. 660 in 1977-78, Rs. 1516 in 1983, Rs. 1952 in 1987-88 and Rs. 2901 in 1993-94. Over the years the amount of debt among the already indebted households also increased.

Average Debt by Source

In the same table we can observe the sources from which the agricultural labour households take loan. According to the 4th, 5th and 6th RLE's, 44 agricultural labourers households took loan from the government, in 1987-88, 70 households, and in 1993-97, 238 households. It can further be seen that 12 agricultural labour households took loan from cooperative societies (1964-65), 31 households in 1974-75, 57 households in 1977-78, 119 households in 1983, 195 households in 1987-88 and 202 households of agricultural labour in 1993-94. Employers are also important source of debt for the agricultural labourers. The table shows out that in the year 1964-65, 48 agricultural labourers families had taken loan from their employers. In 1974-75, 59 such households got debt from the employers, 46 households in 1977-78, 211 households in 1983, 204 households in 1987-88 and 355 households in 1993-94.

Taking loan from the moneylenders is a common phenomenon in the rural areas. It can be observed that 75 households of agricultural labour took loan from the moneylenders in 1964-65, 279 households in 1974-75, 246 households in 1977-78, 282 households in 1983, 429 households in 1977-78, 282 households in 1983, 429 households in 1987-94.

The table shows that from shopkeepers, 18 agricultural labour households took loan in 1964-65, 39 households in 1974-75, 44 households in 1977-78, 70 households in 1983, 151 households in 1987-88 and 199 households to agricultural wage labour in 1993-94.

Agricultural labourers also take loan from their relatives and friends in their time of need. Here we can see that in 1983, 164 agricultural labour households borrowed from their relatives and friends, 268 households in 1987-88 and 373 households in 1993-94.

There are other sources apart from the above mentioned ones, from which agricultural labourers borrowed. As could be seen in the table, 91 agricultural labour families borrowed in 1964-65 from others, 155 households in 1974-75, 227 households in 1977-78, 121 households in 1983, 176 households in 1987-88 and 82 households in 1993-94.

Household Consumption

The table highlights that in 1964-65 during the 1st RLE, 130 agricultural labourers households took loan to meet their consumption needs. Similarly, 281 agricultural labour households took loan for same purpose in 1974-75, 293 households in 1977-78, 461 households in 1983, 670 households in 1987-88 and 937 agricultural labourers families in 1993-94.

Productive Purposes

It can be noted from the table that for productive purposes, 29 agricultural labour households took loan in 1964-65, 74 households in 1974-75, 138 households in 1977-78, 628 households in 1983, 567 households in 1987-88 and 821 households of agricultural labourers in 1993-94.

Marriage and Other Ceremonies

For marriage, *mundan* and death ceremonies, the agricultural wage labours often take loan to meet out the social demands. This is reflected in the table also. We can observe that 59 households belonging to agricultural labour took loan for it in 1964-65, 110 households in 1974-75, 147 agricultural labour households in 1977-78. 222 households in 1983, 270 households in 1987-88, and 496 such households in 1993-94.

Purchase of Land and Construction of Building

The table shows that for this purpose 96, 166 and 290 agricultural labourers households took loan in 1983, 1987-88 and 1993-94, respectively as reported in 4th, 5th, and 6th RLE survey.

Repayment of Debt

The 5th and 6th Rural Labour Enquiry reports show that 23 and 50 households of agricultural labourers took loan for repaying their earlier debt in 187-88 and 1993-94 respectively.

Others (more than one purpose)

The agricultural labourers borrow money for more than one purpose. The data indicate that 26 agricultural labour households took loan for more than one purpose in 1964-65, 118 households in 1974-75, 82 households in 1977-78, 109 households in 1983, 256 households in 1987-88 and 308 agricultural labour households borrowed money in 1993-94.

It can be noted in the table that majority of the agricultural labourers took loan to meet their survival needs. This clearly indicates the fact that agricultural labourers in our country are not paid minimum wages as prescribed by the State. Non-payment of minimum wages and rising prices in the market have made the life of casual wage workers miserable. Agricultural labourers do not get work round the year, because in agriculture the work period strentches upto four months. The underemployment increases poverty. To meet both ends the labourers enter into debt-bondage. This ultimately leads to their oppression and exploitation.

WAGES

Agricultural Labourers are basically a group which is extremely vulnerable as compared to other groups. In many parts of the country their wages have been lower than the minimum wages prescribed by the government. We are presenting here data on wages of agricultural labourers, particularly the ploughman for the years 1991 and 1994-95.

It can be noted in Table 6.11 that in Orissa wage for male ploughman was Rs. 14.48/- in 1991 which rose to Rs. 23.28 in 1994. This was lowest in the country as compared to other states. The highest wage for a ploughman was in Punjab. In 1991 it was Rs. 37.11 which rose to Rs. 61.51 in 1994-95. The detailed wage rate for field labour/ploughman (for male) prevailing in various states at two points of time i.e. in 1990-91 and 1994-95 could be seen in the table. Here it can be also seen that though wages have increased, but the increased wage did not cover their increasing need for food and other substantial items.

Table 6.12 provides Minimum Wages under the Minimum Wages Act, 1948 for the scheduled employment. Table 6.13 provides daily wage for minimum wages for agricultural workers fixed by different States/Union Territories under the Minimum Wages Act, 1948. Table 11 provides minimum rates of wages for the unskilled workers in different States/Union Territories (see Table 6.14 also).

Table 6.11 : Average Daily Wage Rates (in Rs.) for Agricultural and Non-agricultural Occupations from October 2001 to December 2001 for Rural Areas in India

Sr. No.	*Occupation*	*Sex*	*October 2001*	*November 2001*	*December 2001*	*Quarterly*
001	Ploughing	Male	70.40	70.43	71.15	70.65
		Female	39.33	44.35	43.33	42.43
002	Sowing	Male	60.10	61.47	61.75	61.12
		Female	43.10	43.57	44.48	43.70
003	Weeding	Male	50.79	51.72	52.81	51.74
		Female	42.22	42.64	44.14	42.94
004	Transplanting	Male	53.59	54.85	54.96	54.45
		Female	45.44	45.98	47.14	46.15
005	Harvesting	Male	54.74	53.52	54.13	54.10
		Female	45.18	44.00	45.47	44.85
006	Winnowing	Male	53.36	51.61	51.71	52.16
		Female	47.03	43.61	44.23	44.82
007	Threshing	Male	54.34	51.15	50.37	51.76
		Female	54.70	44.82	42.80	44.22
008	Picking					
(1)	Cotton	Male	49.36	43.44	45.33	45.81

	Female	36.41	34.63	31.09	33.70

(Contd.) Table 6.10

(9) Others	Male	59.75	64.40	61.94	62.14
	Female	42.68	43.32	44.97	43.65
009 Herdman	Male	37.21	37.57	38.06	37.61
	Female	28.67	29.31	29.22	29.06
010 Well digging	Male	83.53	82.80	83.63	83.31
	Female	44.43	44.48	45.89	44.90
011 Cane crushing	Male	60.99	60.78	55.47	59.03
	Female	42.96	45.05	44.04	44.07
012 Carpenter	Male	100.99	101.58	102.80	101.78
	Female	—	—	—	—
013 Blacksmith	Male	79.39	79.99	80.99	80.11
	Female	—	—	—	—
014 Cobbler	Male	57.90	59.62	57.74	58.42
	Female	—	—	—	—
015 Mason	Male	110.05	110.96	111.86	100.98
	Female	—	—	—	43.08
016 Tractor driver	Male	81.68	79.39	80.87	80.63
	Female	—	—	—	—
017 Sweeper	Male	53.46	54.31	55.30	54.35
	Female	51.94	50.02	53.53	51.98
018 Unskilled labour	Male	55.57	55.51	56.10	55.72
	Female	41.45	41.53	42.78	41.91

Source : National Sample Survey Organisation.

7

Generating Employment among Agricultural Labourers

Toward a Strategy for Generating Employment

Investment

The main prerequisite for creating quality employment for agricultural labourers is to enhance the level of investment in agriculture by introducing appropriate technology mix to raise productivity keeping the present and future employment needs of the agricultural labourers in view.

For this to happen, specific policy measures, keeping the agricultural labourers in the centre stage, will have to be formulated and implemented. The earlier approach that rural development would take the responsibility of the development of agricultural labourers automatically, did not yield any notable result. Hence, the approach should be based on a perspective that development of agricultural labourers would lead to the development of rural areas. The focus should be, first and foremost, the agricultural labourers as they constitute the most vulnerable section and also comprises the largest group of people living below the poverty line. Investment pattern should be so integrated and converged that it takes into account various aspects of life and livelihood of the agricultural labourers (Mahajan).

Participation

The level of participation of agricultural labourers should be enhanced by fostering and devising strategic organisations, not only through panchayati raj institutions which have failed to take into account the realities of the agricultural labourers. Imaginative and innovative organisational models like workers cooperatives at village, panchayat and block levels will have to be promoted and their representatives will be part of the existing institutional set-up to represent the agricultural labourers' interests. This process will also raise the class-consciousness of the agricultural labourers which will ultimately help them organise on class line to envision and struggle for an egalitarian governance. The existing trade union can include in their charter of demand that at local level especially at block and district level trade union representatives are invited when various programmes are launched, funds allocated and implemented. Despite all limitations, trade unions still can better represent the agricultural labourers' interest. The B.K.M.U. being the country's first and largest union of agricultural labourers can initiate such activities (UNDP, 2001).

In-Situ Development

It is now quite well known, at micro-level, abut the existence, magnitude and characteristics of agricultural labourers. Hence, when any programme is launched a micro-level planning strategy can be attempted to examine in-situ resource base, its level of utilisation vis-a-vis the employment requirements of the agricultural labourers along with exploring alternative and sustainable avenues of new employment opportunties for growing agricultural labourers.

Land Reforms for Generating Employment

As noted earlier, most of the agricultural labourers are landless and hence assetless. And land is the most productive asset. Given this, land reform programme has to be given the paramount importance. After the second world war many countries in the world in addition to launching other programmes for alleviating poverty, have given land reform its due place and importance. As a result, countries like, Japan, Taiwan, Egypt, China, Vietnam, etc. have been able to eradicate poverty to a great extent. In India, in West Bengal State, the land reform measures adopted by the left front government have triggered tremendous growth potentials of the erstwhile landless agricultural labourers (El-ghoneny, 1990).

Special Employment Programme

Given the massive unemployment and under employment among the agricultural labourers special programmes to enhance their wage earning and self-employment opportunities have to be created at micro-level. This could be done by credit and creating employment through building infrastructure. Edgren & Muqtada rightlyvisualise this approach : "Whether development is achieved through rural industrialization or "ruralization" of industries, concurrent measures and incentives should be provided with appropriate princing and credit/subsidy policies for development of transportation, infrastructure, and linkages with the agriculture as well as formal sectors.

While the various forms of macro-and local-level planning are most often directed toward growth and productivity, their short-term impact on the levels of living of the poor are negligible. Therefore, special employment creation schemes should be promoted. SECs, either through wage-based employment or self-employment, are economically justified and politically expedient.

Because of the limitations of special employment schemes as currently practiced, future planning should be directed toward creating productive and viable employment opportunities. The SECs should not be considered simply as 'reservoirs' for employment which are neither linked to growth nor allow permanence of employment entitlements. Wage-based employment promotion, through public works and food-for-work programmes require strict administrative control in order to avoid waste and corruption as well as to reach intended beneficiaries. In addition, the growing trend to allow rural workers a share of the physical assets created should be encouraged. The Maharashtra Employment Guarantee Scheme (MEGS), through its efficient administration provides an example of how wage-based employment schemes can generate substantial benefits to the target population.

The promotion of self-employment schemes among the rural poor through provision of collateral-free credit, subsidies and other inputs is gradually evolving as a major policy thrust in economies with high poverty ratios. Such schemes vary in size, depending on the objective and resource position of the public or non-government organisation that administers the scheme. Schemes also vary according to the composition of the target group. One important objective of such programmes has been to reach the rural female labour force, who have had limited access to employment opportunities beyond household activities. The design of such schemes should concentrate on the viable and productive nature of the activities. Complete packages, which include skill-building and marketing techniques should be encouraged.

Because self-employment schemes are relatively new and are currently ad hoc and uncoordinated, an institutional mechanism should be developed. Supervision as well as more accessible rural banking should be extended to self-employment schemes. Finally, a cost-effectiveness analysis of these schemes should be conducted (ILO, 1987).

Livestock

Livestock are an important source of livelihood for rural labour households. However, due to dwindling pastures, rising cost of rearing of livestock, many economically weaker households find it difficult to raise and rear livestock.

Government may make special credit provision for purchasing livestock and provide ancillary facilities to the below poverty level agricultural labour households so that this provide them alternative employment.

Education and Training

Agricultural labourers though they possess traditional knowledge and skills of many occupations, still they may not be in a position to manage and plan their activities properly. This can be tackled by providing education and training in various skills.

8

Micro-Level Planning - Strategy and Technique

Introduction

Planning has so far been an experience from the top. Despite five decades of experience in planning in the country, the concept of planning has not percolated down to grassroots level institution, for instance, village panchayat. The immediate consequence which comes to our notice is the lack of development of our villages, manifested in growing poverty, unemployment, under-employment, absence of proper development of social and economic infrastructure.

One of the causes which appears prominently while one analyses the existing scenario, is the absence of peoples' participation in the process of development. The Panchayat Raj Institution is intended to make up this gap.

The Panchayati Raj Institution is indeed a revolutionary concept and an important mechanism through which people's participation is being sought for various development activities at grassroots level. But despite this concept's revolutionary potential, the actualisation process has been more often dismal and sometimes tardy. In some cases, its potential has, sagnated or became a negative and conflicting factor.

Hence, a question arises : how the institution could be made more dynamic and responsive to the emerging needs of the people in general and people living in poverty and oppression in particular. Hence we suggest a micro-level planning model which will help the Institution to initiate planning process from below by involving people themselves for their betterment.

- The first task is a to create symbiosis between the Panchayati Raj Institution and other grassroots level people's organisations, for example, Trade Unions, Non-governmental Organisations (NGO), Self Help Group (SHG) and others.
- Second the Panchayati Raj Institution should devise its strategy in such manner that other organisations becomes partners in the process of development rather than becoming competitors. This could be done by co-opting them in various standing committees created by it for operational activities.

This process of building symbiosis could be called convergence of mechanisms/agencies

- Once the convergence of mechanisms are achieved, a philosophy for guidance has to be evolved by participating bodies in the symbiosis. *We suggest the following philosophical ideas:*
- That people are centre of planning. By this we mean that a sustainable development idea, where people and nature would work harmoniously.
- That problems of the people are embedded in exploitation, poverty and their weakened situation. And people are aware about it and they can solve it though action and reflection.
- That people have in their disposal, knowledge, skill and information to solve their problems once an ambience is created where they are provided with space, opportunity and support.
- That the problems people face are not perceived as problems but challenges which could be turned into opportunities by their redressal and resolution.
- That centering development process on people means assisting them in unleashing their potential for collective growth and sustainable development.
- Acceptance of this perspective means changing one's attitude and action-framework which calls for democratisation from below.

The next step is devising operational strategy. Figure 1 presents various steps in the planning process.

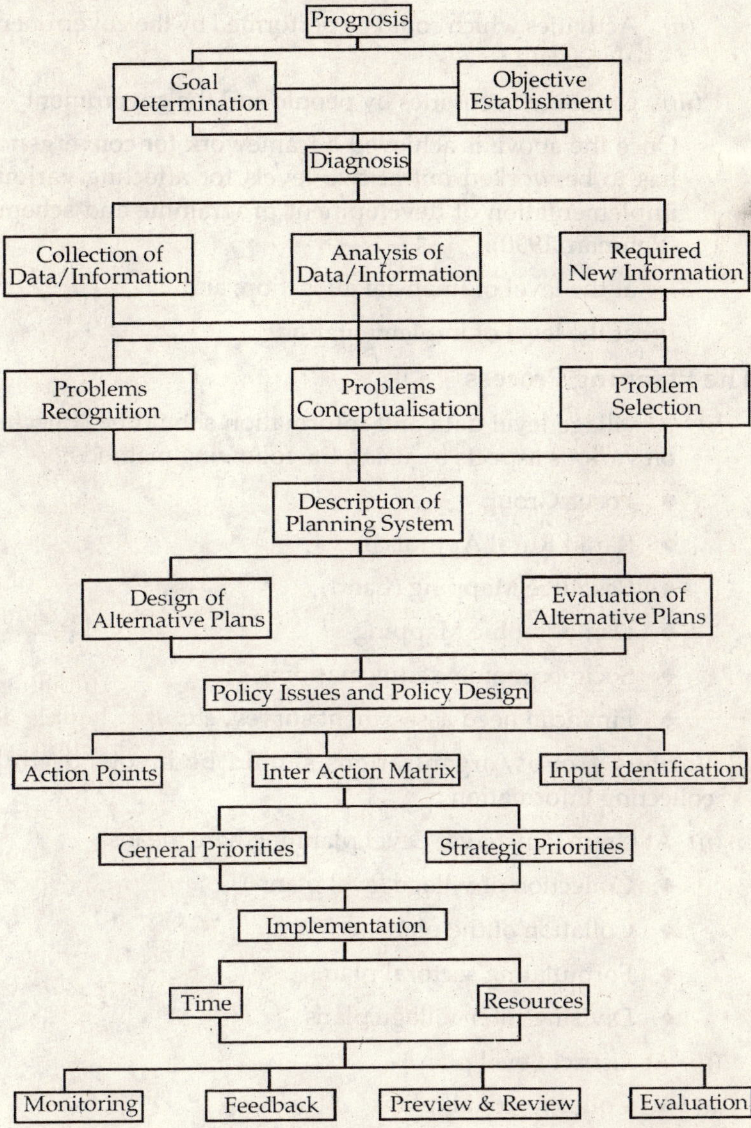

- The next step is regrouping of functions and functionaries on the basis of subjects in the Eleventh Schedule. The activities could be grouped in the following category.

(i) Activities which could be performed by people themselves;

(ii) Activities which could be performed by the government alone; and

(iii) Combined activities by people and the government

Once the above is achieved a framework for convergence has to be worked out at two levels for affecting various implementation of development programme and scheme (Rehman, 1990):

(i) at the level of financial allocation; and

(ii) at the level of implementation

The Planning Process

(i) At village level data and information should be collected on various aspects by using the following methods:

- Focus Group
- Rapid Rural Appraisal
- Resource Mapping (Land)
- Demographic Mapping
- Socio-economic status mapping
- Financial need assessment survey, etc.

Various groups/organisations should be involved while collecting information :

(ii) At Gram Panchayat Level planning here means.

- Collection of village level plans
- Collation of the plans
- Formulating sectoral plan
- Divising Inter-village plans

(iii) At district Level plan

- Collection of all plans
- Combining them into an integrated plans
- Designing sectoral plan

Division of Plans : The plans prepared for the villages and the gram panchayats will have to focus on what can be achieved in the short run first. The village plans and the gram panchayat plans will provide all the required interventions in the four sectors, namely, People's Sector, Bank Sector, Government Sector and Combined Sector.

The People's Sector will contain all development inverventions which the people can do themselves. For example, maintenance of community tanks, village path or preservation of sacred groves. The Bank Sector will include development interventions which is possible by availing of credit from the bank, which could include creation of income generating assets, livestock, etc.

The Government Sector will include activities or projects which can be executed by Government funding. This could include construction of roads, bridges, check dams, infrastructure, running of schools, etc. The Combined Sector is a residual sector, where all development activities that require people's contribution, flow of credit and government financing as also private sector investment as appropriate. These could be in the nature of setting up an agro-processing unit (Bandyopadhyay, 2002).

Time Schedule

Many activities are to be performed for igniting development potentials. Some have to be performed in short time span while some in medium and long term time span. Hence, activities have to be prioritised judiciously and chronologically which would ultimately contribute to achieving goals and realising objectives.

Child Labour in Micro-Planning

Child labour is a serious problem. Its existence also indicates deplorable socio-economic condition of

- a child
- its parents
- its family
- its family's socio-economic condition
- its family's
  - poverty
  - under employment

— unemployment, etc.

At micro-level planning, when action points are prioritised families with incidence of child labour could be brought within the fold of poverty alleviation continuum first, for such families are always at the bottom of deprivation.

This can be done by according priority in terms of :

- Providing employment to the families,
- Providing ancillary benefits to the child concerned.

The problem of incidence of child labour could be tackled at the grassroots level by the PRI in collaboration with other organisations.

For achieving better results, a framework for convergence focusing the child labour vis-a-vis family be worked out which is illustrated in the following diagram:

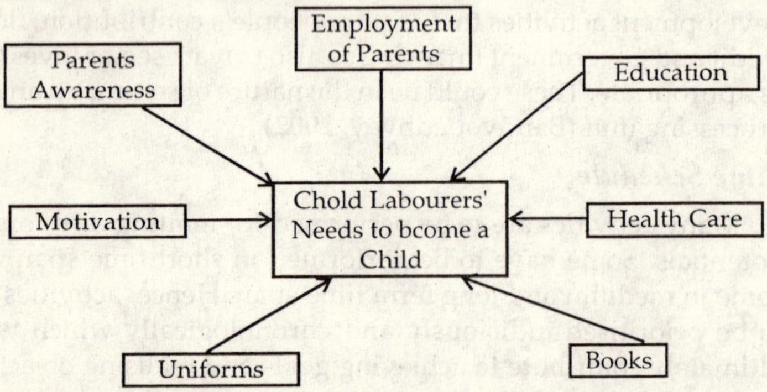

By focusing all the above simultaneously a child labour could be freed from the 'suffix' labour, which erodes the child's childhood and preparatory potential to grow up as a capable adult worker.

The above framework could be put into action only by convergence of various agents, government, non-government, self-help groups, PRI, different departments under different agencies.

Epilogue

A village is a world in itself. It is not populated by one category. Heterogeneity and hierarchical orders are its main characteristics. This characteristics touch every aspect and area of life. Some aspects are natural and some are human made. In fact, human interventions, because of myriad existing and emerging needs, have greatly altered many orders of thing both in material and psychological terms.

Moreover, experiences gained over millennia have also left its indelible marks on every aspect of life in every village. And these experiences, either in the forms of knowledge, skill and information or in the form of practice, have not properly been recorded with a humanistic perspective. More often, what have been recorded and preserved, are in the category of reactions among groups with camouflaged nomenclatures. As a result, human history has become sectarian tell tale.

Against this background the prerequisite of the day is to build up a micro-level data base at village level covering every aspect of life-demographic, environmental, flora, fauna, geographic, etc. The knowledge thus gathered would eventually help in identifying the problems and underlining their resolution in proper and sustainable manner.

Hence, very village should have a village *Information Centre*. Which will be working as the centre for *'thinking, acting, and reflecting'* for envisioning and designing a better sustainable village and the world.

REFERENCES

1. Bandhyopadhyay, D. et al. (2002) 'Convergence of Programmes by Empowering SHGS and PKIs. In *Economic and Political Weekly*, Vol. XXXVII, No. 26, June.
2. Rehman, M.M. (1990) *Political Economy of Institutional Planning in Education*. New Delhi, Commonwealth Publishers.

9

Organising Rural Workers : an Experience

Introduction

After independence, India embarked on a massive development effort with a clear emphasis on rural development; for majority of its population lived in villages and many of them were below the poverty line. Through its five year plans the Government has been launching a plethora of programmes and schemes to alleviate the poverty of the rural masses. The approaches followed were by generating employment and creating asset base in rural areas.

Initially, it was a top-down approach, i.e., decisions were taken at the top of the administrative hierarchy and then the decisions were pushed down to implementation level without the participation of the beneficiaries. As a result, the intended benefits did not reach the beneficiaries to a desired extent. There were a number of reasons behind the emergence of this situation. However, one of the most important reasons was the lack of organisation of the exploited rural labourers. This was especially pointed out by international organisations like Food and Agricultural Organisation (FAO) and International Labour Organisation (ILO). Quoting from a report, ILO highlights the importance of rural workers organisation which reads:

"In developing Asia economic growth is straining at the leash of an iniquitous and outmoded social system. The extension of trade unionism to the countryside is necessary in order to apply much needed pressure for economic and social reforms and their effective implementation, to democratize the process of economic development, and to ensure the willing participation and involvement of the people, so crucial for its success. Nothing less than a thorough going social and cultural transformation of the rural scene and the restructuring of rural society will meet the needs of the situation. The obvious need of the hour in almost all spheres of economic activity is thus organisation-organisation of planning to make possible the marriage of peoples' needs with available resources; organisation of work to make possible the full utilisation of labour; organisation of education to usher in institutional change; and above all, organisation of the masses to secure their participation in the economic effort and to ensure the equitable distribution of the fruits of growth" (See Box 9.1).

Box 9.1Trades' Unions: Their Past, Present And Future

(a) Their past.Capital is concentrated social force, while the workman has only to dispose of his working force. The contract between capital and labour can therefore never be struck on equitable terms, equitable even in the sense of a society which places the ownership of the material means of life and labour on one side and the vital productive energies on the opposite side. The only social power of the workmen is their number. The force of numbers, however, is broken by disunion. The disunion of the workmen is created and perpetuated by their unavoidable competition amongst themselves.

Trades' Unions originally sprang up from the spontaneous attempts of workmen at removing or at least checking that competition, in order to conquer such terms of contract as might raise them at least above the condition of mere slaves. The immediate object of Trades' Unions was therefore confined to everyday necessities, to expediencies for the obstruction of the incessant encroachments of capital, in one word, to questions of wages and time of labour. This activity of the Trades' Unions is not only legitimate, it is necessary. It cannot be dispensed with so long as the present system of production lasts. One the contrary, it must be generalised by the formation and the combination of Trades' Unions throughout all countries. On the other hand, unconsciously to themselves, the Trades' Unions were forming centres of organisation of the working class, as the medieval municipalities and communes did for the middle class. If the Trades' Unions are required for the guerilla fights between capital and labour, they are still more important as organised agencies for superseding the very system of wages labour and capital rule.

(b) Their present.Too exclusively bent upon the local and immediate struggles with capital, the Trades' Unions have not yet fully understood their power of acting against the system of wages slavery itself. They therefore kept too much aloof from general social and political movements. Of late, however, they seem to awaken to some sense of their great historical mission, as appears, for instance, from their participation, in England, in the recent political movement from the enlarged views taken of their function in the United States, and from the following resolution passed at the recent great conference of Trades' delegates at Sheffield.

"That this conference, fully appreciating the efforts made by the International Association to unite in one common bond of brotherhood the working men of all countries, most earnestly recommend to the various societies here represented, the advisability of becoming affiliated to that body, believing that it is essential to the progress and prosperity of the entire working community."

(c) Their future.

Apart from their original purposes, they must now learn to act deliberately as organising centres of the working class in the broad interest of its complete emancipation. They must aid every social and political movement tending in that direction. Considering themselves and acting as the champions and representatives of the whole working class, they cannot fail to enlist the non-society men into their ranks. *They must look carefully after the interests of the worst paid trades, such as the agricultural labourers, rendered powerless by exceptional circumstances* (emphasis is ours). They must convince the world at large that their efforts, far from being narrow and selfish, aim at the emancipation of the downtrodden millions.

Source : Marx,.K. and F. Engels (1963) *Selected Workers,* Vol.Two, Moscow, Progress Publishers.

Some Lessons from Rural Labour Camps

Rural Labour constitutes the largest segment of the workforce of the country. The problem of rural labour is therefore equally multi-dimensional and highly complicated in nature. However, the apparent and striking face of the problem is always conceptualized and construed as poverty. And more often the search for solution of poverty was the intended goal of every action. The search, however, remains as elusive as ever. It did not yield any tangible solution either delineating the causes of or remedies for poverty.

In this perspective NLI envisioned an imaginative programme in the form of holding rural labour camp with a view to conscientising the rural labourers. The purpose was to assist the rural labourers, particularly the largest component constituted by landless agricultural labourers, petty agricultural producers, sharecroppers and rural artisans, belonging especially to the vulnerable sections, to critically examine the nature and character of reality through a conscious reflection of the reality of their existence for transforming it through the process of praxis.

This attempt has yielded commendable result. For, example, the Government of West Bengal had adopted this innovative programme during identification and recording of bargadars (sharecroppers) under operation Barga. Besides, wherever such camps were held there a sense of regeneration among the vulnerable sections had emerged. These camps have also provided some very important lessons for us.

First, the problem of rural labour should not be conceptualised merely as that of poverty. What emerged from the diverse experiences gained from camps organised at different places with rural labour belonging to different socio-cultural backgrounds, is that lack of empathy on the part of rural labourers themselves and on the part of people who are involved in the process of solving their problems as well, is one of the major obstacles to their development.

This resulted in a situation where, apart from conceptual complication, the understanding of causes of and remedies for poverty remained a half-hearted reflection and action for transformation. Second, the socio-economic structure, designed and perpetuated by the socio-economically powerful and privileged sections was viewed as if emerging from without. Many policy, programmes and actions were mostly formulated and launched without disturbing the skewed nature of control over productive assets. In the existing socio-economic structure, the rural poor is unfavourably placed. As a result, they have been denied of their due share in the gains from the development process. This denial is quite often not clearly understood by the deprived rural labourer nor any comprehensive effort has been made to educate them as to why they are deprived, how and what they have been deprived of. What is perhaps more disturbing is that majority of the rural labourer is unaware of their hidden potential as collective. Their understanding of their potential that if they are organised, a vast regenerative capability would unfold and help them create a new reality thereby liberating them from poverty.

Third, it was amply clear that lack of organisation is the most serious obstacle on their part to taking up any conscious decision and decisive action on the part of the rural labour. For instance, we have not come across any organisational frameworks among the rural labour, to redress and resolve their problem-the problem either communitarian or isolated.

Imparting organisational knowledge and skill has enhanced the collective capability of the rural labourers. This is perhaps one of the important lessons for us as well as for those who are concerned with the development of the rural labourers.

Fourth, it was also felt that mere conceptual awareness and imbibing organisational skills and information are not enough. What is required is to assist them understanding issues on which they should reflect upon for taking action for transformation. Therefore, the clarity of issues, which might range from social, political, economic, cultural and psychological and understanding their interconnectedness and dynamics are more important for any organisation to form and sustain and it getting it institutionalised. More often, it is being felt that the rural labourers are prone to expectation from above and accept their reality as given rather than to act upon it. For example, during a training programme organised for the development of leadership capability of the group leaders of Development of Women and Children in Rural Areas (DWCRA) scheme (an important programme launched by the government for the benefit of families, particularly women living poverty line) it was observed that the assistance channeled through this scheme was accepted more as a dole than as a due.

This very feeling did not allow them to organise themselves into a collective entity. As a result, a large chunk of the intended assistance was siphoned off by the delivery system.

This clearly reveals how important it is to develop consciousness about one's due through conscientisation which would help the rural labour to educate themselves for realising their potential through building organisations and taking up action for transforming the existing reality into a new reality.

One more important lesson for us is that, more often than not, one finds it difficult to prioritize issues for undertaking action. This lack of clarity frequently runs counter to what is being intended and what is achieved. As we have mentioned earlier, what, therefore, is required is to delineate the interconnectedness of various issues and strategies that are intended to be evolved to resolve problems. This clarity will perhaps help reach the goal of "empowering the rural labour" more effectively and efficiently. Any strategy to empower the rural labour should have the above imperative as the essential component.

> The word conscientization (based on the Brazilian *conscientizacao*), the process by which human beings participate critically in transforming act, should not be understood as an idealistic manipulation. Even if our vision in conscientization is dialogical, not subjective or mechanistic, we cannot attribute to this consciousness a role that it does not have, that of transforming reality. Yet we also must not reduce consciousness to a mere reflection of reality.
>
> *Paulo Freire*

The philosophical context has to be more clearly enunciated against the backdrop of existing socio-economic and political situations. Because, from time immemorial, human beings have been striving to achieve higher quality of life and its existence on this earth. The striving has not been always an easy task – it has been a process strewn with innumerable upheavals. Even the very fact of comprehending the process itself has remained unaccomplished. There have been interpretations of this process, the process in which the human beings find themselves. However, the interpretations have yet to change the existing situation – a situation where materials and relations are unequal, dominated by exploitation, perpetuated by traditions, customs and 'faiths' which again are the results of intended perpetuation of inequity and exploitation.

It has continued to exist in different intensity and magnitude for millennia because the interpretations have often not been put in practice. For practice means change - turning existential problematic topsy-turvy and creating a new order of things. Marx epitomised this situation more clearly: "philosophers have only interpreted the world, in various ways, the point is, however, to change it."

The change has indeed been a difficult task because changing means sharing space and opportunity. And the beginning of the change process is to begin to talk, begin to reflect, and begin to initiate dialogue. Freire explains this more eloquently: Human existence cannot be selient, nor can be nourished by false words, but only true words, with which humans transform the world. To exist, humanly, is to name the world, to change it. Once named, the world in turn reappears to the names as a problem and requires of them a new naming. [humans] are not built in silence but in word, in work, in action-refection.... If it is in speaking their word that humans transform the world by naming it, dialogue imposes itself as the way in which [humans] achieve significance as [humans]. Dialogue is thus an existential necessity".

The process of initiating dialogue is not episodic – it is a contemplated and concrete decision, it is praxis. It is the process of unrolling the 'mysterious' nature of existing iniquitous ideological apparatus and simultaneously creating an equitous and humane existential framework of socio-economic and political structure. This can be done only by 'organic' intellectual pursuit from conception to action. Today this 'organic' intellectual pursuit has gained currency by Participatory Action Research (PAR).

"The ideology of PAR is that a self-conscious people, those who are currently poor and oppressed, will progressively transform their environment by their own praxis. In this process others may play a catalytic and supportive role but will not dominate" (Rahman, 1991: 13).

This is needed. This is needed because democracy and humanism cannot co-exist with socio-economic and political system which fosters sectarianism and polarisation and which consequently and subsequently ensures exploitation, inequality and disharmony. Hence more concretely PAR means generation and practice of knowledge by people, for the people and of the people.

It was in this background that VVGNLI initiated a participatory research with emphasis on organising rural workers. Before this initiative the Rural Labour Camps organised by NLI were only one time activity and it did not involve continued efforts of follow-up and other such activities to help building the organisation and making it emerge as an influential force in rural areas.

This is for the first time that VVGNLI initiated the present action research project with a clear cut orientation of organising of rural labourers and with a clear cut plan for follow-ups and other training programmes to help the organisation emerging as an influential force. The aim was to develop self-action among rural labour for sustainable development. The specific objectives were:

1. To promote relevant interest organisations of the people through motivation, education and awareness programmes.
2. To facilitate and promote processes among rural labour through their organisations for identifying, planning and implementing need-based social, psychological and material development action programmes.
3. To organize need-based interface programmes between newly developed people's organisations and other governmental agencies.
4. To motivate, reorient and sensitize local administration and other development agencies for extending their support to organisations of rural workers.
5. To understand and record the processes of emergence and growth of people's organisations and the processes by which such organisations bring about the subjective and objective development of the members.

The principles and philosophy behind the project were to raise the level of collective consciousness among the rural labourers by their collective self-enquiry and reflection about their present existence, what they understood about development, their oppression and their problems and its causes and finally its resolution. The perspective against which the process of conscientising of the rural workers was taken up has been illustrated in Fig. 1.

Selection of the Area

VVGNLI had already conducted Rural Labour Camps in certain villages of district Tikamgarh Development Block, Tikamgarh in Madhya Pradesh, earlier. Therefore, it was decided to select certain other development block of the distt. for the action research intervention. It was decided by the research team that specific area for intervention i.e. specific development block should be selected on the basis of well defined socio-economic indicators such as:

(1) Existence of a significant number of rural labourers;

(2) Visible scars of neglect by development authorities;

(3) Absence of any organisation of he rural labourers; and

(4) There should exist potential for greater employment and income generation and other development activities.

A visit was made by research team to a development Block, namely, Niwari for intervention. Niwari block is one of the most underdeveloped areas and also politically sensitive area of the district. Bureaucratic apathy, corruption, unbridled politicking and under utilisation of natural resources are some of the characteristic features of the area.

The Setting

Tikamgarh District: The district of M.P. is situated near Jhansi and as such lies between latitude 24 26 and 25 40 North and longitude 78 26 East. It is part of Sagar revenue division and located in the Northern part of the State. The district is bounded by Jhansi and Lalitpur districts in the north, Chattarpur district of M.P. in the east and the southern edge of district touches Sagar district of M.P.

During the pre-independence period, it was a princely state and the original capital of this territory was Orcha. But later, in 1783, the capital was transferred to Tehri or Tikamgarh (Named in 1887 as Tikamgarh in the honour of lord Krishna).

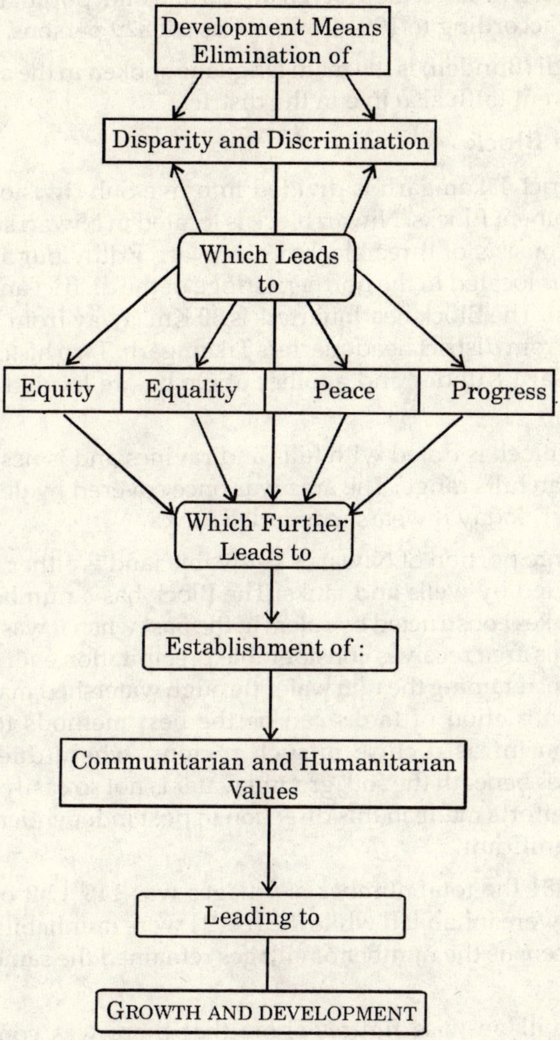

Fig. 9.1 : Basis of Praxis : The Theoretical Foundation of Action-research Intervention

The total area of the district is 5048 89 Sq.km. and the district headquarters is located at Tikamgarh. Total population of the district according to 1991 Census was 940829 persons.

Hindi (Bundeli) is the main language spoken in the area people of different faith also live in the district.

Niwari Block

District Tikamgarh is divided into five Sub-divisions and six development Blocks. Niwari block is located in Niwari subdivision which consists of three blocks i.e. Niwari, Prithviour and Palera. Niwari is located in the northern fringe of the district and adjacent to Jhansi. The Block headquarters is 30 Km. away from Jhansi and 80 Km. from district headquarters Tikamgarh. Two historical forts, are at Garh Kundar and another at Orcha are located in Niwari block.

The Block is doted with hills and ravines and is nestled in the Vindhyan hills range. The area was once covered by dense forest. However, today it wears a denuded look.

A large portion of Niwari's cultivable land is either rained fed or irrigated by wells and tanks. The Block has a number of large tanks/lakes constructed by rulers in the past when it was a princely state. This area receives considerable precipitation every year and therefore, retaining the rain water through watershed management and construction of tanks can be the best methods to develop irrigation infrastructure in such regions, where due to rocky structures beneath the soil, ground water is not so easily available. But the efforts made in this direction in post independence period are insignificant.

In 1981 the total number of villages was 148. Out of this, 127 villages were inhabited while the rest 21 were uninhabited *jungles*. In 1991 census the number of villages remained the same as it was in 1981.

The village-wise figures show that there was considerable increase in the number of households as well as in population. For example, in 1991, the number of households registered an increase of 50 percent in 1991 over 1981. Correspondingly, the population also increased at a very high rate thus putting a lot of stress on the already stressed services and facilities available in the Block. In 1981, the total number of population in the block was 97,461. This increased to 1,26,378 in 1991 which worked out to 29.67 percent increase over 1981 in 1991.

Demographic Profile

According to 1991 census the population of Niwari Block was 126,378 with 20,682 occupied residential households. Of the total population 67,733 (53.39%) and 58,545 (46.40%) were males and females respectively.

Caste Configuration

Out of the total population 26.02 and 3.64 percent are Scheduled Castes and Scheduled Tribes. Together they constituted about 30.00 percent of the total population. Schedule castes are not homogeneous groups. They are divided into as many as three dozens groups. Similarly, the tribes are also divided. But basically they belong to *saur* tribal group of Madhya Pradesh.

Literacy

1991 Census reported that literacy rate in the Block was depressingly low. It was 32.59 per cent for all and for female it was 7.98 per cent. Although almost all the villages of the Block and primary schools, and just a few years ago the National Literacy Mission appeared to have made considerable effort but the participation of people had remained as dismal as ever. In fact, here are some villages where primary schools are still non-existence.

Literacy is an important indicator for measuring development of people. By this yardstick Niwari Block presents a dismal look. Out of its total population only 24.61 and 7.98 percent males and females are literate respectively. The figures are below the national averages.

Occupational Profile

It may be noted that the total main workers, in 1991, was 43,918 of which 3,474 and 10,444 were males (76.21) and females (23.78), respectively. Industry-wise distribution shows that out of the total 43,918 workers 31,335 were cultivators (71.34%), 6,780 were agricultural labourers (15.43%), 360 were engaged in livestock, forestry, fishing, hunting and plantations, orchards and allied activities (0.8%).

It could be noted that there were 7622 marginal workers, in Niwari Block in 1991. The most interesting point which could be noted is that 97.03 per cent were female marginal workers.

Landholding Pattern in Niwari

There are 22,669 holding in Niwari. A size-class wise distribution of holdings shows that 43.12 percent holdings were marginal, 27.24 percent small, 19.90 percent semi-medium, 8.91 percent medium and 0.81 per cent were large holdings. The important point which could be noted here is the fact that more than 70 per cent holdings were in the category of marginal and small holdings.

With regards to the area under various size classes of holding, it could be seen that 12.20 per cent area were under the operation of marginal holdings, 31.84 per cent are under small holdings, followed by 31.07 per cent under semi-medium, 28.78 per cent under medium, and 6.08 per cent under large-size class of holdings.

Problems

The rural labourers are beleaguered with a number of problems which cut across different aspects such as political, social, economic, education, employment, etc.

The problems were conceptualised by the workers during various camps and other village level meetings and interventions. WE have classified them under the following categories:

1. Economic Problems
2. Social Problems
3. Political Problems

A brief details of the problems is being provided here in the following paragraphs:

Economic Problems

Unemployment: This has been the most frequently cited problem by the participants of all the rural labour camps and people with whom we had interacted during our visits to different villages in the Block. As we have noted earlier, very less had been done to develop agriculture in the block.

Irrigation facilities have not been adequately provided. As a result, it is only during the monsoon that some crops are raised.

This does not provide employment for more than three months. Consequently, either people migrate to other areas or remain idle, and to fend off during the lean period they borrow and thus many of them become debt-bonded. Another cause of unemployment is the slow but steady disappearance of village crafts in which a fair number of people used to remain engaged and eked out their livelihood. Hence, unemployment has become the single most factor that is devasting a large number of families.

Low Wages: Another problem that emerged more often in the list of problems is the low wage level in the area. On average, the wage rate ranged from Rs.25 to 30, being slightly higher during the peak season. In the days of galloping price rise, the low-wage further eats into their precarious existence by making them less capable of buying essential items.

Landlessness: Most of the households are marginal farmers or landless agricultural labourers. Due to growth of population and consequent fragmentation of existing holdings and alination of land and lack of development, landlessness or semi-landlessness phenomenon among a large section of population is increasing quite fast.

Indebtedness: This is another problem which was cited quite often by the people. Indebtedness is the outcome of unemployment and resultant dependency of the working people on the landed classes and moneylenders. Non-availability of institutional credit and lack of income generating activities have contributed to the his a phenomenon of indebtedness.

Social Problems

Untouchability: Despite 50 years of independence and a number of enactments, the phenomenon of untouchability still exists in Niwari and that to a large extent. Still drinking wells in the villages are segregated on the basis of caste. This has been causing demoralisation among the gradually conscious sections of the Scheduled Castes and Scheduled Tribes. Even today the Scheduled Castes and Scheduled Tribes are not allowed to enter village temples. It was also reported that children belonging to Scheduled Castes and Scheduled Tribes communities are were allowed to study in schools on many occasions.

Alcholism: Another most insidious problem emerging in the rural areas is the mass consumption of liquor, and rural workers are becoming its most chosen victims. Drug is also making inroads into the villages. Niwari's villages are pockmarked by liquor shops known in local parlance "madhusala".

Lack of education: Schools especially, the primary ones, were almost dysfunctional. Teachers did not come regularly. The ambience in most of the schools was non-conducive. The drop-out rates were very high especially among girls and SC and ST children.

Political Problems: Participation of rural workers at various political level had not been free from interference of the local well off people, even at panchayat level their voice was often ignored.

Other problems are listed briefly as below:

(i) Rampant corruption at all levels;

(ii) Lack of information about different development schemes and projects;

(iii) Atrocities against women are quite frequent; and

(iv) Prevatence of Political factionalism in the village

Methodology of Action Research Intervention:

VVGNLI's Action Research Intervention Strategy is based on the unique democratic method of education of the people, commonly known as dialogical conscientisation. This intervention involved the following steps (See Fig. 2):

Step 1 : Pre-camp surveys and actual selection of participants: Selection of Participants was done at village level meetings of rural labourers conducted by the research team to explain the purpose or objectives of the project. It was ensured while selecting the participants case should be taken so that: *(i)* he or she was young; *(ii)* he or she possessed some articulating power; *(iii)* he or she was a wage worker; and *(iv)* he or she had some apparent leadership qualities.

Step 2 : Establishing necessary rapport with the participants and to some extent with the people of area during pre-camp surveys and village level meeting conducted for selection of participants. The purpose to make the people at large to realize that this intervention was in their interests.

Step 3: The Camp: Camp process was based on the method of dialogical concientisation. The role of faculty members was restricted to the level of a facilitator. Problem themes were developed by participants and thereafter they were facilitated and persuaded to find out he root causes of the problems and ways to resolve those problems.

Lastly, they were facilitated to think and search out the social and political forces, which could solve their problem. From this point they gradually came to realize the importance of the organisation. The time taken to reach this final point depended upon the articulating power of the participants which in our experience depended on the two factors: education and mobility of labourers. The camp duration was fixed to be four days and he final objective of the camp was to foster an organisation of rural labourers emerging from within by taking an initial shape in the camp itself or thereafter. Various behavioural games are employed to develop their articulation if articulating power was found low.

Step 4: A strategy based on interface with government functionaries was employed to ensure the proper participation of poorer sections in development process. To facilitate such relations between government functionaries and representatives of poorer sections, an interface programme with government functionaries was conducted at the last day of the camp when participants had already imbibed the value of collective organisation and prepared their plan of action.

Step 5: After the camp, the social organizers of the project area helped the participants in conducting village level meetings of rural labourers. They were also responsible for training the rural labour activists about how to broaden the base of the organisations among rural labourers and how to mobilize the people, prepare the charter of demands and lead different legal forms of struggles. The social Organizers were also responsible for documenting various organisational and psychological processes that were emerging in the area.

Step 6: Reorientation-cum-training programmes for the emerging rural labour activists were organised in VVGNLI and also

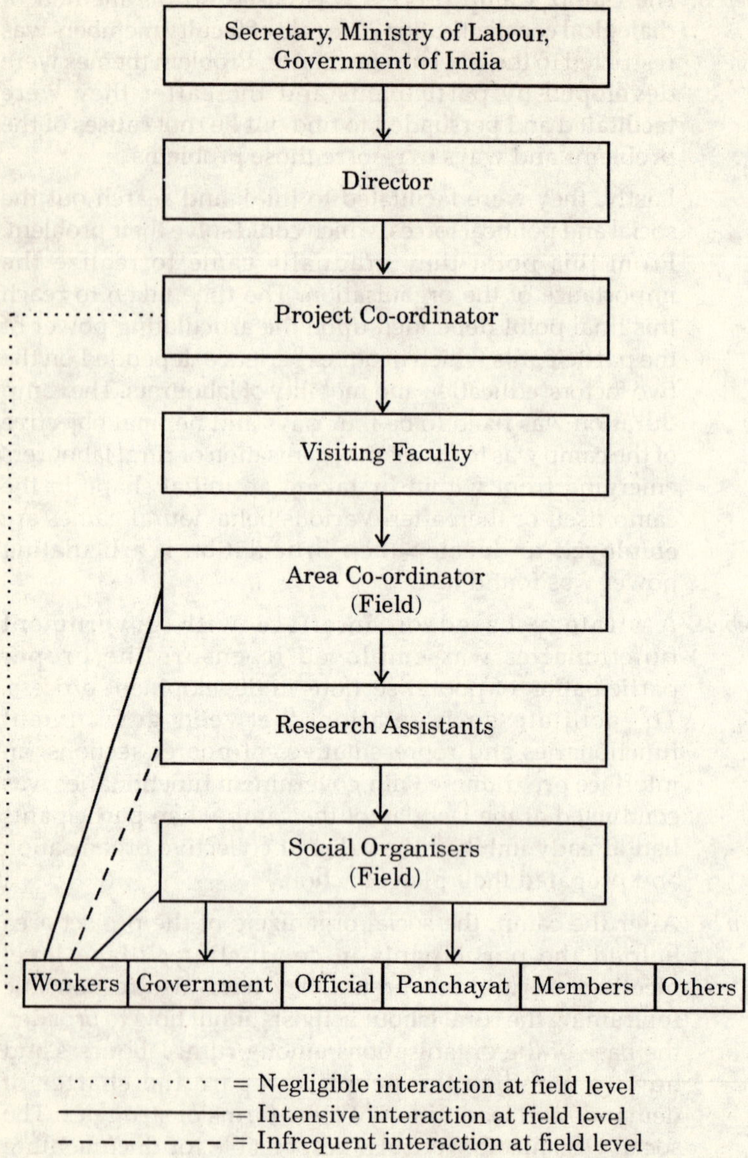

Fig. 9.2 : Role of Animators/Actors in the Field

in project area from time to time. Initial training programmes covered basic aspects of how to build an organisation and how to mobilize the people for sustainability. It also provided them an orientation about history of peasant movements and labour movements. The training programmes of later phase basically trained them about the structure and functioning of trade unions.

Step 7: A special interface programme at block level was organised in which on the one side there were the leading activists of the rural labour organisations emerging in the block, and the district government functionaries were on the front facing the rural labour activists. This interface programme was organised when the rural labour organisation emerged at the Block level and there emerged a group of rural labour activists playing active role in mobilising the rural labourers. In addition. In this interface programme, the rural labour activists clearly put the demands of the poorer sections of the area before the government functionaries and made them to realize the intensity of suffering of rural poor because of exploitation and oppression. This interface between the two sides helped a lot in developing a cooperation between rural labour organisation and the government functionaries. (The details of action-intervention process have been presented in Figs. 3&4).

The Outcome

The action research intervention had produced two tangible results: one, the level of consciousness and awareness among rural labourers have substantially increased. For example, it was quite difficult for the workers to approach the government officials for any activity. Today it is quite common among the workers that they do not hesitate to face any authority.

Second, emergence of two major organisations, whose membership has been growing gradually. Almost one third of the Block's villages are linked with the organisations. The organisations are, namely:

1. Bundelkhand Gramin Mazdur Union; and
2. Bundelkhand Khet Mazdur Union

Some important impacts of the organisations/and its activities are summarised in the following pages.

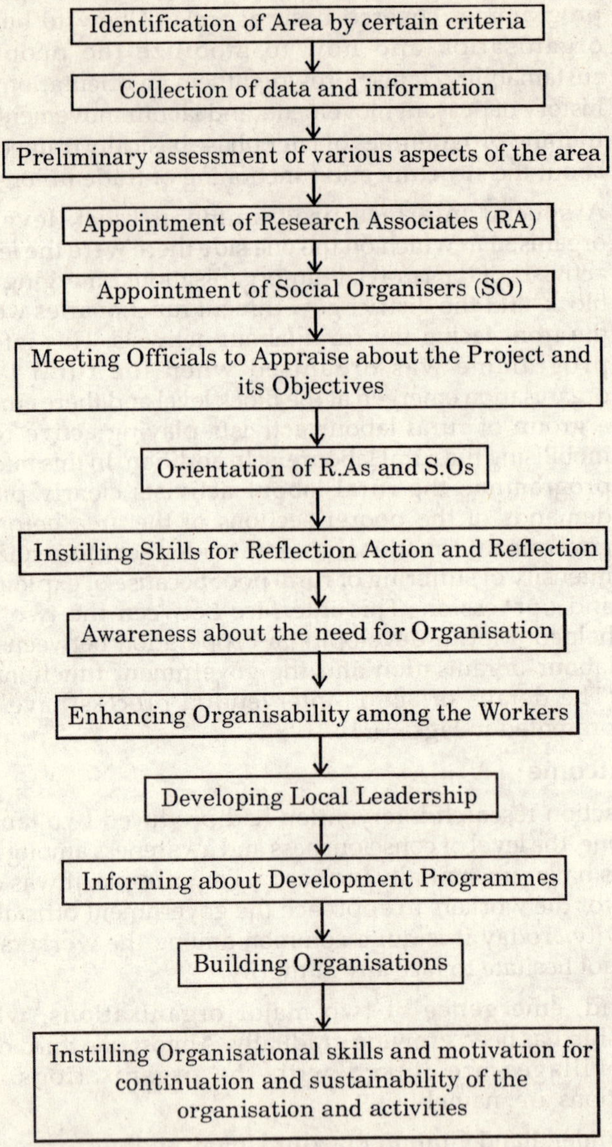

Fig. 9.3 : Action Research Intervention Process

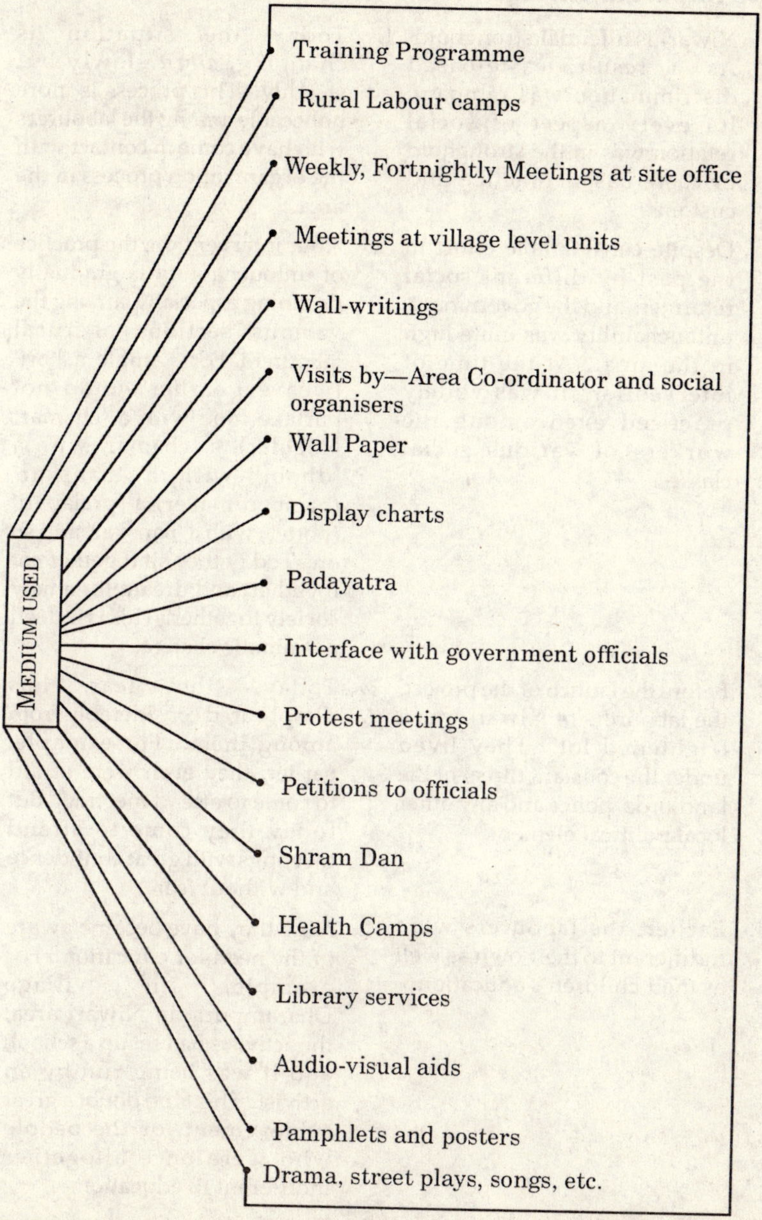

Fig. 9. 4 : Various Medium Used in the Intervention Process

The Impact of Intervention

1.	Niwari is a feudal stronghold. As a result, caste-based discrimination was rampant. Its every aspect of social relation was in the stronghold of caste-based practice and customs.	1.	Today the situation is changing, *albeit* slowly but steadily. This process is more noticeable among the labourers who have come in contact with the organization process in the area.
2.	Despite considerable effort in the past by different social reformers and the government, untouchability was quite high in the area. At the time of intervention, it was widely practiced even among the workers of various social classes.	2.	After intervention, the practice of untouchability is gradually declining especially among the various sections of rural labourers. For example, a 'kori' (weaver) earlier would not partake food with a 'chamar' (cobbler), a 'chamar' with a 'dhobi' with a 'banskar' (bamboo maker) a 'prajapati' (potter) with a 'banskar' and so on. Today they sit together eat together, and dream for a new society together. This is indeed a dramatic change.
3.	Before the launch of the project, the labourers of Niwari was a frightened lot. They lived under the constant threat of the landlords, police and any other local political element.	3.	Today, the fear has disappeared considerably from among them. For example, earlier, they even were afraid to come to attend meeting. But today they come to attend meetings with great confidence and without fear.
4.	Earlier, the labourers were indifferent to their own as well as their children's education	4.	Now they have become aware of the need for education. For example, in village Dharampura, in Niwari area, the activists had set up a school; and it was being run by an activist. This is no doubt a great achievement for the people who were once altogether indifferent to education.
5.	Before the intervention, social economic and political	5.	Today the situation has considerably changed. For

oppression was rampant. The labourers meekly accepted it.	example, in village Thona and Gidkhini, the labourers put up a challenge when they were oppressed by the landlords and advantaged classes.
6. Before the conscientisation process, the exploitation of the labourers were accepted by them as the dicate of their fate. They thought it was ordained. Hence, they never protested.	6. Now the situation has change dramatically. They had understood who were their exploiters, and how the exploitation took place. For example, their demand for minimum wages in several villages was an indication of their understanding and desire for the change.
7. Earlier, they were altogether unaware about their rights.	7. Today they are aware about heir constitutional as well as legal rights. This has enhanced their confidence. For example in the month of June, 2000 a demonstration of the workers of the Niwari Block was held in front of the S.D.O. revenue's office. They submitted a charter of demand to the S.D.O. It was for the first time that they themselves conversed together to demand their due from the state which had not been responsive to them earlier.
8. The labourers were completely ignorant about the evolution of society and its dynamics. How it has evolved and how it has adversely affected their lives, all these were altogether absence in the recesses of their minds.	8. Today they are clear about its structure and evolution and their placement in the society. They have understood that they had been deprived and relegated to the position of chattel. As a result of this realisation, today they are contemplating to change it for a better society based on equality and justice.
9. The gender-based discrimination was quite pervasive	9. Today, the situation has been gradually changing and the

	among the labourers. They followed the same yardstick of the landlords while treating their women.		growing level of participation women in various organising activities is an indication. For example, earlier, they hardly came to any meeting. Today they are participating in substantial number. Their involvement in the demonstration against liquor and demand for employment were a few examples. Earlier, they never used to sit together with men. Today the barrier has broken and men have began to accept them as their equals.
10.	Consumption of liquor has become endemic in the area, especially among the labourers. So is the gambling.	10.	Today both the vices have been slowly disappearing especially among the workers who are becoming the union members. The pressure and persuasion of fellow members helping those who are in the stranglehold of liquor. The labourers are also realizing that the habit of consumption of liquor and gambling has been responsible for their dependence on landlords and moneylenders, to a great extent.
11.	As usual, the level of employment is not very much of longer duration. As a result, the wage level has always been low and below the minimum wage. Besides, the labourers were unaware even about the minimum wage fixed by the government.	11.	During the period succeeding after the continuous camp based orientation in many villages, the labourers began to demand minimum wages. They also had been succeeded in obtaining minimum wages. For instance, the labourers in Murara, Lachanpura and Deuri Nayak villages, after a brief protest, received minimum wages.
12.	Earlier, the pressure of the employers on labourers in	12.	With the unionization process, the pressure has been dwindling

	many places was very high. They were at the beck and call of the employers.		though slowly. For example, in village Murara, one couple was forced to work for a landlord but was not paid any wage. When the couple protested, they were thrashed badly by the landlord and his henchman. When the activists of the union came to know about the incident they took the couple to the police station and lodged an FIR. About 40 activists accompanied the affected couple. The landlord apologized to the couple and thereafter the case was withdrawn. This incident had helped boosting the morale of the union activists.
13.	Ignorance and conservatism was very high among the labourers. They were prone to accept the gimmicks of the local soothsayers and quacks.	13.	After intervention the situation has changed considerably. The labourers now scoop at such conservatism. For example, belief in 'ghost' and other super natural phenomena once dominated their lives. When anyone suffered any illness they went to the village quacks first. But today they believe that consulting a doctor is the best alternative.
14.	Earlier, the labourers believed in bigotry. Their life was a cycle of rituals and customs. Both men and women assiduously adhered to such rituals which caused a great deal of economic loss to them, either in cash or in kind.	14.	Today they indulge less in rituals. They have understood the futility of many such practices.
15.	Earlier the labourers never imagined that there was anything beyond their caste framework. They thought that the caste based identities were divine and irredeemable.	15.	Today, the myopic identity crisis has been slowly disappearing and on its place "class consciousness" is appearing. The struggle for building and sustaining the unions is an example of their effort at raising the class consciousness.

Lessons

The chronicle of the experiments and experiences provide us a number of important lessons – the lessons in hopes and disappointment and also insights into eventual initiatives which would be taken up for correction and further experimentation.

The whole process provides us the following lessons:

First, the action research has shown that organising the diverse groups of rural labour is not difficult. It is within the range of possibility provided strategic measures are taken on the basis of ground realities.

Second, the process of action research has made it amply clear to us that rural labourers could be organised in a common platform on issues such as employment, exploitation, caste based oppression, corruption, various development programmes meant for the rural labourers, shortage of water, lack of educational opportunities, etc.

Third, the organisation process should not be made in haste. It has to be gradual without attracting much attention of the adversary parties. Initially issues, which are communitarian in nature, should be taken up of for redressal.

Fourth, awakening the adversaries at the inception about their possible erosion of power might put undue pressure on the nascent organisational possibilities of the rural labour. Hence, every effort should be made to strengthen collectivity of the labourers, thereby gradually putting up challenges to the adversaries.

Fifth, the most important lesson is that the tactics are to be based on the premise that rural labourers who have been oppressed and exploited for centuries, understand the process of their oppression and exploitation against the perspective of an expected socio-political structure based on justice, equality and human rights.

Sixth, given the situation in under developed rural areas, Frerian conscientisation process has to be adhered of *albeit* changing its connotation, in the Indian context and social milieu.

Seventh, rural labour camp, which is one of the important techniques for conscientisation of rural labour for building organisation, should be more frequently held by locally emerging leaders to give local activists a chance to do their own work.

Eighth, old, decadent and divisive social orders have to be attacked and challenged as these are often hindrances to building class-consciousness among the working masses. It was found that in a camp where such discussion took place, the participants understood more clearly their oppressive status and identified the main causes of their exploitation and were inspired of take corrective steps.

Ninth, the animators have to be clearly selected keeping in view the philosophy of organising the working masses and building a new society based on equality and humanness. Hence, rigorous training of the animators is needed before introducing them to the fields. The philosophy and principles of the project have to be made clear to them.

Tenth, conscientisation should also be simultaneously supplemented by information regarding various means, ways and methods of development. Today we find a strange situation. Though the activists have become quite articulate, but when it comes to do their work, they balk or expect that government apparatus should do it as they lack resources. They may be right in the given situation. But if their capacity is reinforced by skills and information, the chances of raising their standard and simultaneous struggle for bringing about a communitarian social structure should be a great possibility.

Elelventh, the contents of the camp should also include inputs on collective leadership skills apart from legal knowledge, developmental skills, interface with activists of similar organisation, exchange of animators, etc.

Twelfth, project proposal should be translated in to vernacular before launching any of such project. Otherwise, the local organisers and activists will remain unclear about the philosophy and principles of the project.

Fals-Borda, Ornaldo & Anisur Rahman (1991) *Action and Knowledge: Breaking the Monopoly with Participatory Action Research.* London. Intermediate Technology Publications.

Bernard, W.T. (2000) 'Participatory Research as Emancipatory Method: Challengs and Opportunities'. In. Burton, Dawn (ed.) *Research Training for Social Scientists: A Handbook for Postgraduate Researchers.* London, Sage Publications.

Melaren, P. & Deter Leonard (ed.) (1993) *Paulo Freire: A Critical Eneounter.* London, Routledge.

Appendix I : Tables

Table 1 : Growth of Rural and Urban Population in India over the Years

Period	*Average annual percentage growth rate of population*		
	Rural	*Urban*	*Total*
1901-11	0.64	0.04	0.58
1911-21	-0.13	0.83	-0.03
1921-31	1.00	1.91	1.10
1931-41	1.18	3.20	1.42
1941-51	0.88	4.14	1.33
1951-61	2.05	2.64	2.15
1961-71	2.19	3.82	2.48
1971-81[a]	1.93	4.61	2.47
1981-91[b]	2.00	3.65	2.39
1991-2001	1.79	3.12	2.13

Source : Office of the Registrar General, India.

a. The 1981 Census could not be held in Assam. The growth rates for 1971-81 and 1981-91 have been worked out on the interpolated population figures for Assam for 1981.

b. The 1991 Census was not held in Jammu & Kashmir Growth rate for 1981-91 is worked out with the projected population.

Table 2 : Percentage distribution of rural population according to village size categories for States, Union Territories and India during 1991

State/Union Territory	Population: Village size category					Total Population	Percentage of Population: Village size category				
	<=500	501-1000	1001-2000	2001-5000	>=5001		<=500	501-1000	1001-2000	2001-5000	>=5001
Andhra	1604596	3514979	9317855	20035361	14148091	48620881	3.30	7.23	19.16	41.21	29.10
Arunachal Pradesh	391499	152881	112448	68920	28182	753930	51.93	20.28	14.91	9.14	3.74
Assam	2610085	4673473	6894017	4962863	786089	19926527	13.10	23.45	34.60	24.91	3.94
Bihar	7113694	11748409	17995085	22853733	15310532	75021453	9.48	15.66	23.99	30.46	20.41
Goa	22271	44879	116156	286914	219821	690041	3.23	6.50	16.83	41.58	31.86
Gurajrat	1139722	3405902	7747243	10066786	4703868	27063521	4.21	12.58	28.63	37.20	17.38
Haryana	292930	1153472	2887478	5140323	2934701	12408904	2.36	9.30	23.27	41.42	23.65
Himachal Pradesh	2528783	1114224	667343	378651	32677	4721678	53.56	23.60	14.13	8.02	0.69
Karnataka	2496803	5357955	8212975	10054293	4947387	31069413	8.04	17.25	26.43	32.36	15.92
Kerala	1143	2455	25504	380282	21008840	21486224	0.01	0.01	0.12	1.77	97.78
Madhya Pradesh	9267549	15353903	15442679	9085777	1692425	50842333	18.23	30.20	30.37	17.87	3.33
Maharashtra	3291605	9027749	14791551	13638230	7646466	48395601	6.80	18.65	30.56	28.18	15.80

Table 2 contd : Percentage distribution of rural population according to village size categories for States, Union Territories and India during 1991

State/Union Territory	Population: Village size category					Total Population	Percentage of Population: Village size category				
	<=500	501-1000	1001-2000	2001-5000	>=5001		<=500	501-1000	1001-2000	2001-5000	>=5001
Manipur	294090	218645	269863	408760	140146	1331504	22.09	16.42	20.27	30.70	10.53
Meghalaya	841967	327477	170918	98282	6087	1444731	58.28	22.67	11.83	6.80	0.42
Mizoram	114372	107093	86606	49165	14574	371810	30.76	28.80	23.29	13.22	3.92
Nagaland	176081	200885	239363	320477	64497	1001323	17.58	20.06	23.90	32.01	6.44
Orissa	6277359	7578624	7847670	5052123	668977	27424753	22.89	27.63	28.62	18.42	2.44
Punjab	1020234	2638592	4385471	4719902	1524545	14288744	7.14	18.47	30.69	33.03	10.67
Rajasthan	4247729	7241020	9838123	9462144	3149861	33938877	12.52	21.34	28.99	27.88	9.28
Sikkim	51571	115691	106919	76509	18761	369451	13.96	31.31	28.94	20.71	5.08
Tamil Nadu	601067	2112681	6756581	14842312	12468713	36781354	1.63	5.74	18.37	40.35	33.90
Tripura	25486	82041	298813	1090951	838193	2335484	1.09	3.51	12.79	46.71	35.89
Uttar Pradesh	11033548	21380913	34391518	34436318	10264075	111506372	9.89	19.17	30.84	30.88	9.21
West Bengal	3467060	6673401	11454941	17502161	10272801	49370364	7.02	13.52	23.20	35.45	20.81

Table 2 contd : Percentage distribution of rural population according to village size categories for States, Union Territories and India during 1991

State/Union Territory	Population: Village size category					Total Population	Percentage of Population: Village size category				
	<=500	501-1000	1001-2000	2001-5000	>=5001		<=500	501-1000	1001-2000	2001-5000	>=5001
Andaman & Nicobar Islands	46943	47617	61065	50081	0	205706	22.82	23.15	29.69	24.35	0.00
Chandigarh	487	1250	8498	24657	31294	66186	0.74	1.89	12.84	37.25	47.28
Dadra & Nagar haveli	3674	11272	23761	68260	19785	126752	2.90	8.89	18.75	53.85	15.61
Daman & Diu	717	3651	8628	16796	24251	54043	1.33	6.76	15.97	31.08	44.87
Delhi	3657	10177	64650	272683	597852	949019	0.39	1.07	6.81	28.73	63.00
Lakshadweep	286	0	0	13185	9122	22593	1.27	0.00	0.00	58.36	40.38
Pondicherry	26315	55339	69991	115971	23184	290800	9.05	19.03	24.07	39.88	7.97
India	58993326	104356650	160293713	185572890	113595797	622812376	9.47	16.76	25.74	29.80	18.24

Source : Office of the Registrar General, India.

Table 3 : Percentage Distribution of Rural Population by size of Village over the years, for India.

Size of village in terms of population	1961	1971	1981	1991[a]
Less than 200	3.83	2.68	1.78	1.69
200-499	12.55	9.91	7.49	7.78
500-999	18.33	16.45	14.21	16.76
1000-1999	19.80	19.90	19.25	25.74
2000-4999	17.22	18.68	20.09	29.80
5000-9999	5.05	5.94	6.90	11.21
10000 & above	2.80	4.07	4.56	7.02
Rural population as percentage of total population	82.03	80.09	76.66	74.27
Total population (figures in million)	439.23	548.16	683.33	838.58

Source : Office of the Registrar General, India.

Note : Size class-wise percentage do not add upto percentage of total rural population as data on Assam are excluded in the size class-wise distribution.

a. Excluding Jammu & Kashmir.

Table 4 : Per thousand distribution of rural households by size class of land cultivated in India during the agriculture year 1986-87, 1992-93 & 1998-99.

Size class of land cultivated (Figures in hectare)	*Households*			*Population*		
	1986-87	*1992-93*	*1998-99*	*1986-87*	*1992-93*	*1998-99*
Up to 0.40	544	575	632	472	509	573
0.41-1.00	173	171	168	179	179	182
1.01-2.00	139	135	112	158	155	128
2.01-4.00	86	76	59	108	95	74
4.01-& above	58	43	30	82	61	43
Total	1000	1000	1000	1000	1000	1000

Source : Employment and Unemployment situation in India, NSS 55th round (July 1999-June 2000)NSS Report No. 458-1.

Table 5 : Structure of Rural/Rural Labour households in the Rural Labour Enquiries

Item		*1st Rural Enquiry 1964-65*	*2nd Rural Labour Enquiry 1974-75*	*3rd Rural Labour Enquiry 1977-78*	*4th Rural Labour Enquiry 1983*	*5th Rural Labour Enquiry 1987-88*	*6th Rural Enquiry 1993-94*
1		2	3	4	5	6	7
1. Estimated number of Rural Households (In Million)		70.4	82.1	95.7	100.5	108.4	119.5
2. Percentage of Rural Labour Households		25.4	30.3	36.8	37.3	39.7	38.3
3. Percentage of Agriculture Labour Households to Rural Households		21.8	25.3	29.9	30.7	30.7	30.3
4. Average size of the household	A	4.5	4.8	4.7	4.6	4.6	4.4
	R	4.5	4.8	4.7	4.6	4.6	4.5
5. Average earning strength	A	2.1	2.3	2.1	2.1	2.0	2.0
	R	2.1	2.3	2.1	2.0	2.0	2.0
6. Average number of wage-earners	A	2.0	2.2	1.8	1.9	1.4	1.7
	R	2.0	2.2	1.7	1.8	1.3	1.6
7. Extent of wage employment (in days) in Agricultural employment							
Male	A	217	193	229	227	231	247P
	R	219	192	229	227	230	237P

1		2	3	4	5	6	7
Female	A	149	138	186	190	157	220P
	R	161	136	186	189	157	215P

A = Agricultural Labour Households
R = Rural Labour Households
P = Provisional

Table 6 : Estimated Number of Rural Households by States and Classes.

(Figure in 000)

Sl. No.	States/ Union Territories	All Classes of Households					
		All Rural House holds		Agricultural Labour House holds		Rural Labour House holds	
		1987-88	1993-94	1987-88	1993-94	1987-88	1993-94
1	2	3	4	5	6	7	8
	Major States						
1.	Andhra Pradesh	10145	11049	4007	4583	4915	5503
2.	Assam	2781	3551	548	816	857	1236
3.	Bihar	12019	12351	4334	4844	5099	5264
4.	Gujarat	4606	5178	1582	1959	2328	2477
5.	Haryana	2053	2293	405	364	551	691
6.	Karnataka	5259	5777	2069	2180	2440	2398
7.	Kerala	3912	3905	1179	1102	1872	1866
8.	Madhya Pradesh	8634	9560	2714	3332	3057	3809
9.	Maharashtra	8560	9563	3308	3937	3977	4746
10.	Orissa	5184	5955	1826	1516	2218	1734
11.	Punjab	2430	2550	683	706	869	888
12.	Rajasthan	5420	5780	686	576	1851	1525
13.	Tamil Nadu	7688	8937	3088	3761	4103	4884
14.	Uttar Pradesh	18098	19992	3636	3061	4630	3849
15.	West Bengal	8329	9984	2989	3252	3623	4276

1	2	3	4	5	6	7	8
	Other States/UTs						
16.	Arunachal Pradesh	208	132	1	5	31	6
17.	Goa*	135	123	20	24	46	39
18.	Himachal Pradesh	848	913	41	26	126	139
19.	Jammu & Kashmir	906	330	51	11	173	49
20.	Manipur	170	208	9	12	15	19
21.	Meghalaya	230	283	20	35	34	51
22.	Mizoram	61	70	1	6	2	7
23.	Nagaland	—	74	—	2	—	3
24.	Sikkim	50	70	5	5	8	7
25.	Tripura	394	501	46	76	128	172
26.	A & N Islands	36	44	3	6	16	21
27.	Chandigarh	11	20	—	—	7	11
28.	D & N Haveli	20	24	8	7	12	17
29.	Daman & Diu	—	13	—	4	—	7
30.	Delhi	98	236	19	27	22	34
31.	Lakshadweep	4	3	—	—	1	1
32.	Pondicherry	70	61	27	27	42	37
	All India	108359	119530	33305	36262	43053	45766

* Include Daman & Diu during 1987-88

Table 7 : Percentage Distribution of Agricultural and Rural Labour Households with & without Cultivated Land during 1993-94 by States & Classes

All Classes Households

Sl. No.	States/ Union Territories	All Rural Households			Rural Labour Households			Agrl. Labour Households		
		With Land	Without Land	Total	With Land	Without Land	Total	With Land	Without Land	Total
1	2	3	4	5	6	7	8	9	10	11
Major States										
1.	Andhra Pradesh	50.54	49.46	100.00	39.43	60.57	100.00	41.91	58.09	100.00
2.	Assam	70.65	29.35	100.00	43.99	56.01	100.00	50.95	49.05	100.00
3.	Bihar	62.53	37.47	100.00	38.37	61.63	100.00	37.81	62.19	100.00
4.	Gujarat	53.66	46.34	100.00	36.36	63.64	100.00	19.13	60.87	100.00
5.	Haryana	48.47	51.53	100.00	12.15	87.85	100.00	14.97	85.03	100.00
6.	Karnataka	61.75	38.25	100.00	45.36	54.64	100.00	47.63	52.37	100.00
7.	Kerala	30.62	69.38	100.00	24.06	75.94	100.00	24.30	75.70	100.00
8.	Madhya Pradesh	75.08	24.92	100.00	54.91	45.09	100.00	56.68	43.32	100.00
9.	Maharashtra	57.00	43.00	100.00	40.34	59.66	100.00	42.16	57.84	100.00
10.	Orissa	64.59	35.41	100.00	56.28	43.72	100.00	58.00	42.00	100.00
11.	Punjab	38.45	61.55	100.00	5.50	94.50	100.00	5.41	94.59	100.00

Table 7 Contd : **Percentage Distribution of Agricultural and Rural Labour Households with & without Cultivated Land during 1993-94 by States & Classes**

All Classes Households

Sl. No.	*States/ Union Territories*	*All Rural Households*			*Rural Labour Households*			*Agrl. Labour Households*		
		With Land	*Without Land*	*Total*	*With Land*	*Without Land*	*Total*	*With Land*	*Without Land*	*Total*
1	2	3	4	5	6	7	8	9	10	11
12.	Rajasthan	81.11	18.89	100.00	64.88	35.12	100.00	51.85	48.15	100.00
13.	Tamil Nadu	36.61	63.39	100.00	23.13	76.87	100.00	24.89	75.11	100.00
14.	Uttar Pradesh	77.08	22.92	100.00	59.72	40.28	100.00	62.14	37.86	100.00
15.	West Bengal	58.36	41.64	100.00	44.12	55.88	100.00	49.28	50.72	100.00
	Other States/UTs									
16.	Arunachal Pradesh	76.66	23.34	100.00	13.82	86.18	100.00	—	100.00	100.00
17.	Goa	39.62	60.38	100.00	41.27	58.73	100.00	42.25	57.75	100.00
18.	Himachal Pradesh	86.72	13.28	100.00	75.31	24.69	100.00	72.27	27.73	100.00
19.	Jammu & Kashmir	83.78	16.22	100.00	66.23	33.77	100.00	57.96	42.04	100.00
20.	Manipur	77.86	22.14	100.00	38.36	64.64	100.00	35.65	64.35	100.00
21.	Meghalaya	94.96	5.04	100.00	81.36	18.64	100.00	83.75	16.25	100.00
22.	Mizoram	94.96	5.04	100.00	81.36	18.64	100.00	83.75	16.25	100.00

Table 7 Contd : **Percentage Distribution of Agricultural and Rural Labour Households with & without Cultivated Land during 1993-94 by States & Classes**

All Classes Households

Sl. No.	States/ Union Territories	*All Rural Households*			*Rural Labour Households*			*Agrl. Labour Households*		
		With Land	*Without Land*	*Total*	*With Land*	*Without Land*	*Total*	*With Land*	*Without Land*	*Total*
1	2	3	4	5	6	7	8	9	10	11
23.	Nagaland	95.57	4.43	100.00	100.00	—	100.00	100.00	—	100.00
24.	Sikkim	67.82	32.18	100.00	74.83	25.17	100.00	96.86	3.14	100.00
25.	Tripura	47.93	52.07	100.00	22.46	77.54	100.00	26.33	73.67	100.00
26.	A & N Islands	28.01	71.99	100.00	17.78	82.22	100.00	35.96	64.04	100.00
27.	Chandigarh	2.88	97.12	100.00	—	100.00	100.00	—	100.00	100.00
28.	D & N Haveli	78.61	21.39	100.00	81.43	18.57	100.00	81.39	18.61	100.00
29.	Daman & Diu	37.84	62.16	100.00	28.29	71.17	100.00	19.52	80.48	100.00
30.	Delhi	2.52	97.48	100.00	—	100.00	100.00	—	100.00	100.00
31.	Lakshadweep	—	100.00	100.00	—	100.00	100.00	—	100.00	100.00
32.	Pondicherry	30.32	69.68	100.00	14.13	85.87	100.00	15.01	84.99	100.00
	All India	61.26	38.74	100.00	41.20	58.80	100.00	43.03	56.97	100.00

Table 8 : Average size of Land Cultivatd and Percentage Distribution of Estimated Number of All Rural Labour Households with Cultivated Land by Size of Land Cultivated 1993-94

Sl. No.	States/ Union Territories	*Average size of* Land Cultivate Per Cultivating Households (in Hectare) 1987-88	1993-94	*Percentage of Households by Size of Land* 0.01 to 0.20 Hecr.	0.21 to 0.40 Hecr.	0.41 to 0.60 Hecr.	0.61 to 0.80 Hecr.	0.81 to 1.00 Hecr.	1.01 to 2.00 Hecr.	2.01 & Above Hecr.	All
1	2	3	4	5	6	7	8	9	10	11	12
	Major States										
1.	Andhra Pradesh	0.32	0.21	33.50	30.00	8.80	12.20	4.00	10.00	1.20	100.00
2.	Assam	0.18	0.13	53.00	27.80	8.50	4.70	2.30	3.20	0.20	100.00
3.	Bihar	0.19	0.13	51.60	24.80	8.30	5.30	3.70	5.30	0.70	100.00
4.	Gujarat	0.41	0.25	13.80	30.80	18.00	16.10	4.30	13.10	3.40	100.00
5.	Haryana	0.13	0.14	23.90	31.60	5.50	14.30	3.10	12.50	8.70	100.00
6.	Karnataka	0.45	0.34	16.10	24.10	10.70	21.50	8.00	14.90	4.00	100.00
7.	Kerala	0.11	0.04	84.40	9.20	3.40	0.60	1.20	0.50	0.40	100.00
8.	Madhya Pradesh	0.52	0.44	13.90	20.20	17.60	13.90	11.50	17.90	4.70	100.00

Table 8(contd.) : **Average size of Land Cultivatd and Percentage Distribution of Estimated Number of All Rural Labour Households with Cultivated Land by Size of Land Cultivated 1993-94**

Sl. No.	States/ Union Territories	*Average size of* Land Cultivate Per Cultivating Households (in Hectare) 1987-88	1993-94	*Percentage of Households by Size of Land* 0.01 to 0.20 Hecr.	0.21 to 0.40 Hecr.	0.41 to 0.60 Hecr.	0.61 to 0.80 Hecr.	0.81 to 1.00 Hecr.	1.01 to 2.00 Hecr.	2.01 & Above Hecr.	All
1	2	3	4	5	6	7	8	9	10	11	12
9.	Maharashtra	0.54	0.42	13.90	14.60	12.50	12.90	9.00	28.30	8.40	100.00
10.	Orissa	0.25	0.27	32.00	27.40	14.60	10.30	7.90	7.20	0.30	100.00
11.	Punjab	0.11	0.04	22.20	34.70	4.80	14.80	9.80	8.90	4.30	100.00
12.	Rajasthan	1.19	0.72	9.70	22.30	18.80	13.00	10.70	12.30	12.90	100.00
13.	Tamil Nadu	0.13	0.09	37.70	31.40	11.90	8.30	4.30	5.50	0.40	100.00
14.	Uttar Pradesh	0.21	0.20	47.20	30.10	11.20	4.90	2.10	3.10	1.00	100.00
15.	West Bengal	0.13	0.10	58.20	28.20	8.90	3.60	0.30	0.20	0.10	100.00
	Other States/UTs										
16.	Arunachal Pradesh	0.07	0.07	—	3.20	18.60	78.10	—	—	—	100.00
17.	Goa	0.16	0.15	68.40	12.40	—	6.50	5.50	6.90	—	100.00

Table 8(contd.) : Average size of Land Cultivatd and Percentage Distribution of Estimated Number of All Rural Labour Households with Cultivated Land by Size of Land Cultivated 1993-94

Sl. No.	States/ Union Territories	Average size of Land Cultivate Per Cultivating Households (in Hectare) 1987-88	1993-94	Percentage of Households by Size of Land: 0.01 to 0.20 Hecr.	0.21 to 0.40 Hecr.	0.41 to 0.60 Hecr.	0.61 to 0.80 Hecr.	0.81 to 1.00 Hecr.	1.01 to 2.00 Hecr.	2.01 & Above Hecr.	All
1	2	3	4	5	6	7	8	9	10	11	12
18.	Hamachal Pradesh	0.21	0.21	57.70	24.30	8.70	5.50	0.70	1.90	0.80	100.00
19.	Jammu & Kashmir	0.44	0.34	16.80	39.70	15.80	10.60	4.80	10.70	1.20	100.00
20.	Manipur	0.24	0.15	28.40	30.80	14.20	26.40	—	—	—	100.00
21.	Meghalaya	0.49	0.12	62.00	23.40	7.20	4.70	10.80	1.60	—	100.00
22.	Mizoram	0.07	1.78	—	4.00	8.70	—	—	46.20	40.90	100.00
23.	Nagaland	—	0.55	20.70	16.00	31.90	14.10	5.60	11.20	—	100.00
24.	Sikkim	0.29	0.24	33.20	46.90	8.60	11.00	—	—	—	100.00
25.	Tripura	0.08	0.09	47.10	30.90	6.10	5.50	5.70	1.90	2.60	100.00

Table 9 (Contd.): Average size of Land Cultivatd and Percentage Distribution of Estimated Number of All Rural Labour Households with Cultivated Land by Size of Land Cultivated 1993-94

Sl. No.	Average size of States/ Union Territories	Land Cultivate Per Cultivating Households (in Hectare) 1987-88	1993-94	Percentage of Households by Size of Land: 0.01 to 0.20 Hecr.	0.21 to 0.40 Hecr.	0.41 to 0.60 Hecr.	0.61 to 0.80 Hecr.	0.81 to 1.00 Hecr.	1.01 to 2.00 Hecr.	2.01 & Above Hecr.	All
1	2	3	4	5	6	7	8	9	10	11	12
26.	A & N Islands	0.14	0.11	42.10	12.40	5.30	7.60	11.80	15.10	5.30	100.00
27.	Chandigarh	0.04	—	—	—	—	—	—	—	—	—
28.	D & N Haveli	0.56	0.45	13.70	32.30	17.70	17.40	12.80	5.30	0.50	100.00
29.	Daman & Diu	—	0.15	17.40	38.80	6.60	29.30	1.70	—	6.00	100.00
30.	Delhi	0.40	—	—	—	—	—	—	—	—	—
31.	Kakshadweep	0.08	—	—	—	—	—	—	—	—	
32.	Pondicherry	0.48	0.03	56.50	43.40	—	—	—	—	—	100.00
	All-India	0.32	0.23	34.30	25.30	11.80	9.90	5.40	10.10	2.90	100.00

* Includes Daman & Diu during 1987-88

Table 10 : Average Daily Intake of Proteins and Calories in India

Year	*Proteins (Figures in grams)*	*Calories (Figures in Kilo Calories)*
1975	63.6	2296
1976	65.4	2396
1977	61.9	2306
1978	62.6	2341
1979	62.3	2366
1980	62.8	2404
1983[a]	63.8	2481
1988-90[b]	61.8	2283
1991-92[c]	54.1	2139
1993-94[d]	55.8	2187
1994-95	55.8	2172
1996-97[e]	54.0	2114
2001[i]	50.7	1955

Source : Annual Reports of National Nutrition Monitoring Bureau (NNMB), Hyderabad.

Note : During 1981 and 1982, the NNMB surveys were incomplete and hence the results not reported.

a. During 1983 the surveys were conducted on a sub-sample of NSSO 'Central' sample in only four states viz., Andhra Pardesh, Gujarat, Orissa and Tamil Nadu.

b. Results are based on Repeat Surveys conducted earlier during 1975-79 to study changes in consumption and nutritional situation.

c. Report of NNMN (1993) During the eyars 1991 & 1992, surveys were conducted on a sub-sample of Gujarat, Orissa and West Bengal.

d. Report of NNMB (1996) represents the simple average at state level estimates of consumption for the State of Kerala, Tamil Nadu, Karnataka, Andhra Pradesh, Maharashtra, Madhya Pradesh, Orissa.

e. During 1996-97 Second Repeat Surveys were conducted in theState of Kerala, Tamil Nadu, Karnataka, Andhra Pradesh, Maharastra, Gujarat and Orissa (NNMB II Prepeat Survey).

f. Figures are based on NNMB survey on "Diet and Nutritional Status of Rural Population" carried out in the year 2000-2001.

Table 11 : Per capita Availability of Foodgrains and other Selected Commodities in India.

	Net availability of foodgrains per day (Figures in grams)[1]			*Per capita availability of*		
Year	*Cereals*	*Pulses*	*Total*	*Edible oil*[2] *(Figures in Kilograms)*	*Sugar (Figures in Kilog-grams)*[3,4]	*Cotton Cloth (Figures in Sq.mtr.)*
1980-81	417.3	37.5	454.8	5.3	7.3	11.0
1989-90	431.5	41.1	472.6	6.5	12.3	14.6
1990-91	468.5	41.6	510.1	6.6	12.7	15.1
1991-92	434.5	34.3	468.8	6.4	13.0	13.7
1992-93	427.9	36.2	4.64.1	6.8	13.7	15.6
1993-94	434.0	37.2	471.2	7.1	12.5	15.9
1994-95	457.6	37.8	495.4	7.8	13.2	15.2
1995-96	443.4	32.8	476.2	8.0	14.1	16.3
1996-97	468.2	37.3	505.5	9.0	14.6	16.2
1997-98	417.3	33.0	450.3	7.6	14.5	15.9
1998-99	433.5	36.9	470.4	9.8	14.9	13.1
1999-2000	428.0	32.2	460.2	10.3	15.6	14.2
2000-2001	390.4[P]	28.0[P]	418.4[P]	9.5	15.8p	14.2

Source :

— Directorate Statistics and Economics, Report of Agricultural Cooperation, Ministry of Agriculture

— Directorate of Vanaspati, Vegitable Oil & Fats, Department of Food and Public Distribution, Ministry of Consumer Affaris, Food & Public Distribution.

— Directorate of Sugar, Department of Food and Public Distribution, Ministry of Consumer Affairs, Food and public Distribution.

— Compendium of Textiles Statistics, Ministry of Textiles.

1. Production figures relate to agriculture year which is July-June.

2. Data related to er capita consumption of edible oil, for the period November to October, corresponding to given years.

3. Relates to actual release for domestic consumption.

4. Upto 1965-66 the sugar season was Nov. -Oct. and after that it has changed to Oct.-Sept.

P Provisional

Table 12 : Per thousand distribution of households and population by MPCE class in India during 1999-2000

Rural			*Urban*		
MPCE Class (Rs)	*House-holds*	*Popula-tion*	*MPCE class (Rs)*	*House-holds*	*Popula-tion*
000-225	44	52	000-3000	38	52
225-255	42	50	300-350	37	50
255-300	87	100	350-425	75	96
300-340	90	100	425-500	86	101
340-380	93	103	500-575	86	99
380-420	92	97	575-665	91	100
420-470	100	102	665-775	96	101
470-525	96	93	775-915	103	100
525-615	111	103	915-1120	113	100
615-775	113	99	1120-1500	130	101
775-950	61	50	1500-1925	67	50
>950	71	50	>1925	77	50
All classes	1000	1000		1000	1000

Source : Employment and Unemployment in India, 1999-2000, NSS 55th Round.

MPCE : Monthly Per Capita Expenditure.

Table 13 : Housing Amenities in India

Facility	*Percentage of households with a specific facility*					
	1993-94		*1998*		*1999-2000*	
	Rural	*Urban*	*Rural*	*Urban*	*Rural*	*Urban*
1. DrinkingWater supply source						
Tap			18.7	70.1		
Tubewell &		50.1	21.3			
handpumps Well			25.8	6.7		
Tanks/pond	NA	NA	1.3	0.2	NA	NA
reserved for						
drinking Other tank/				0.6	0.1	
pond River/canal/				1.3	0.2	
lake Spring			1.7	0.1		
Tanker			0.2	1.0		
Other			0.2	0.1		
All			**100.0**	**100.0**		
2. Lighting						
No Lighting	0.2	0.2			0.5	0.3
Kerosene	62.1	16.5			50.6	10.3
Other oil	0.3	0.1			0.2	0.1
Gas	0.0	0.1			0.1	0.1
Candle	0.1	0.1	NA	NA	0.1	0.0
Electricity	37.1	82.8			48.4	89.1
Other	0.1	0.1			0.1	0.1
Not recorded	0.1	0.1			0.0	0.0
All	**100.0**	**100.0**			**100.0**	**100.0**
3. Toilet facility						
No latrine			82.5	25.5		
used Service			2.7	5.9		
latrine Speptic		NA	NA	7.5	35.2	
tank Pour flush			2.9	8.4		
Sewerage			0.8	22.5	NA	NA
system Other			3.5	2.5		
Not recorded			0.0	0.0		
All			**100.0**	**100.0**		

Source : National Sample Survey Organisation, 50th round (July 1993-June 1994), 54th round (January-June 1998), 55th round (July 1999-June 2000).

NA : Not available

Table 14 : Labour force Participation Rates by Sex and Sector for States, Union Territories and India

State/Union Territory	1987-88				1993-94				1999-2000			
	Rural		Urban		Rural		Urban		Rural		Urban	
	Male	Female	Male	Female	Male	Female	Male	Female	Male	Female	Male	Female
Andhra Pradesh	60.4	48.6	52.9	22.5	63.5	52.1	56.0	20.7	61.1	48.0	53.2	18.4
Arunachal Pradesh	52.4	30.5	55.3	14.4	50.6	41.0	52.5	10.9	42.5	31.0	40.6	11.0
Assam	53.2	16.8	53.7	10.2	54.1	17.2	55.9	12.4	54.6	16.1	56.5	13.8
Bihar[1]	50.7	19.5	47.5	8.2	52.1	17.3	47.1	7.6	50.3	17.4	46.6	8.2
Goa	a	a	a	a	62.3	30.9	55.1	23.5	57.8	21.5	58.5	15.9
Gujarat	56.6	38.5	53.2	11.3	58.1	39.7	55.1	14.8	58.7	41.3	54.7	13.8
Haryana	49.2	30.2	57.5	12.9	47.0	27.2	53.2	15.7	48.1	20.2	X	10.1
Himachal Pradesh	54.7	48.2	49.5	17.1	59.5	52.0	50.5	20.2	54.6	47.4	53.3	14.2
Jammu & Kashmir	54.2	34.8	55.4	15.8	52.4	39.3	52.2	14.3	55.4	33.0	50.0	6.8
Karnataka	57.7	38.1	52.0	20.3	60.9	43.2	55.8	19.1	60.1	38.1	56.2	18.6
Kerala	55.8	33.6	59.0	26.1	56.8	26.4	59.9	25.0	58.7	27.3	59.1	25.4
Madhya Pradesh1	54.9	41.3	49.9	15.0	57.6	41.1	49.8	14.8	54.0	38.3	50.9	13.6
Maharashtra	55.2	46.6	52.6	16.7	55.8	47.8	54.9	17.7	54.2	43.7	56.3	14.6
Manipur	44.2	19.4	39.1	13.1	48.3	31.1	45.6	23.0	50.6	25.7	47.8	22.5
Meghalaya	58.3	51.2	52.5	35.6	62.2	49.3	50.5	19.6	55.9	41.9	40.7	21.1

Table 14 (Contd) : **Labour force Participation Rates by Sex and Sector for States, Union Territories and India**

State/Union Territory	1987-88				1993-94				1999-2000			
	Rural		Urban		Rural		Urban		Rural		Urban	
	Male	Female	Male	Female	Male	Female	Male	Female	Male	Female	Male	Female
Mizoram	59.1	40.9	51.0	35.9	53.7	31.8	48.6	26.6	56.3	44.1	48.7	26.5
Nagaland	b	b	60.5	7.7	44.8	21.6	40.6	10.5	53.2	45.1	43.3	21.7
Orissa	57.9	28.6	52.4	13.6	57.7	31.9	54.6	16.1	56.4	30.2	51.1	15.3
Punjab	57.1	32.1	56.5	13.3	55.4	22.3	57.1	9.9	54.3	28.2	56.5	12.8
Rajasthan	52.2	45.5	49.1	19.3	54.2	45.8	49.8	16.3	50.3	38.9	49.9	14.1
Sikkim	49.9	30.4	50.2	12.9	56.6	19.4	58.8	14.8	51.9	24.5	55.7	22.5
Tamil Nadu	60.4	47.7	59.5	24.3	61.3	48.1	60.1	24.7	61.0	43.4	58.5	22.7
Tripura	53.0	14.2	51.2	12.1	53.0	13.6	52.9	15.0	50.7	7.6	52.2	8.1
Uttar Pradesh[1]	52.4	22.1	50.4	9.6	52.7	21.9	49.8	10.3	48.6	20.1	51.2	9.7
West Bengal	56.0	20.7	58.3	14.5	56.7	18.9	58.7	16.7	54.9	16.5	61.2	12.9
A & N Islands	54.8	18.4	57.2	12.1	62.9	43.0	59.8	21.7	56.0	19.3	65.3	24.9
Chandigarh	62.8	12.2	54.3	19.5	55.0	11.9	65.8	20.9	79.0	12.8	65.6	15.3
D & N Haveli	57.0	49.0	c	c	55.8	54.6	61.8	28.0	59.2	35.4	66.4	11.2
Daman & Diu	53.9	25.0	51.4	16.4	61.6	26.6	51.5	13.9	66.5	30.0	55.7	20.3

Table 15 : Labour force Participation Rates by Sex and Sector for States, Union Territories and India

State/Union Territory	1987-88				1993-94				1999-2000			
	Rural		Urban		Rural		Urban		Rural		Urban	
	Male	Female	Male	Female	Male	Female	Male	Female	Male	Female	Male	Female
Delhi	45.3	5.1	56.7	9.9	58.6	9.8	54.6	10.2	54.1	3.6	54.6	10.9
Lakshadweep	45.9	18.2	39.1	19.2	52.1	20.4	54.0	15.1	55.1	19.9	46.0	22.1
Pondicherry	54.9	36.9	52.6	19.0	52.1	28.2	55.4	19.0	58.7	29.4	57.4	18.1
India	**54.9**	**33.1**	**53.4**	**16.2**	**56.1**	**33.0**	**54.3**	**16.5**	**54.0**	**30.2**	**54.2**	**14.7**

Source : National Sample Survey Organisation

Note : Figures relate to usual status of individuals. Labour force covers thos involved in gainful activity regularly + those involved in gainful activity occasionally + those unemployed. The figures represent the size of labour force as percentage of population.

1. Due to creation of new states after 1991, the data for the eyars prior to 2001 for the states of Bihar, Madhya Pradesh and Uttar Pradesh include the data of newly created states namely Jharkhand, Chattishgarh and Uttaranchal respectively.

a. Included with Daman & Diu. Figures for 1993-94 are exclusive of Goa.

b. No survey

c. No urban area

Appendix II

NATIONAL AGRICULTURE POLICY

(1) Agriculture is a way of life, a tradition, which, for centuries, has shaped the thought, the outlook, the culture and the economic life of the people of India. Agriculture, therefore, is and will continue to be central to all strategies for planned socio-economic development of the country. Rapid growth of agriculture is essential not only to achieve self-reliance at national level but also for *household food security and to bring about equity in distribution of income and wealth resulting in rapid reduction in poverty levels.*

(2) Indian agriculture has, since Independence, made rapid strides. In taking the annual foodgrains production from 51 million tonnes of the early fifties to 206 million tonnes at the turn of the century, it has contributed significantly in achieving self sufficiency in food and in avoiding food shortages in our country. *The pattern of growth of agriculture has however, brought in its wake, uneven development, across regions and crops as also across different sections of farming community* and *is characterized by low levels of productivity, and degradation of natural resources in some areas.* Capital inadequacy, lack of infrastructural support and demand side constraints such as *controls on movement storage and sale of agricultural products,* etc., have continued to affect the economic viability of agriculture sector. Consequently, the growth of agriculture has also tended to *slacken during the nineties.*

(3) Agriculture has also become a relatively unrewarding profession due to generally unfavourable price regime and low value addition, causing abandoning of farming and increasing migration from rural areas. The situation is likely to be exacerbated further in the wake of integration of agricultural trade in the global system, unless immediate corrective measures are taken.

(4) Over *200 million Indian farmers and farm workers* have been the backbone of *India's agriculture.* Despite having achieved national food security the well being of the farming community continues to be a matter of grave concern for the planners and policy makers in the country. The establishment of an agrarian economy which ensures food and nutrition to India's billion people, raw materials for its expanding industrial base and surpluses for exports, and a fair and equitable reward system for the farming community for the services they provide to the society, will be the mainstay of reforms in the agriculture sector.

(5) The *National Policy on Agriculture seeks to actualise* the vast untapped growth potential of Indian agriculture, strengthen rural infrastructure to support faster agricultural development, promote value addition, accelerate the growth of agro business, create employment in rural areas, secure a fair standard of living for the farmers and agricultural workers and their families, discourage migration to urban areas and face the challenges arising out of economic liberalization and globalisation. Over the next two decades, it aims to attain :

- A growth rate in excess of *4 per cent per annum* in the agriculture sector;
- Growth that is based on *efficient use of resources* and conserves, our soil, water and bio-diversity;
- *Growth with equity,* i.e., growth which is widespread across regions and farmers;
- Growth that is *demand driven* and caters to domestic markets and maximises benefits from exports of agricultural products in the face of the challenges arising from economic liberalization and globalisation;
- Growth that is sustainable technologically, environmentally and economically.

Sustainable Agriculture

(6) The policy will seek to promote technically sound, economically viable, environmentally non-degrading, and socially acceptable use of country's natural resources—land, water and genetic endowment to promote sustainable development of agriculture. Measures will be taken to contain biotic pressures on land and to control indiscriminate diversion of agricultural lands

for non-agricultural purposes. The unutilized wastelands will be put to use for agriculture and afforestation. Particular attention will be given for increasing cropping intensity through multiple-cropping and inter-cropping.

(7) The Government accords abiding importance to improving the quality of the country's land and soil resources. Reclamation of degraded and fallow lands as well as problem soils will be given high priority to optimize their productive use. Special emphasis will be laid on conserving soils and enriching their fertility. Management of land resources on watershed basis will receive special attention. Areas of shifting cultivation will also receive particular attention for their sustainable development. Integrated and holistic development of *rainfed areas* will be promoted by *conservation of rain water* by vegetative measures on watershed basis and augmentation of biomass production through agro and farm forestry with the involvement of the watershed community. All spatial components of a watershed, i.e. arable land, non-arable and drainage lines will be treated as one geo-hydological entity. Management of grazing land will receive greater attention for augmenting availability of animal feed and fodder. A long-term perspective plan for sustainable rainfed agriculture through *watershed approach* will be vigorously pursued for development of *two thirds of India's cropped area which is dependent on rains.*

(8) Rational utilization and conservation of the country's abundant water resources will be promoted. *Conjunctive use* of surface and ground water will receive highest priority. Special attention will be focused on water quality and the problem of receding ground water levels in certain areas as a result of over-exploitation of underground aquifers. Proper on-farm management of water resources for the *optimum use of irrigation potential* will be promoted. Use of in situ moisture management techniques such as mulching and use of micro overhead pressured irrigation systems like drip and sprinkler and green house technology will be encouraged for *greater water use efficiency* and improving productivity, particularly of horticultural crops. Emphasis will be placed on *promotion of water harvesting structures* and suitable water conveyance systems in the hilly and high rainfall areas for rectification of regional imbalances. Participatory community irrigation management will be encouraged.

(9) Erosion and narrowing of the base of India's plant and animal genetic resources *in the last few decades* has been affecting the food security of the country. Survey and evaluation of genetic resources and safe conservation of both indigenous and exogenously introduced genetic variability in crop plants, animals and their wild relatives will receive particular attention. The use of bio-technologies will be promoted for evolving plants which consume less water, are drought resistant, pest resistant, contain more nutrition, give higher yields and are environmentally safe. Conservation of bio-resources through their *ex situ* preservation in Gene Banks, as also *in situ* conservation in their natural habitats through bio-diversity parks, etc., will receive a high priority to prevent their extinction. Specific measures will also be taken to conserve indigenous breeds facing extinction. There will be a time bound programme to list, catalogue and classify country's vast agro bio-diversity.

(10) Sensitization of the farming community with the environmental concerns will receive high priority. Balanced and conjunctive use of bio-mass, organic and inorganic fertilizers and controlled use of agro chemicals through integrated nutrients and pest management (INM & IPM) will be promoted to achieve the sustainable increases in agricultural production. A nation-wide programme for utilization of rural and urban garbage, farm residues and organic waste for organic matter repletion and pollution control will be worked out.

(11) Agro forestry and social forestry are prime requisites for maintenance of ecological balance and augmentation of bio-mass production in the agricultural systems. Agro-forestry will receive a major thrust for efficient nutrient cycling, nitrogen fixation, organic matter addition and for improving drainage. Farmers will be encouraged to take up farm/agro-forestry for higher income generation by evolving technology, extension and credit support packages and removing constraints to development of agro and farm forestry. Involvement of farmers and landless labourers will be sought in the development of pastures/forestry programmes on public wastelands by giving financial incentives and entitlements to the *usufructs* of trees and pastures.

(12) The history and traditional knowledge of agriculture, particularly of tribal communities, relating to organic farming and preservation and processing of food for nutritional and medicinal

purposes is one of the oldest in the world. Concerted efforts will be made to pool, distil and evaluate traditional practices, knowledge and wisdom and to harness them for sustainable agricultural growth.

Food and Nutritional Security

(13) Special efforts will be made to raise the productivity and production of crops to meet the increasing demand for food generated by unabated demographic pressures and raw materials for expanding agro-based industries. A regionally differentiated strategy will be pursued, taking into account the agronomic, climatic and environmental conditions to realize the full growth potential of every region. Special attention will be given to development of new crop varieties, particularly of food crops, with higher nutritional value through adoption of bio-technology particularly, genetic modification, while addressing bio-safety concerns.

(14) A major thrust will be given to development of rainfed and irrigated horticulture, floriculture, roots and tubers, plantation crops, aromatic and medicinal plants, bee-keeping and sericulture, for augmenting food supply, exports and generating employment in the rural areas. Availability of hybrid seeds and disease free planting materials of improved varieties, supported by network of regional nurseries, tissue culture laboratories, seed farms will be promoted to support systematic development of horticulture having emphasis on increased production, post-harvest management, precision farming, bio-control of pests and quality regulation mechanism and exports.

(15) Animal husbandry and fisheries also generate wealth and employment in the agriculture sector. Development of animal husbandry, poultry, dairying and aqua-culture will receive a high priority in the efforts for diversifying agriculture, increasing animal protein availability in the food basket and for generating exportable surpluses. A national livestock breeding strategy will be evolved to meet the requirements of milk, meat, egg and livestock products and to enhance the role of draught animals as a source of energy for farming operations and transport. Major thrust will be on genetic upgradation of indigenous/native cattle and buffaloes using proven semen and high quality pedigreed bulls and by expanding artificial insemination network to provide services at the farmer's doorstep.

(16) Generation and dissemination of appropriate technologies in the field of animal production as also health care to enhance production and productivity levels will be given greater attention. Cultivation of fodder crops and fodder trees will be encouraged to meet the feed and fodder requirements and to improve animal nutrition and welfare. Priority attention will also be given to improve the processing, marketing and transport facilities, with emphasis on modernisation of abattoirs, carcass utilization and value addition thereon. Since animal disease eradication and quarantine is critical to exports, animal health system will be strengthened and disease free zones created. The involvement of co-operatives and the private sector will be encouraged for development of animal husbandry, poultry and dairy. Incentives for livestock and fisheries production activities will be brought at par with incentives for crop production.

(17) An integrated approach to marine and inland fisheries, designed to promote sustainable aquaculture practices, will be adopted. Biotechnological application in the field of genetics and breeding, hormonal applications immunology and disease control will receive particular attention for increased aquaculture production. Development of sustainable technologies for fin and shell fish culture as also pearl-culture, their yield optimization, harvest and post-harvest operations, mechanization of fishing boats, strengthening of infrastructure for production of fish seed, berthing and landing facilities for fishing vessels and development of marketing infrastructure will be accorded high priority. Deep sea fishing industry will be developed to take advantage of the vast potential of country's exclusive economic zone.

Generation and Transfer of Technology

(18) A very high priority will be accorded to evolving new location-specific and economically viable improved varieties of agricultural and horticultural crops, livestock species and aquaculture as also conservation and judicious use of germplasm and other biodiversity resources. The regionalisation of agricultural research, based on identified agro-climatic zones, will be accorded high priority. Application of frontier sciences like bio-technology, remote sensing technologies, pre and post-harvest technologies, energy saving technologies, technology for environmental protection through national research system as well as proprietary

research will be encouraged. The endeavour will be to build a well organized efficient and result- oriented agriculture research and education system to introduce technological change in Indian agriculture. Upgradation of agricultural education and its orientation towards uniformity in education standards, women empowerment, user-orientation, vocationalization and promotion of excellence will be the hallmark of the new policy.

(19) The research and extension linkages will be strengthened to improve quality and effectiveness of research and extension system. The extension system will be broad based and revitalized. Innovative and decentralized institutional changes will be introduced to make the extension system farmer-responsible and farmer accountable. Role of Krishi Vigyan Kendras (KVKs), Non-Governmental Organizations (NGOs), Farmers Organizations, Cooperatives, corporate sector and para-technicians in agricultural extension will be encouraged for organizing demand driven production systems. Development of human resources through capacity building and skill upgradation of public extension functionaries and other extension functionaries will be accorded a high priority. The Government will endeavour to move towards a regime of financial sustainability of extensions services through affecting in a phased manner, a more realistic cost recovery of extension services and inputs, while simultaneously safeguarding the interests of the poor and the vulnerable groups.

(20) Mainstreaming gender concerns in agriculture will receive particular attention. Appropriate structural, functional and institutional measures will be initiated to empower women and build their capabilities and improve their access to inputs, technology and other farming resources.

Inputs Management

(21) Adequate and timely supply of quality *inputs such as seeds, fertilizers, plant protection chemicals, bio-pesticides, agricultural machinery and credit* at reasonable rates to farmers will be the endeavour of the Government. Soil testing and quality testing of fertilisers and seeds will be ensured and supply of spurious inputs *will be checked*. Balanced and optimum use of fertilizers will be promoted together with use of organic manures & bio-fertilizers to optimize the efficiency of nutrient use.

(22) Development, production and distribution of improved varieties of seeds and planting materials and strengthening and expansion of seed and plant certification system with private sector participation will receive a high priority. *A National Seed Grid* will be established to ensure supply of seeds especially to areas affected by natural calamities. The National Seeds Corporation (NSC) and State Farms Corporation of India (SFCI) will be restructured for efficient utilization of investment and manpower.

(23) Protection to plant varieties through a *sui generies* legislation, will be granted to encourage research and breeding of new varieties particularly in the private sector in line with India's obligations under TRIPS Agreement. The farmers will, however, be allowed their traditional rights to save, use, exchange, share and sell their farm saved seeds except as branded seeds of protected varieties for commercial purpose. The interests of the researchers will also be safeguarded in carrying out research on proprietary varieties to develop new varieties.

(24) Integrated pest management and use of biotic agents in order to minimize the indiscriminate and injudicious use of chemical pesticides will be the cardinal principle covering plant protection. Selective and eco-friendly farm mechanization through appropriate technology will be promoted, with special reference to rainfed farming to reduce arduous work and to make agriculture efficient and competitive as also to increase crop productivity.

Incentives for Agriculture

(25) The Government will endeavour to create a favourable economic environment for increasing capital formation and farmer's own investments by removal of distortions in the incentive regime for agriculture, improving the terms of trade with manufacturing sectors and bringing about external and *domestic market reforms*, backed by *rationalisation of domestic tax structure.* It will seek to bestow on the agriculture sector in as many respects as possible benefits similar to those obtaining in the manufacturing sector, *such as easy availability of credit and other inputs*, and infrastructure facilities for development of agri-business industries and development of effective delivery systems and *freeing movement of agro produce.*

(26) Consequent upon dismantling of Quantitative Restrictions on imports as per WTO Agreement on Agriculture, Commodity-

wise strategies and arrangements for protecting the grower from adverse impact of undue price fluctuations in world markets and for promoting exports will be formulated. Apart from price competition, other aspects of marketing such as quality, choice, health and bio-safety will be promoted. Exports of horticultural produce and marine products will receive particular emphasis. A two-fold long term strategy of diversification of agricultural produce and value addition enabling the production system to respond to external environment and creating export demand for the commodities produced in the country will be evolved with a view to providing the farmers incremental income from export earnings. A favourable economic environment and supportive public management system will be created for promotion of agricultural exports. Quarantine, both of exports and imports, will be given particular attention so that Indian agriculture is protected from the ingress of exotic pests and diseases.

(27). In order to protect the interest of farmers in context of removal of Quantitative Restrictions, *continuous monitoring of international prices* will be undertaken and *appropriate tariffs protection will be provided.* Import duties on manufactured commodities used in agriculture will be rationalized. The domestic agricultural market will be liberalized and all controls and regulations hindering increase in farmers' income will be reviewed and abolished to ensure that agriculturists receive prices commensurate with their efforts, investment. Restrictions on the movement of agricultural commodities throughout the country will be progressively dismantled.

(28) The structure of taxes on foodgrains and other commercial crops will be reviewed and rationalized. Similarly, the excise duty on materials such as farm machinery and implements, fertilizers, etc., used as inputs in agricultural production, post harvest storage and processing will be reviewed. Appropriate measures will be adopted to ensure that agriculturists by and large remain outside the regulatory and tax collection systems. Farmers will be exempted from payment of capital gains tax on compulsory acquisition of agricultural land.

Investments in Agriculture

(29) The Agriculture sector has been starved of capital. There has been a decline in the public sector investment in the agriculture

sector. Public investment for narrowing regional imbalances, acceleration developments of supportive infrastructure for agriculture and rural development particularly rural connectivity will be stepped up. A time-bound strategy for rationalisation and transparent pricing of inputs will be formulated to encourage judicious input use and to generate resources for agriculture. Input subsidy reforms will be pursued as a combination of price and institutional reforms to cut down costs of these inputs for agriculture. Resource allocation regime will be reviewed with a view to rechannelizing the available resources from support measures towards asset formation in rural sector.

(30) A conducive climate will be created through a favourable price and trade regime to promote farmers' own investments as also investments by industries producing inputs for agriculture and agro based industries. Private sector investments in agriculture will also be encouraged more particularly in areas like agricultural research, human resource development, post-harvest management and marketing.

(31) Rural electrification will be given a high priority as a prime mover for agricultural development. The quality and availability of electricity supply will be improved and the demand of the agriculture sector will be met adequately in a reliable and cost effective manner. The use of new and renewable sources of energy for irrigation and other agricultural purposes will also be encouraged.

(32) Bridging the gap between irrigation potential created and utilized, completion of all on-going projects, restoration and modernization of irrigation infrastructure including drainage, evolving and implementing an integrated plan of augmentation and management of national water resources will receive special attention for augmenting the availability and use of irrigation water.

(33) Emphasis will be laid on development of marketing infrastructure and techniques of preservation, storage and transportation with a view to reducing post-harvest losses and ensuring a better return to the grower. The weekly periodic markets under the direct control of panchayat raj institutions will be upgraded and strengthened. Direct marketing and pledge financing will be promoted. Producers markets on the lines of

Ryatu Bazars will be encouraged through out the width and the breadth of the country. Storage facilities for different kinds of agricultural products will be created in the production areas on nearby places particularly in the rural areas so that the farmers can transport their produce to these places immediately after harvest in shortest possible time. The establishment of cold chains, provision of pre cooling facilities to farmers as a service and cold storage in the terminal markets and improving the retail marketing arrangements in urban areas will be given priority. Upgradation and dissemination of market intelligence will receive particular attention.

(34) Setting up of agro-processing units in the producing areas to reduce wastage, especially of horticultural produce, increased value addition and creation of off-farm employment in rural areas will be encouraged. Collaboration between the producer cooperatives and the corporate sector will be encouraged to promote agro-processing industry. An inter-active coupling between technology, economy, environment and society will be promoted for speedy development of food and agro-processing industries and build up a substantial base for production of value added agro-products for domestic and export markets with a strong emphasis on food safety and quality. The Small Farmers Agro Business Consortium (SFAC) will be energized to cater to the needs of farmer entrepreneurs and promote public and private investments in agri-business.

Institutional Structure

(35) Indian agriculture is characterized by pre-dominance of small and marginal farmers. Institutional reforms will be so pursued as to channelize their energies for achieving greater productivity and production. The approach to rural development and land reforms will focus on the following areas :

- Consolidation of holdings all over the country on the pattern of north western States;
- Redistribution of ceiling surplus lands and waste lands among the landless farmers, unemployed youth with initial start up capital;
- Tenancy reforms to recognize the rights of the tenants and share croppers;

- Development of lease markets for increasing the size of the holdings by making legal provisions for giving private lands on lease for cultivation and agri business;
- Updating and improvement of land records, computerization and issue of land pass-books to the farmers; and
- Recognition of women's rights in land.

(36) The rural poor will be increasingly involved in the implementation of land reforms with the help of Panchayati Raj Institutions, Voluntary Groups, Social Activists and Community Leaders.

(37) Private sector participation will be promoted through contract farming and land leasing arrangements to allow accelerated technology transfer, capital inflow and assured markets for crop production, especially of oilseeds, cotton and horticultural crops.

(38) Progressive institutionalization of rural and farm credit will be continued for providing timely and adequate credit to farmers. The rural credit institutions will be geared to promote savings, investments and risk management. Particular attention will be paid to removal of distortions in the priority sector lending by Commercial Banks for agriculture and rural sectors. Special measures will be taken for revamping of cooperatives to remove the institutional and financial weaknesses and evolving simplified procedure for sanction and disbursement of agriculture credit. The endeavour will be to ensure distribution equity in the disbursement of credit. Micro-credit will be promoted as an effective tool for alleviating poverty. Self Help Group-Bank linkage system, suited to Indian rural sector, will be developed as a supplementary mechanism for bringing the rural poor into the formal banking system, thereby improving banks outreach and the credit flows to the poor in an effective and sustainable manner.

(39) The basic support to agriculture has been provided by the cooperative sector assiduously built over the years. The Government will provide active support for the promotion of cooperative-form of enterprise and ensure greater autonomy and operational freedom to them to improve their functioning. The thrust will be on:

- Structural reforms for promoting greater efficiency and viability by freeing them from excessive bureaucratic control and political interference;
- Creation of infrastructure and human resource development;
- Improvement in financial viability and organisational sustainability of cooperatives;
- Democratisation of management and increased professionalism in their operations; and
- Creating a viable inter-face with other grass-root Organizations.

(40) The Legislative and regulatory framework will be appropriately amended and strengthened do achieve these objectives.

Risk Management

(41) Despite technological and economic advancements, the condition of farmers continues to be unstable due to natural calamities and price fluctuations. National Agriculture Insurance Scheme covering all farmers and all crops throughout the country with built in provisions for insulating farmers from financial distress caused by natural disasters and making agriculture financially viable will be made more farmer specific and effective. Endeavour will be made to provide a package insurance policy for the farmers, right from sowing of the crops to post-harvest operations, including market fluctuations in the prices of agricultural produce.

(42) In order to reduce risk in agriculture and impart greater resilience to Indian agriculture against droughts and floods, efforts will be made for achieving greater flood proofing of flood prone agriculture and drought proofing of rainfed agriculture for protecting the farmers from vagaries of nature. For this purpose, contingency agriculture planning, development of drought and flood resistant crop varieties, watershed development programmes, drought prone areas and desert development programmes and rural infrastructure development programmes will receive particular attention.

(43) The Central Government will continue to discharge its

responsibility to ensure remunerative prices for agricultural produce through announcement of Minimum Support Prices policy for major agricultural commodities. The food, nutrition and other domestic and exports requirements of the country will be kept in view while determining the support prices of different commodities. The price structure and trade mechanism will be continuously reviewed to ensure a favourable economic environment for the agriculture sector and to bring about an equitable balance between the rural and the urban incomes. The methodology used by the Commission on Agricultural Costs & Prices (CACP) in arriving at estimates of costs of production will be periodically reviewed. The price structure of both inputs and outputs will be monitored to ensure higher returns to the farmers and bring about cost effectiveness throughout the economy. Domestic market prices will be closely monitored to prevent distress sales by the farmers. Public and cooperative agencies undertaking marketing operations will be strengthened.

(44) The Government will enlarge the coverage of futures markets to minimize the wide fluctuations in commodity prices as also for hedging their risks. The endeavour will be to cover all important agricultural products under futures trading in course of time.

Management Reforms

(45) Effective implementation of policy initiatives will call for comprehensive reforms in the management of agriculture by the Central and the State Governments. The Central Government will supplement/complement the State Governments' efforts through regionally differentiated Work Plans, comprising crop/area/target group specific interventions, formulated in an inter-active mode and implemented in a spirit of partnership with the States. The Central Government will move away from schematic approach to Macro-Management mode and assume a role of advocacy, articulation and facilitation to help the States in their efforts towards achieving accelerated agricultural development.

(46) The Government will focus on quality aspects at all stages of farm operations from sowing to primary processing. The quality of inputs and other support services to farmers will be improved. Quality consciousness amongst farmers and agro processors will be created. Grading and standardization of agricultural products

will be promoted for export enhancement. Application of science and technology in agriculture will be promoted through a regular system of interface between S & T institutions and the users/potential users, to make the sector globally competitive.

(47) The database for the agriculture sector will be strengthened to ensure greater reliability of estimates and forecasting which will help in the process of planning and policy making. Efforts will be made to significantly improve and harness latest remote sensing and information technology to capture data, collate it, add value and disseminate it to appropriate destinations for managing the risk and in accelerating the growth process. The objective will be to engage in a meaningful continuous dialogue with the external environment in the changing scenario and to have on-line and real time system of 'Agriculture on line' capacity to analyze the signals emanating from the farms and the markets for the benefit of the farmers.

(48) The Government of India trust that this Statement of National Agriculture Policy will receive the fullest support of all sections of the people and lead to sustainable development of agriculture, create gainful employment on a self sustaining basis in rural areas, raise standards of living for the farming communities, preserve environment and serve as a vehicle for building a resurgent national economy.

Appendix III

THE PATH AHEAD*

Opportunities in Agriculture

5.1.173 The Tenth Plan is being formulated at a time when agriculture faces challenges from both domestic and external sources. The challenge before policy makers is not only to reverse the slowdown of agricultural growth in the 1990s but to ensure that the gains of agriculture in alleviating rural poverty are not lost and the estimated 200 million under-nourished population get access to food.

5.1.174 Agriculture strategies and policies will have to be redefined to benefit all regions by increasing investments and maintenance in irrigation, power, roads, post harvest, handling, processing and marketing infrastructure.

5.1.175 Forward and backward linkages will have to be established and strengthened to give a better deal to farmers.

5.1.176 The Tenth Plan envisages an overall GDP growth rate of 8 per cent per annum. The National Agricultural Policy has envisaged:

- Growth that is based on efficient use of resources and conserves our soil, water and bio-diversity;
- growth with equity; i.e., growth which is widespread across regions and benefits all farmers;
- growth that is demand-driven and caters to domestic markets as well as maximises benefits from exports; and
- growth that is sustainable technologically, environmentally and economically;
- growth rate in excess of 4 per cent.

* *Government of India, Planning Commission, Tenth Plan Document.*

5.1.177 The strategy to achieve the envisaged growth rate of 3.97 per cent in the sector during the Tenth Plan, would be a regionally differentiated on based on agro climatic conditions and land and water resources of different regions.

5.1.178 Thrust would be given for the development of the eastern and northeastern regions together with other eco-fragile regions—hill areas, coastal areas, etc. by further expanding the On—farm Water Management scheme which has been introduced to exploit the rich ground water potential. The Technology Mission on Horticulture has become operational in the northeastern region and backward and forward linkages will be ensured.

5.1.179 States where there is stagnation/deceleration of growth due to environmentally unsustainable practices, will be encouraged to improve management practices and diversity to crops which will restore soil health.

5.1.180 The thrust areas during the Tenth Plan would include

- Increasing cropping intensity;
- diversification to high value crops/activities;
- development of minor irrigation and utilisation of created irrigation potential;
- rainwater harvesting and conservation for the development of rainfed areas watershed approach;
- reclamation/development of problem soils/lands;
- utilisation of unutilised/under-utilised wastelands and degraded lands by allocation/leasing;
- timely and adequate availability of inputs like seeds, fertilisers, implements;
- thrust on seed production - breeder, foundation and certified—to achieve the desired seed replacement rate;
- bridging the gap between research and farmer's yields;
- encouragement to the private sector for effective extension and input support services;
- promotion of a farming system approach;
- cost effectiveness while increasing productivity;
- promotion of organic farming, with the use of organic waste, IPM and INM;

- strengthening of marketing, processing and value-addition infrastructure;
- upgradation of indigenous cattle and buffalo using certified semen/high quality pedigreed bulls and providing services at farmer's door;
- conservation of threatened breeds of livestock and improvement of breeds used for draught and pack;
- creation of disease-free zones and a national immunisation programme against most prevalent animal diseases;
- adequate availability of fodder seeds and improvement of pasture lands;
- increase in fish production from both culture and capture resources; and
- emphasising the quality and safety aspects of produce in agriculture, animal husbandry, and the dairy and fisheries sector.

5.1.181 With increasing population, land holdings are getting fragmented and becoming unviable. The average size of holdings has decreased from 2.28 ha in 1970-71 to 1.57 ha in 1990-91. To deal with problems of fragmented and small holdings:

- A clear policy regarding transfer of agricultural land has to be implemented.
- Transfer to land has to be made easy to enable the farmers to augment their holdings to viable size units.
- Stamp duty on transactions of land for agriculture to be rationalised.
- Leasing of land and contract farming to be allowed/ promoted and made easy which will help generate income for both lessee and lessor/contractor.
- Legislation needs to be enacted to facilitate land utilisation - transfer, leasing contract farming.
- Technologies suited for small holdings have to be developed to increase the productivity and returns of small holdings.
- States would be asked to take up the consolidation of holdings and computerisation of land records.

5.1.182 While, on the one hand, the per capita availability of land has declined, there are vast areas which are unutilised or under-utilised. If such lands are put to productive uses, the production will increase and millions of farm families will get livelihood support and their income will increase. For utilisation of unutilised/under-utilised degraded/wastelands, States would be persuaded to consider the following:

- Allotment/leasing of Government/panchayat lands for production purposes to landless and weaker sections.
- Providing access to grasses and fodder from forest area and allowing growing of grasses/fodder and medicinal and aromatic plants.
- Wastelands which require huge financial resources for development will be earmarked and used for generating raw material for industry in partnership with the private sector.

5.1.183 Sustainable development of natural resources would be given a major thrust through watershed approach and appropriate measures like:

- Formulation of a perspective plan for the development of rainfed/degraded land;
- implementation of watershed development programme as a single national initiative;
- thrust on people's participation in planning and execution of field activities in the implementation of the watershed development programme;
- emphasis on rain water harvesting and conservation;
- development of minor irrigation, especially in the eastern region having abundance of ground water;
- promotion of on-farm water management, water-saving technologies and devices for increasing water use efficiency;
- increasing forest/tree cover to facilitate recharge of ground water;
- completing irrigation projects expeditiously and ensuring maintenance of canals and other irrigation projects;
- setting up of water user associations and recovery of water

charges so that there is better maintenance; ensuring that there is sufficient water for drinking, agriculture and other uses. Enaction of legislation on use of ground water will be followed up with the States;

- as electricity is an important input for agriculture, effort will be made to link pricing/tariff as a policy reform for providing adequate power;
- special thrust on research for efficient water utilisation and conservation - promotion of water saving methods and devices such as diggi, drip/sprinkler irrigation;
- encouraging water conservation and recycling of water by households, urban local bodies and industry.

5.1.184 The strategies for the development of horticulture and plantation crops would include:

- Improving production, productivity, reducing cost of production, supply of good quality, disease-free, high yielding seeds and planting material and promotion of inter-cropping/multi story cropping;
- value addition and quality improvement through propagation of latest technologies and improved farm practices (micro-irrigation, fertigation, integrated nutrient/pest management and promotion of protected/green house cultivation, precision farming, etc.);
- strengthening of organisational support, promotion of human resource development, capacity building and enhancement of the knowledge base of farmers and other functionaries engaged in the horticulture/plantation sector;
- promotion of bee-keeping and medicinal and aromatic plants on a large scale;
- promotion of re-plantation, gap filling, rejuvenation, and expansion of coverage in new areas;
- shift towards credit linked subsidy regime in favour of planters and processors through commodity boards, NABARD, commercial/cooperative banks;
- market development and export promotion by way of improving international market intelligence and promotion of Indian brands abroad.

5.1. 185 Measures to increase the availability of quality agricultural inputs in adequate quantities would include:

- Thrust on seed production and distribution to achieve higher seed replacement rate (SRR)
- Emphasis on bio-technology for development of high yielding seeds.
- Restructuring of the NSC and SFCI to operate as a single agency.
- Replacement of the Seed Act, 1966 for development of the seed sector.
- Promotion of the balanced use of fertilisers and INM with emphasis on the use of organics together with management/utilisation of crop residues.
- Encouragement to organic farming.
- Strengthening of testing facilities for seeds, fertilisers, soil, water, pesticides, pesticides residues, etc.
- Emphasis on adoption of IPM with emphasis on natural controls, need-based use of pesticides and strengthening of pest surveillance and forecasting facilities for the promotion of the IPM concept.
- Creation and strengthening of plant quarantine facilities at all entry points to check the entry of exotic pests and diseases.
- Promotion of efficient and energy saving implements and machines through involvement of the private sector in mass production of quality implements.
- Development of facilities to import agri machines/implements and study these for the development of models suited to Indian conditions.

5.1.186 Over the years the established credit infrastructure has provided a valuable support to the farmers in adopting improved production technologies. But, of late, the system has been under strain and the availability of credit to the farm sector has remained inadequate. Against the recommended 18 per cent share of agriculture in priority sector lending by banks, the relative share in the net bank credit stood at 15.8 per cent in March 2000 and

15.7 per cent in March 2001. The following efforts will be made to increase the flow of agriculture credit.

- Ensuring that Kisan Credit Cards are issued to all entitled farmers by the end of the Tenth Plan.
- States would not be eligible for funding by cooperative sector/NCDC till they adopt the Multi-State Cooperative Act for providing more functional and financial autonomy.
- Cooperative banks will be strengthened through recapitalisation.
- Micro financing would be encouraged through self-help groups/women's groups.

5.1.187 The present agriculture extension system has become outmoded and ineffective. It is not able to effectively meet the present-day demands of farmers. Therefore, the following steps will be taken:

- Agricultural extension will be reformed and strengthened to make it demand driven, using the print and electronic media to disseminate information;
- private sector involvement will be encouraged in extension and services support such as agri-clinics;
- IT and the print media will be used to reach information to farmers;
- linkages between KVKs of ICAR and State/district extension services will be strengthened together with that of private sector/NGOs involved in agriculture extension;
- utilisation of infrastructure available with KVKs/ICAR Institutes and SAUs for providing input support services to the farmers, including testing and certification of inputs and farm produce.

5.1.188 Efforts to create and strengthen storage/cold storage infrastructure would include:

- Enhanced back-ended credit-linked financial incentives for taking up storage/cold storage, post-harvest processing and value-addition infrastructure;
- encouragement to the private sector in the creation of agriculture infrastructure by way of reduction in fiscal levies

(excise, custom, central sales tax levied by the Central Government and reduction/rationalisation of sales tax and other local levies by the State Governments) on equipment, machinery, etc.; and

- review and abolition of statutory controls to the extent possible to attract private sector and investment.

5.1.189 Indian agriculture has undergone a change from subsistence farming to commercial production. Marketing infrastructure and prices play a very important role in the development of a crop commodity and the development of a particular area or region. No appreciable growth can be visualised without adequate marketing support. States will, therefore, be persuaded to amend their respective APMC Acts to provide for:

- Phasing out of all the remaining restrictions on movement, stocks, credit, exports and processing,
- development of integrated agricultural markets in private and cooperative sectors;
- direct marketing of agricultural produce by setting up farmers' markets;
- contract farming involving a commitment on the part of the farmers to produce a specific commodity and commitment on the part of the contractor to purchase the produce at a pre-determined price;
- abolishing all restrictions in various Acts which impinge on free trade of agriculture commodities; and
- enlargement of commodity coverage under forward contracts/future trading.

5.1.190 Besides the development of domestic markets for agri-commodities, adequate thrust will also be given for export promotion through:

- Formulation of a produce-wise strategy;
- phasing out all restrictions on exports;
- promotion and setting up of with adequate financial incentives and facilities;
- incentives for modernisation of processing facilities and promotion of value-added products;

- rationalisation and improvement of the export inspection system, sanitary and phyto-sanitary measures with adequate strengthening and appropriate interventions in terms of education, training, upgradation of skills, knowledge, etc.,
- undertaking comprehensive international market intelligence and development of product profiles for identified agricultural products, having potential in different countries, keeping in view quality standards, price competitiveness, etc.; and
- promotion of Indian brands abroad for identified products.

Food Security and Diversification of Agriculture

5.1.191 As on 1 April 2002, there was 55.95 mt of foodgrains stock with Government agencies (24.91 mt of rice and 26.04 mt of wheat). The Expenditure Reforms Commission has recommended a buffer stock of 10 mt (4 mt of wheat and 6 mt of rice). Keeping in view environmental considerations and consumer demand, it would be necessary to encourage horticulture, livestock/dairy products. This would require a holistic approach to issues relating to:

- targetting food subsidies properly and providing access of food to the poor in an efficient manner;
- review of pricing and procurement operations under MSP to make them more effective;
- integration of marketing, value-addition and exports to deal with marketable surplus of cereals, fruits, vegetables and livestock products.

Research for Increasing Productivity and Quality

5.1.192 The growth in total factor productivity seems to be decelerating, suggesting a decline in the force of technology. In some areas like that of pulses and some other crops, there has not been any research breakthrough. The thrust and strategies for research would include:

- Thrust on modern technologies like development of transgenics, space technology and sustainable development of natural resources together with preservation and exploitation of rich biodiversity;

- reorientation of research in the context of diversified agriculture, value addition, agri-business;
- thrust on technologies for sustainable development of natural resources and cost reduction and quality improvement technologies;
- emphasis on research on mechanisation of small farms, hill agriculture, energy management and use of renewable sources of energy in agriculture;
- thrust on research to achieve a breakthrough in pulses and oilseeds, management of coconut wilt, seed spices, medicinal and aromatic plants etc.;
- review of ICAR/agriculture research.

Reforms and Opportunities in Agriculture

5.1.193 There will be a fresh look at agricultural subsidies, pricing and procurement operation under MSP for:

- Rationalisation of agricultural subsidies, especially those adversely affecting natural resources;
- utilising MSP and procurement operations as a tool to bring in desired diversification in the cropping/farming system;
- quality control of inputs and produce;
- encouraging crop production for alternative use - ethanol, feed, starch etc.;
- Convergence of Central sector and Centrally sponsored schemes of various departments and also in schemes being implemented under State Plans for the efficient utilisation of financial and manpower resources.

Appendix IV

THE KERALA AGRICULTURAL WORKERS ACT, 1974

(ACT 18 OF 1974)

Law Department

NOTIFICATION

No.16662-K1/72/Law

Dated, Trivandrum,
the 6th August, 1974/
Sravana 15, 1896 (Saka)

The following Act of the Kerala State Legislature is hereby published for general information. The Bills passed by the Legislative Assembly received the assent of the President on the 31st day of July, 1974.

By order of the Governor,
M. Sekharan,
Law Secretary.

ACT 18 OF 1974

THE KERALA AGRICULTURAL WORKERS ACT? 1974*

An act to provide for the welfare of agricultural workers in the State of Kerala and to regulate the conditions of their work.

Preamble—Whereas it is expedient to provide for the welfare of agricultural workers in the State of Kerala and to regulate the conditions of their work;

Be it enacted in the Twenty-fifth year of the Republic of India as follows:-

---

* Published as Extraordinary Gazette No. 591 dated 6-8-1974. 25 /4560/B.

CHAPTER-I

Preliminary

(1) Short title, extend and commencement :

(1) This Act may be called the Kerala Agricultural Workers Act, 1974.

(2) It extends to the whole of the State of Kerala.

(3) It shall come is to force on such as the Government may, by notification in the Gazette, appoint, and different dates may be appointed for different areas and for different provisions of this Act.

(2) Definitions

In this Act, unless the context otherwise require,

(a) "adult" means a person who has completed his eighteenth year of age;

(b) "adolescent" means a person who has completed his fifteenth year of age but has not completed his eighteenth year of age,

(c) "agricultural dispute" means any dispute or difference between landowners and landowners or between landowners and agricultural workers or between agricultural workers and agricultural workers which is connected with the employment or non-employment or the terms of employment or with the conditions of labour, of any person.

Explanation : Where any landowner discharges, dismisses, retrenches of otherwise terminates the services of, or denies employment to, an individual agricultural worker, any dispute or difference between that agricultural worker and his employer connected with, or arising out of, such discharge, dismissal, retrenchment, termination or denial of employment shall be deemed to be an agricultural dispute notwithstanding that no other agricultural worker nor any union of agricultural workers is a party to the dispute:

(d) "agricultural land" means any land used for cultivation, but does not include any plantation as defined in the Plantation Labour Act, 1951 (Central Act 69 of 1951);

(*e*) "agricultural Tribunal" means, in relation to any area, the Agricultural Tribunal constituted under this Act for that area;

(*f*) "agricultural worker" means a person who, in consideration of the wages payable to him by a landowner, works on, or does any other agricultural operation in relation to the agricultural land of such landowner;

(*g*) "board" means the Agricultural workers' Provident Fund Board constituted under section 11;

(*h*) "child" means a person who has not completed his fifteenth year of age;

(*i*) "Conciliation Officer" means, in relation to any area, the Conciliation Officer appointed under this Act for that area;

(*j*) "family" means husband, wife and their unmarried minor children or such of them as exist;

(*k*) "Fund" means the fund established in pursuance of subsection (1) of section 8;

(*l*) "Inspector" means an Inspector appointed under subsection (I) of section 5 or deemed, under subsection (3) or that section, to be appointed for the purposes of this Act;

(*m*) "landowner" means :

(*i*) in relation to a land personally cultivated, the owner of such land;

(*ii*) in relation to a land held by a cultivating tenant, such cultivation tenant;

(*iii*) in any other case, the person in actual possession of the land, and includes his heirs, assignees and legal representatives.

Explanation I : For the purposes of this clause:-

(*i*) "cultivating tenant" shall have the same meaning as in clause (8) of section 2 of the Kerala Land Reforms Act, 1963 (1 of 1964); and

(*ii*) "personally cultivate" means cultivate either solely by one's own labour or with the help of the members of his family or hired labourers or both, or personally direct or supervise cultivation by such members or hired labourers or both, provided that such members or hired labourers have not agreed to pay or to take any fixed proportion of the produce of the land they cultivate as compensation for being allowed to cultivate it or as remuneration for cultivating it.

Explanation II : For the avoidance of doublc it is hereby clarified that the Government shall be deemed to be the landowner, where the land referred to in sub-clause (I) or sub-clause (iii) is land owned by or, as the case may be, in the actual possession of, the Government;

(n) "prescribed wages" means-

(i) Wages at such rate, not being-

(A) less than the minimum rate of wages fixed or revised under the Minimum Wages Act, 1948 (Central Act 11 of 1948); or

(B) more than fifteen percent in excess of such minimum rate of wages,

as may be specified by the Government by notification in the Gazette;

(ii) the agreed rate of wages, which ever is higher.

Explanation : For the purposes of this clause, the rate or wages decided by an Industrial Relations Committee constituted for any area or the rate of wages agreed at conferences held by the Government in respect of any area shall be deemed to be the agreed rate of wages for that area during the period covered by such decision;

(o) "prescribed" means prescribed by rules made under this Act;

(p) "Scheme" means the Agricultural Workers' Provident Fund Scheme framed under subsection (I) of section 8,

(q) "Wages" means all remuneration, whether payable in cash or in kind, which would, if the terms of employment, express or implied, were fulfilled, by payable to a person employed in respect of his employment or of work down in such employment but does not included-

(i) the value of :

(A) Any house accommodation, supply of light water or medical attendance; or

(B) Any other amentty or any service excluded by general or special order of the Government; or

(ii) any contribution paid by the employer under any scheme framed under any law for the time being in force;

(iii) any sum paid to the person employed to defray special expanses entailed on him by the nature of his employment.

CHAPTER-II

Officers and Agricultural Tribunal

(3) Appointment of Conciliation Officers

The Government may, by notification in the Gazette, appoint for any area specified therein any officer of the Labour Department not below the rank of Assistant Labour Officer to be a Conciliation officer for the purpose of performing the functions entrusted to a Conciliation Officer by a or under this Act.

(4) Constitution of Agricultural Tribunals :

(1) The Government may, by notification in the Gazette, constitute for any area specified therein an agricultural Tribunal for the purpose of performing the functions of the Agricultural Tribunal under this Act.

(2) An Agricultural Tribunal shall consist of sole member, who shall be an officer not below the rank of Deputy Collector, appointed by the Government.

(5) Inspectors :

(1) The Government may by notification in the Gazette, appoint:

(a) Such officers, or

(b) Such person as possess, the prescribed qualification, as they think fit, to be Inspectors for the purposes of this Act and define the local limits within which they shall exercise their powers.

(2) Subject to any rules made in this behalf, an Inspector may, within the local limits for which he is appointed:

(a) enter, at any time after sunrise and before sunset with such assistant (if any), being persons in the service of the Government or any local or other public authority, as he thinks fit, premises or places where agricultural workers are employed or where he has reasons to believe that records are kept, for the propose of examining any register or record of wages required to be kept under this Act or the rules made thereunder and require the production thereof for inspection;

(b) examine any person whom he finds in any such promises or place and whom he has reasonable cause to believe to be a agricultural worker;

(c) seize or take copies of such register or record or portions thereof as he may consider relevant in respect of any offence under this Act which he has reason to believe has reason to believe has been committed by a landowner; and

(d) exercise such other powers as may be prescribed.

(3) until Inspectors are appointed under this Act, the Inspectors appointed under the Minimum Wages Act, 1948 (Central Act 1.1 of 1948), shall be deemed to be Inspectors appointed under this act for the area in which they exercise jurisdiction under the said Act.

(6) Facilities to be afforded to Inspectors

Every Landowner shall afford an Inspector all reasonable facilities for making an entry, inspection, examination or inquiry under the Act.

CHAPTER-III

Security of Employment and Welfare

(7) Preference for employment as agricultural workers:

(1) The landowner shall not employ any agricultural worker other than an agricultural worker who has worked in the same land during the previous agricultural seasons.

Provided that preference shall be given to agricultural workers employed for the previous agricultural operation in the same agricultural and during the same agricultural season:

Provided further that where there are permanent workers of the landowner, such workers shall be given preference over other agricultural workers.

Explanation : For the purpose of this subsection, "permanent worker", in relation to a landowner, means an agricultural worker who is bound by custom or contract or otherwise to work in the agricultural land of that landowner.

(2) Notwithstanding anything contained in subsection (1), where any agricultural worker has worked in the land of a landowner during three consecutive agricultural seasons, prior to the previous agricultural seasons, he shall not be denied employment merely on the ground that he has not worked during the previous agricultural season, provided his absence during that season was due to reasons beyond his control.

(3) Nothing contained in subsection (1) or subsection (2) shall be deemed to enable the landowner to refuse employment during an agricultural season to an agricultural worker eligible to be employed by the landowner under either of those subsections but who has not offered himself for employment on any previous day of that agricultural season.

(4) Where the agriculture workers mentioned in subsection (1) or subsection (2) or subsection (3) are not available or the number of such agricultural workers available is less than the number required by the landowner for the agricultural operation in his land, nothing in those subsections shall be deemed to prevent him from employing other agricultural workers.

(5) Notwithstanding anything contained in the foregoing provisions of this section, no landowner shall be under an obligation to employ any agricultural worker.

(a) who does not offer himself for employment; or

(b) who is more than sixty-five years of age in the case of a male worker or sixty years of age in the case of a female worker; or

(c) who is incapacitated and is unable to do the work; or

(d) who has intentionally caused damage of crops belonging to the landowner or caused any other loss to the landowner.

(8) Establishment of Agricultural Worker's Provident Fund

(1) The Government may, by notification in the Gazette, frame a scheme to be called the Agricultural Worker's Provident Fund Scheme for the establishment of a provident fund under this Act

and there shall be established, as soon as may be after the framing of the Scheme, a fund in accordance with the provisions of this Act and the Scheme.

(2) The fund shall vest in and be administered by a Board constituted under section 11.

(3) Subject to the provisions of this Act, the Scheme framed under subsection (1) provide for or any of the matters specified in the Scheduled.

(4) The Scheme framed under subsection (1) shall be laid as soon as may be after it is framed, before the Legislative Assembly while it is in section for a total period of fourteen days which may be comprised in one session or in two successive sessions, and if before the expiry of the session in which it is so laid or the session immediately following, the Legislative Assembly makes any modification in the Scheme, the Scheme shall thereafter have effect only in such modified form; so however that any such modification shall be without prejudice to the validity of anything previously done under the Scheme.

(9) Contributions to the Fund:

(1) The landowner shall pay Contribution to the Fund at the rate of five per cent of the wages paid by him to each agricultural worker employ by him.

(2) Each agricultural worker shall also pay contribution to the Fund of an amount equal to the amount of contribution payable by the landowner under subsection (1).

(3) Where the wages are payable in kind, the amount of contribution for the purposes of subsections (1) and (2) shall be calculated at such commutation rate as may be notified by the Government in that behalf from time to time.

(10) Modification of scheme:

(1) The Government may, by notification in the Gazette, add to, amend or vary the scheme.

(2) Every notification under subsection (1) shall be laid, as soon as may be after it is issued, before the legislative Assembly which it is in session for a total period of fourteen days which may be comprised in one session or in two successive sessions, and if before the expiry of the session in which it is so laid or the session

immediately following, the Legislative Assembly makes any modification in the notification or decides that the notification should not be issues, the notification shall thereafter have effect only in such modified form or be of no effect, as the case may be, so however that any such modification or annulment shall be without prejudice to the validity of anything previously done under that notification.

(11) Constitution of Board:

(1) The Government shall, by notification in the Gazette, constitute with effect from such date as may be specified in the notification a Board to be called the Agricultural Workers' Provident Fund Board for the Administration of the Fund.

(2) The Board shall be a body corporate by the name aforesaid having perpetual succession and a common seal and shall by the said name sue and be sued.

(3) The Board shall consist of such number of members as the Government may determine and they shall be chosen in such manner as may be prescribed:

Provided that the number of members representing the Government' the landowners and the agricultural workers shall be equal.

(4) The Government shall appoint one of the members of the Board to be its Chairman.

(5) The term of office or, and the manner of filling casual vacancies among, the members of the Board shall be such as may be prescribed.

(6) The names of members and the Chairman shall be published in the Gazette.

(7) The Board shall administer the Fund in such manner as may be specified in the Scheme.

(12) Appointment of officers for assisting the Board:

(1) The Government may appoint such number of officers as they think fit for assisting the Board in the administration of the Fund.

(2) The officers appointed under subsection (1) shall exercise such powers and discharge such duties as may be prescribed.

(13) Directions by the Government:

(1) The Government may after consultation with the Board give to the Board general instructions to be followed by the Board, and such instructions may include directions relating to the recruitment, conditions of service and training of its employees and the wages to be paid to the employees.

(2) In the exercise of its powers and performance of its duties under this Act or the Scheme the Board shall not depart from any general instructions issued under subsection (1), expect with the previous permission of the Government.

(3) Any amount standing to the credit of a member in the Fund at the time of his or her ceasing to be agricultural worker, whether on the ground that he or she is over sixty-five or sixty years of age, as the case may be, as on the ground that he or she is incapacitated and is unable to work or on any other ground, shall, subject, to any deduction authorised by the Scheme, be paid to him or her and shall be free from any debt or other liability incurred by that member before his or her ceasing to be an agricultural worker.

(15) Landowner not to reduce wages, etc :

No landowner shall by reason only of his liability for the payment, of any contribution to the Fund reduce whether directly or indirectly the wages of any agricultural worker to whom the scheme applies.

CHAPTER-IV

Hours and Limitations of Employment and Wages

(16) Hours of work

Save as otherwise expressly provided in this Act, no adult agricultural worker shall be required to work for more than eight hours in any day and no adolescent or child for more than six hours in any day:

Provided that nothing contained in this section shall be deemed to prohibit an agreement between the landowner and the agricultural workers for working for less than eight hours or six hours, as the case may be, on any particular day or days or on all days of Employment or to affect any custom or practice prevailing in the locality under which the agricultural workers is required to work for less than eight hours or six hours, as the case may be.

(17) Daily intervals for rest

The period of work on each day shall be so fixed that no period shall exceed four hours and that no agricultural worker shall work for more than four hours, before he has had an interval for rest for at least half an hour.

(18) Wages Payable to agricultural workers:

(1) Every landowner shall pay to any agricultural worker employed by him the prescribed wages for each day of work done.

(2) The Government may from time to time by notification in the Gazette, fix the number of hours of work which shall constitute a normal working day for the purpose of subsection (1) either for the whole State of any part thereof:

Provided that where the Government have fixed the number of hours work which shall constitute a normal working day in respect of any of the categories of agricultural workers in the employment in agricultural under section 13 of the Minimum Wages Act, 1948 (Central Act 11 of 1948), the hours of work so fixed shall, until a notification is issued under this subsection, be deemed to have been fixed under this subsection.

(19) Wages for harvest:

(1) The prescribed wages for harvest shall be paid at the threshing floor on which the threshing takes place and no portion of the produce shall be removed from the threshing floor without payment of the prescribed wages to the agricultural worker concerned.

(2) Notwithstanding anything contained in subsection (1), where the quantum of prescribed wages is in dispute and such quantum cannot be determined without setting the dispute under the provisions of this Act, an officer not below the rank of a Tahsildar authorised in this behalf by the Government by notification in the Gazette shall, if he is satisfied that the harvested produce of kept in the threshing floor till the settlement of the dispute will perish or be otherwise lost, take such action as he thinks expedient in each case to ensure that the harvested produce does not perish or is not otherwise lost till the settlement of the dispute.

(20) Enforcement of payment of prescribed wages:

(1) The Conciliation Officer shall, after giving the applicant and the land owner an importunity of being heard and after such inquiry, if any, which he may consider necessary, direct:

(a) in the case of a claim arising out of the payment of less than the prescribed wages, the payment to the agricultural worker of the amount by which the prescribed wage payable to him exceeds the amount actually paid by the landowner;

(b) in the case of claim arising out of non-payment of prescribed wages, the payment of the prescribed wages to the agricultural worker.

(3) If as a result of a direction under subsection (2), any amount of the prescribed wages becomes payable to an agricultural worker, the Conciliation Officer may:

(a) in the case of harvest:

(i) recover in kind such amount of the prescribed wages at the threshing floor from out of the harvested paddy; and

(ii) if the harvested paddy or any portion thereof has been removed from the threshing floor in contravention of the provisions of section 19, recover in kind the amount of prescribed wages from the land owner concerned and if such recovery is not possible, the Conciliation Officer shall make a report to the Collector specifying the full particulars regarding the amount of cash value of the prescribed wages due to the agricultural worker concerned and on receipt of such report, the collector shall proceed to recover the same from the landowner concerned as if it were an arrear of public revenue due on land;

(B) In the case of any work other than harvest, recover in kind the amount of prescribe wages from the landowner concerned and if such recovery is not possible, the Conciliation Officer shall make a report to the Collector Specifying the full particulars regarding the amount or cash value of the prescribed wage due to the agricultural worker concerned and on receipt of such report, the Collector shall proceed to recover the same from the landowner concerned as if it were an arrear of public revenue due on land.

Explanation—In this subsection, "Collector" means the District Collector or any other Officer appointed by the Government to exercise the powers and perform the functions of a Collector under the Kerala Revenue Recovery Act, 1968 (15 of 1968).

(4) The Conciliation Officer shall have such powers as are necessary to effect the payment of the prescribed wages to be the agricultural worker, including the power to enter upon any land on which, or into any building in which, the harvested crop is kept.

(21) Wages for over-time Work

Where an agricultural worker is required by the landowner to work for more than the number of hours of work fixed or deemed to have been fixed under subsection (2) of section 18, he shall be entitled in respect of each hour of such over-time work to wages at the rate of twice his ordinary rate of wages for one hour.

Provided that nothing contained in this section shall apply in respect of harvest or any work connected therewith.

CHAPTER-V

Disputes

(22) Settlement of agricultural disputes:

(1) Where an agricultural dispute exists or is apprehended, the Conciliation Officer may hold conciliation proceedings and shall for the purpose of bringing about a settlement of the dispute, without delay investigate the same and all matters affecting the merits and the right settlement thereof any may do all such things, as the thinks, fit, for the purpose of inducing the parties to come to a fair and amicable settlement of the dispute.

(2) If a settlement of the dispute or of any of the matters in dispute is arrived at in the course of conciliation proceedings, the Conciliation Officer shall send a report thereof to the District Labour Officer together with a memorandum of settlement signed by the parties to the dispute.

(3) If no such settlement is arrived at, the Conciliation Officer shall, as soon as practicable after the close of the investigation, send to the District Collector through the District Labour Officer a full report setting forth the steps taken by him for ascertaining the facts and circumstances relating to the dispute and for bringing

about a settlement thereof, together with a full statement of such facts and circumstances, and the reasons on account of which, in his opinion, a settlement could not be arrived at:

Provided that in a case where the agricultural dispute relates to an agricultural land situate within the local limits of more than one revenue district, the Conciliation Officer shall send the report to the District Collector in whose jurisdiction the major portion of such land is situate.

(4) If on a consideration of the report referred to in subsection (3), the District Collector is satisfied that there is a case for reference to an Agricultural Tribunal: he may, by order in writing, refer the agricultural dispute to the said tribunal for adjudication and where the District Collector does not make such a reference, he shall record and communicate to the parties concerned his reasons therefore.

(5) Where an agricultural dispute has been referred to an Agricultural Tribunal under subsection (4), the Tribunal shall hold its proceedings expeditiously and shall, as soon as practicable after the conclusion of the proceedings, but not later than thirty days from the data of receipt of the reference by the Tribunal submit its award to the District Collector.

(6) The District Collector shall, within a period of fifteen days from the date of receipt of the award referred to in subsection (5), cause the same to be published in his office an in the office of the Agricultural Tribunal shall be final and shall be given effect to by the parties to the agricultural dispute.

(7) An award referred to in subsection (5) shall, subject to any order of the Government under section 26, become enforceable on the expiry of ten days from the date of its publication in the manner provided in subsection (6).

(8) Every memorandum of settlement referred to in subsection (2) and, subject to any order Government under section 26, every award of an Agricultural Tribunal shall be final and shall be given effect to by the parties to the agricultural dispute.

(23) Appeal:

(1) Against any order passed by a Conciliation Officer under section 20, an appeal shall lie to the Agricultural Tribunal within a period of thirty days from the date of the order appealed against,

and the decision of the Agricultural Tribunal on such appeal shall be final.

(24) Decision in Appeal in Respect of Prescribed Wages to be Given Effect to:

(1) Where the amount of prescribed wages paid to an agricultural worker under section 18 or recovered under section 20 for payment to an agricultural worker is less than the amount of prescribed wages payable as a result of the decision in appeal, the balance shall be recovered from the landowner concerned as if it were an arrear of public revenue ...on land and paid to the agricultural worker concerned.

(2) Where the amount of prescribed wages paid to an agricultural worker under section 18 or recovered under section 20 for payment to an agricultural worker is in excess of the amount of prescribed wages payable as a result of the decision in appeal such excess shall be recovered from the agricultural worker concerned for payment to the landowner concerned and the provisions of section 39 shall apply to such recovery.

(25) **Reference or Decision of Disputes by Government:**

(1) Notwithstanding anything contained in section 22, where any agricultural disputes exists or is apprehended, the Government may, by order in writing and for reasons to be stated therein:

(a) refer the dispute to the Agricultural Tribunal constituted for the area in which the dispute exists or is apprehended, for adjudication; or

(b) decide the dispute themselves' and pass an award.

(2) Where a dispute is referred to an Agricultural Tribunal under clause (2) of subsection (1), the provision of subsections (5), (6), (7) and (8) of section 22 shall apply as if the reference to the Tribunal were made by the District Collector under subsection (4) of that section.

(3) The Government shall cause every award passed by them under clause (b) of subsection (1) to be published in the Gazette and in such other manner as may be prescribed.

(4) An award referred to in subsection (3) shall be final, shall be given effect to by the parties to the agricultural dispute and

shall be enforceable on the expiry of five days from the date of its publication in the Gazette.

(26) Power of Government as respects awards:

(1) If the Government are of opinion that it is inexpedient on public grounds affecting national economy or social justice to give effect to the whole or any part of an award referred to in subsection (5) of section 22, they may by notification in the Gazette, declare that the award shall not become enforceable on the expiry of the period mentioned in subsection (7) of the said section.

(2) Where any declaration has been made in relation to an award under subsection (1), the Government may, within thirty days from the date of publication of the award under subsection (6) of section 22, make an order rejecting or modifying the award, and such order shall be published in the Gazette.

(3) Where no order has been passed by the Government under subsection (2), the award shall become enforceable on the expiry of the period of thirty days mentioned in that subsection.

(4) Where an order has been made by the Government under subsection (2), the award shall not be enforceable or, as the case may be, the award as modified shall be enforceable on the expiry of a period of five days from the date of publication of such order in the Gazette.

CHAPTER-VI

Penalties and Procedure

(27) Penalty for obstructions, etc:

(1) Whoever obstructs any Inspector or Conciliation Officer in the discharge of his duties under this Act or refuses or willfully neglects to afford any Inspector reasonable facilities for making an inspection, examination or inquiry authorised by or under this Act, shall be punishable with imprisonment for a term which may extend to six months, or with fine which may extend to one thousand rupees, or with both.

(2) Whoever willfully refuses to produce on the demand of an Inspector any register or other document kept in pursuance of this Act or prevents or attempts to prevent or does anything which he has reason to believe is likely to prevent any person from appearing

before, or being examined by, an Inspector acting in pursuance of his duties under this Act, shall be punishable with imprisonment for a term which may extend to six months, or with fine which may extend to one thousand rupees, or with both.

(28) Penalty for Making False Statements, etc:

Whoever for the purpose of avoiding any payment to be made by him under this Act or under the scheme or for enabling any other person to avoid such payment, knowingly makes or causes to be made any false statement or false representation, shall be punishable with imprisonment for a term which may extend to six months, or with fine which may extend to one thousand rupees, or with both.

(29) Penalty for Breach of Settlement or Award:

Any person who commits a breach of any term of any settlement or awards shall be punishable with imprisonment for a terms which may extend to one year, or with find which may extend to one thousand rupees, or with both and where the breach is a continuing one, with a further fine which may extend to one hundred rupees for every day during which the breach continues after conviction for the first such breach, and the curt trying the offence may direct that the whole or any part of the fine realised from him shall be paid by way of compensation to any person who in its opinion has been injured by such breach.

(30) Other penalties:

Whoever contravenes or makes default in complying with any of the provisions of this Act or the Scheme of any rule made under this Act shall, if no other penalty is elsewhere provided by or under this Act for such contravention or non-compliance, be punishable with imprisonment for a term which may extend to six months, or with fine which may extend to one thousand rupees, or with both and, in the case of a continuing contravention, with an additional fine which may extend to one hundred rupees for every day during which such contravention continues after conviction for the first such contravention.

(31) Enhanced Penalty after Previous Conviction:

If any person who has been convicted of any offence punishable under this Act is again found guilty of an offence involving a contravention of the same provisions, he shall be punishable on a subsequent conviction with imprisonment for a term which shall not be less than one month, but which may extend to six months and with fine which shall not be less than five hundred rupees, but which may extend to two thousand rupees.

Provided that for the purposes of this section, no cognizance shall be taken of any conviction made more than five years before the commission of the offence which is being punished.

(32) Offences by Companies:

(1) Where an offence under this Act has been committed by a company, every person who at the time the offence was committed was in charge or, and was responsible to the company for the conduct of the business of the company, as well as the company, shall be deemed to be guilty of the offence and shall be liable to be proceeded against and punished accordingly:

Provided that nothing contained in this subsection shall render any such person liable to any punishment if he proves that the offence was committed without his knowledge or that he exercised all due deligen to prevent the commission of such offence.

(2) Notwithstanding anything contained in subsection (1), where an offence under this Act has been committed by a company and it is proved that the offence has been committed with the consent or connivance of, or is attributable to any neglect on the part of any director, manager, secretary or other officer of the company, such director manager, secretary or other officer shall also be deemed to be guilty to that offence and shall be liable to be proceeded against and punished accordingly.

Explanation: For the purposes of this section:

(a) "Company" means anybody corporate and includes a firm or other association of individuals; and

(b) "director", in relation to a firm, means a partner in the firm.

(33) Cognizance of offences: No court shall take cognizance of any offence punishable under this Act, except on complaint made by, or with the previous sanction in writing of, the Government or an officer authorised by the Government in this behalf by notification in the Gazette, and no court inferior to that of a Magistrate of the First Class shall try any offence punishable under this Act..

(34) Limitation of prosecutions: No Court shall take cognizance of an offence punishable under this Act unless complaint theories is made within three months from the date on which the alleged commission of the offence comes to the knowledge of the Government or the officer authorised under section 33.

CHAPTER-VII

Miscellaneous

(35) Register of agricultural workers:

(1) The executive authority or every local authority shall prepare a register of agricultural workers residing within the jurisdiction of that local authority.

(2) The register shall contain each particulars may be prescribed.

(3) The register shall be maintained by the executive authority in such manner as may be prescribed.

(36) Maintenance of Registers and Records by Landowners:

(1) Every landowner shall maintain such registers and records as may be prescribed.

(2) The registers and records referred to in subsection (1) shall contain such particulars and shall be kept in such place, as may be prescribed.

(37) Bar of jurisdiction of civil courts: No civil court shall entertain any suit or other proceedings to set aside or modify any order or decision passed by any authority or officer under this Act in respect of any of the matters falling within its or his scope.

(38) Power to take evidence on oath, etc: Any authority or officer exercising powers under this Act shall have the same powers as are vested in a civil court under the code of Civil Procedure, 1908 (Central Act 5 of 1908), when trying a suit, in respect of the following matters, namely:

(a) enforcing the attendance of any person and examining him on oath;

(b) requiring the discovery and production of documents,

(c) receiving evidence on affidavit;

(d) issuing commissions for the examination of witness; and

(e) such other matters as may be prescribed;

And any proceeding before such authority or officer shall be deemed to be a judicial proceeding within the meaning of sections 193 and 228 and for the purposes of section 196, of the Indian Penal Code (Central Act 45 of 1860).

(39) Recovery of money due from landowners:—(1) where any money is due to an agricultural worker from a landowner under a settlement referred to in subsection (2) of section 22, or an award under sub-section (5) of that section or under clause (b) of subsection (1) of section 25 or an award as modified by the Government under subsection (2) of section 26, the agricultural worker himself or any other person authorised by him in writing in that behalf or, in the case of the death of the agricultural worker, his assignees or heirs may within prejudice to any other mode of recovery make an application to the District Collector for the recovery of the money due to him and if the District Collector is satisfied that any money is so due, he shall proceed to recover the same as if it were an arear of public revenue due on land:

Provided that every such application shall be made within one year from the date on which the money became due to the agricultural worker from the landowner:

Provided further that any such application may be entertained after the expiry of the said period of one year if the District Collector is satisfied that the applicant had sufficient cause for not making the application within the said period.

(2) Any amount due from a landowner as contribution to the Fund and any other amount due from a landowner under this Act or the Scheme may, if the amount is in arrear, be recovered as if it were an arrear of public revenue due on land.

(40) Proper to recover damages: Where a landowner makes default in the payment of any contribution to the fund, the Government may recover from him such damages, not exceeding twenty-five per cent of the amount of arrears. As they thinkfit.

(41) Effect of laws and agreements inconsistent with this Act and Scheme:

(1) The provisions of this Act and the Scheme shall have effect notwithstanding anything inconsistent therewith contained in any other law or in the terms of any award agreement or contract of service, whether made before or after the commencement of this section.

Provided that where under any such award, agreement, contract of service custom or otherwise, any agricultural worker was enjoying immediately before the commencement of this section benefits in respect of any matter, which are more favourable to him than those to which he would be entitled under this Act, the agricultural worker shall be entitled to the more favourable benefits in respect of other matters under this Act.

(2) Nothing contained in this Act shall be construed as precluding any agricultural worker from entering into an agreement with a landowner for granting him rights or privileges in respect of any matter, which are more favourable to him than those to which he would be entitled under this Act.

(3) For the avoidance of double it is hereby declared that nothing contained in subsection (1) or subsection (2) shall be deemed to enable a landowner to enter into any agreement in contravention of the provisions of section 7.

(42) Exemption:

(1) Nothing contained in this Act other than sections 18, 20, 23, 24, clause (b) of subsection (1) and subsections (3) (4) of section 25 and subsection (1) of section 41 shall apply in relation to a landowner who does not hold more than one hectare in extent of land.

Explanation:—Where the landowner is a member of family, the extent of land held individually by any member of his family or joint by some or all of the members of such family shall, for the purposes of this subsection, be deemed to be held by the landowner.

(2) The Government may, by notification in the Gazette, for reasons to be recorded in writing, exempt any landowner or class of landowners or any agricultural land or class of agricultural lands from all or any of the provisions of this Act.

(43) Delegation of Powers

The Government may, by notification in the Gazette direct that any power exercisable by them under this Act of the rules made thereunder shall, is relation to such matters and subject to such conditions, if any, as may be specified in the direction be exercisable also by such officer or authority subordinate to the Government as may be specified in the notification.

(44) Members of Board, etc., to be Public Servants

Every of the Board and every officer appointed under this Act shall be deemed to be a public servant within the meaning of section 21 of the Indian Penal Code (Central Act, 45 of 1960).

(45) Power of Remove Difficulties

If any difficulty arises in giving effect to the provisions of this Act or the Scheme or any award or settlement under this Act, the Government may, by order, do anything not inconsistent with such provisions which appears to them necessary or expedient for the purpose of removing the difficulty.

(46) Protection of Action Taken in Good Faith

Done or intended to be done in pursuance of this Act or the Scheme or any rule or order made under this Act.

(47) Power to make rules:

(1) The Government may, by notification in the Gazette, make rules to carry out the purposes of this Act.

(2) In particular, and without prejudice to the generality of the foregoing power, such rules to carry out the purposes of this Act.

(a) The procedure to be followed by the conciliation Officer and the Agricultural Tribunal.

(b) The foes to be paid for applications and appeals under this Act;

(c) The powers of the Conciliation Officer necessary for the effective enforcement of the provisions of this Act;

(d) The manner of estimating the cash value of the prescribed wages in kind;

(e) The procedure to be followed by the Government under sections 25 and 26;

(f) Any other matter which has to be, or may be, prescribed under the provisions of this Act.

(3) Every rule made under this section and every notification issued under section 45 shall be laid, as soon as may be after it is made or issued, before the Legislative Assembly while it is in session for a total period of fourteen days which may be comprised in one session or in two successive sessions, and if before the expiry

of the session in which it is.....or the session immediately following, the Legislative Assembly makes any modification in the rule or notification or decides that the rule or notification should not be made or issued, the rule or notification shall there should not be made or issued, the rule or notification shall there after have effect only in such modified form or be of no effect, as the case may be; so however that any such modification or annulment shall be without prejudice to the validity of anything previously done under that rule or notification.

The Schedule

(See subsection (3) of section 8)

(1) The time and manner in which the contributions shall be paid to the Fund by the employers.

(2) The manner in which the employees' contributions may be collected by the employers and remitted to the Fund.

(3) The number of members of the Agricultural Workers' Provident Fund Board and their term of office.

(4) The manner in which the members are to be appointed and removed.

(5) The manner in which the Chairman of the Board is to be appointed.

(6) The constitution of the committees for assisting the working of the Board.

(7) The manner in which the accounts shall be kept, the accumulation in the fund invested, the accounts audited, etc.

(8) The manner in which periodical reports are to be submitted to the Government by the Board regarding the working of the Board.

(9) Conditions under which withdrawal from the Fund and any deduction or forfeiture therefrom may be made and the maximum amount of deduction or forfeiture.

(10) The fixation of annual rate of interest payable to the members of the Fund by the Board in consultation with the Government.

(11) The form in which the employees shall furnish particle of

himself and his family.

(12) The communication of any person or persons to receive the amount at the credit of a member on his death and the conciliation or alteration of such nomination.

(13) Registers and records to be maintained by the employer and the returns to be furnished by them.

(14) The powers, if any, which may be exercised by the officers appointed under this Act for the administration of the Scheme.

(15) The conditions of service, duties and remuneration of officers working under the Board.

(16) Any other matter which is to be provided for in the Scheme for the purpose of implementing the Scheme.

Appendix V

THE TRIPURA AGRICULTURAL WORKERS ACT, 1986

No. F.2(11)-Law/Leg/84 Dated, Agartala, the 26th June, 1986.

The following Act of the Tripura Legislative Assembly received assent of the Governor on 10-4-1986 and is hereby published for general information.

TRIPURA ACT NO. 9 OF 1986

THE TRIPURA AGRICULTURAL WORKERS ACT, 1984

AN

ACT

to provide for welfare of agricultural workers in the State of Tripura and to regulate the conditions of their works.

Whereas it is expedient to provide for the welfare of Agricultural workers in the State of Tripura and to regulate the conditions of their works;

BE it enacted in the Thirty Seventh Year of the Republic of India as follows:

CHAPTER-I

Preliminary

(1) Short title, Extent and Commencement:

(1) This Act may be called the Tripura Agricultural Workers' Act, 1986.

(2) It extends to the whole of the State of Tripura.

(3) It shall come into force on such date as the State Government may, by notification in the Official Gazette, appoint, and different dates may be appointed for different areas and for different provisions of this Act.

(2) Definitions

In this Act, unless the context otherwise requires,—

(a) "adult" means a person who has completed his eighteenth year of age;

(b) "agricultural dispute" means any dispute or difference between landowners and landowners or between landowners and agricultural workers or between agricultural workers and agricultural workers which is connected with the employment or non-employment or the terms of employment or with the conditions of labour of any agricultural workers;

Explanation:—Where any landowner discharges, dismisses, retrenches or otherwise terminates the services of, or denies employment to, an individual agricultural worker, any dispute or difference between that agricultural worker and his employer connected with, or arising out of such discharge, dismissal, retrenchment, termination or denial of employment shall be deemed to be an agricultural dispute notwithstanding that no other agricultural worker nor any Union of agricultural workers is a party to the dispute.

(c) "agricultural land" means any land used for cultivation, but does not include any Plantation as defined in the Plantations Labour Act, 1951 (Central Act 69 of 1951);

(d) "Agricultural Tribunal" in relation to any area, means the Agricultural Tribunal constituted under this Act for that area;

(e) "agricultural worker" means a person who, in consideration of the wages payable to him by a landowner, works on, or does any other agricultural operation including maintenance of livestock in relation to the agricultural land of such landowner;

(f) "Conciliation officer" means in relation to any area, the conciliation Officer appointed under this Act for that area;

(g) "family" means husband, wife and their unmarried children or any of them as may exist;

(h) "Inspector" means an Inspector appointed under sub-section (1) of section 5 or deemed, under sub-section (3) of that section to be appointed for the purposes of this Act.

(*i*) "landowner" means:

(*i*) in relation to a land under personal cultivation, the owner of such land;

(*ii*) in relation to a land held by a Bargadar or under Raiyat, such Bargadar or under Raiyat as defined in the Tripura Land Revenue and Land Reforms Act, 1960 (Act 43 of 1960);

(*iii*) in any other case, the person in actual possession of the land, and includes his heirs, assignees and legal representatives.

Explanation-I—In the purpose of this clause—

"Personal cultivation", with its grammatical variation and cognate expressions, means cultivation by a person on his own account—

(*i*) by his own labour, or

(*ii*) by the labour of any member of his family, or

(*iii*) by servants or by hired labour on wages, payable in cash or in kind but not as a share of produce, under his personal super-vision or the personal supervision of any member of his family;

Explanation-II:—For the avoidance of doubts it is hereby clarified that the Government shall be deemed to be the landowner, where the land referred to in sub-clause (i) or sub-clause (iii) is land owned by, or as the case may be, in the actual possession of, the Government;

(*j*) "Minor" means a person who has not completed the age of eighteen years;

(*k*) "prescribed wages" means wages at such rate, not being—

(*a*) less than the minimum rate of wages fixed or revised under the Minimum Wages Act, 1948 (Central Act II of 1948); or

(*b*) more than fifteen percent in excess of such minimum rate of wages, as may be specified by the Government by notification in the Gazette; or

(*c*) the agreed rate of wages, whichever is higher.

(*l*) "Prescribed" means prescribed by rules made under this Act;

(m) "wages" means all remunerations, whether payable in cash or in kind, which would, if the terms of employment, express or implied were fulfilled, by payable to a person employed in respect of his employment or of work done in such employment but does not include.

(i) the value of

(a) any house accommodation, supply of light, water or medical attendance; or

(b) any other amenity or any service excluded by general or special order of the Government; or

(ii) any sum paid to the person employed to defray special expenses entailed on him by the nature of his employment.

CHAPTER-II

Officers and Agricultural Tribunal

(3) Appointment of Conciliation Officer

The Government may, by notification in the Official Gazette, appoint for any area specified therein any officer of the Labour Department, not below the rank of Labour Officer, to be a Conciliation Officer for the purpose of performing the functions entrusted to a Conciliation Officer by or under this Act.

(4) Constitution of Agricultural Tribunals

(1) The Government may, by notification in the Officiai Gazette, constitute for any area specified therein an Agricultural Tribunal for the purpose of performing the functions of the Agricultural Tribunal under this Act.

(2) An Agricultural Tribunal shall consist of a sole member, who shall be an officer not below the rank of **Deputy Collector,** appointed by the Government.

(5) Appointment of Inspector:

(1) The Government may, by notification in the official Gazette, appoint:

(a) such officers, or

(b) such person as possess, the prescribed qualification, as they think fit, to be Inspectors for the purposes of this Act and

define the local limits within which they shall exercise their powers.

(2) Subject to rules made in this behalf, an Inspector may, within the local limits for which he is appointed:

(a) enter, at any time after sunrise and before sunset with such assistants, being persons in the service of the Government or any local or other public authority, as he thinks fit, premises or places where agricultural workers are employed or where he has reasons to believe that records are kept, for the purpose of examining any register or record of wages required to be kept under this Act or the rule made thereunder and require the production thereof for inspection;

(b) examine any person whom he finds in any such premises or place and whom he has reasonable cause to believe to be an agricultural worker;

(c) seize or take copies of such register or record or portions thereof as he may consider relevant in respect of an offence under this Act which he has reason to believe has been committed by a landowner; and

(d) exercise such other powers as may be prescribed,

(3) Until Inspectors are appointed under this Act the Inspectors appointed under the Minimum Wages Act (Central Act II of 1948), shall be deemed to be Inspectors appointed under this Act for the area in which they exercise jurisdiction under the said Act.

(6) Facilities to be Afforded to Inspectors

Every landowner shall afford an Inspector all reasonable facilities for making an entry, Inspection, examination or enquiry under this Act.

CHAPTER-III

Security of Employment and Welfare

(7) Preference for Employment as Agricultural Workers:

(1) The landowner shall not employ any agricultural worker other than an agricultural worker who has worked in the same land during the previous agricultural season:

Provided that preference shall be given to agricultural workers employed for the previous agricultural operation in the same agricultural land during the same agricultural season:

Provided further that where there are permanent workers of the landowner, such workers shall be given preference over other agricultural workers.

Explanation:—For the purpose of this sub-section "permanent worker", in relation to a land owner, means an agricultural worker who is bound by contract or otherwise to work in the agricultural land of that landowner.

(2) Notwithstanding anything contained in sub-section (1) where any agricultural worker has worked in the land of a landowner during three consecutive agricultural seasons, prior to the previous agricultural season, he shall not be denied employment merely on the ground that he has not worked during the previous agricultural season, provided his absence during that season was due to reasons beyond his control.

(3) Nothing contained in sub-section (1) or sub-section (2) shall be deemed to enable the land owner to refuse employment, during an agricultural season, to an agricultural worker eligible to be employed by the land owner under either of those sub-sections but who has not offered himself for employment on any previous day of that agricultural season.

(4) Where the agricultural workers mentioned in sub-section (1) or sub-section (2) or sub-section (3) are not available or the number of such agricultural workers available is less than the number required by the landowner for the agricultural operation in his land, nothing in those sub-section shall be deemed to prevent him from employing other agricultural workers.

(5) Notwithstanding anything contained in the foregoing provisions of this section, no landowner shall be under an obligation to employ any agricultural worker:

(a) who does not offer himself for employment; or

(b) who is more than sixty-five years of age in the case of male worker or sixty-years of age in the case of a female worker; or

(c) who is incapacitated and is unable to do the work; or

(*d*) who has intentionally caused damage of crops, belonging to the landowner or caused any other loss to the landowner.

(8) Framing of Welfare Schemes for Agricultural Workers:

(1) The State Government may, by one or more Notification frame one or more schemes, namely Tripura Agricultural Workers Contributory Provident Fund Scheme, Tripura Agricultural Workers Group Insurance Scheme, Tripura Agricultural Workers (Old-age and Invalid) Pension Scheme or any other beneficial schemes of whatever nomenclature as may be found expedient for the agricultural workers on terms and conditions as may be specified in the Notification and different schemes, may be framed for different areas or for different classes of agricultural workers and different date may be appointed for different schemes for different areas.

(2) Any scheme framed by the State Government under sub-section (1) shall provide the mode of administration of such scheme and all other matters incidental thereto.

(3) Every Notification publishing any scheme under sub-section (1) shall be laid as soon as may be after it is made, before the Legislative Assembly, while it is in session for a total period of fourteen days which may be comprised in one session or in two successive sessions, and if, before the expiry of the session it is so laid, or session immediately following, the House agrees in making any modification in the scheme, or the House agrees that the scheme should not be made, the scheme shall thereafter have effect only in such modified form or be of no effect, as the case may be, so however, that any modification or annulment shall be without prejudice to the validity of anything done under that scheme.

CHAPTER-IV

Hours and Limitations of Employment and Wages

(9) Hours of Work

Save as otherwise expressly provided in this Act, no adult agricultural worker shall be required to work for more than eight hours in any day and no minor for more than six hours in any day:

Provided that nothing contained in this section shall be deemed to prohibit an agreement between the land-owner and the agricultural workers for working for less than eight hours or six hours, as the case may be, on any particular day or days or on all days of Employment or to effect any custom or practice prevailing in the locality under which the agricultural worker is required to work for less than eight hours or six hours, as the case may be.

(10) Daily Intervals for Rest

The period of work on each day shall be so fixed that no period shall exceed four hours and that no agricultural worker shall work for more than four hour before he has had an interval for rest for at least half an hour.

(11) Wages Payable to Agricultural Workers:

(1) Every landowner shall pay to any agricultural worker employed by him the prescribed wages for each day of work done;

(2) The Government may, from time to time by notification in the Official Gazette, fix the number of hours of work which shall constitute a normal working day inclusive of one or more specified intervals for the purpose of sub-section (1) either for the whole State or any part thereof:

Provided that where the Government have fixed the number of hours of work which shall constitute a normal working day in respect of any of the categories of agricultural workers in the employment in agriculture under section 13 of the Minimum Wages Act, 1948 (Central Act, II of 1948), the hours of work so fixed shall, until a notification is issued under this sub-section, be deemed to have been Fixed under this sub-section.

(12) Wages for Harvest:

(1) The prescribed wages for harvest shall be paid at the thrashing floor on which the thrashing takes place and no portion of the produce shall be removed from the thrashing floor without payment of the prescribed wages to the agricultural worker concerned;

(2) Notwithstanding anything contained in sub-section (1) where the quantum of prescribed wages is in dispute and such quantum cannot be determined without settling the dispute under the provisions of this Act, an officer not below the rank of a Labour Inspector authorised in this behalf by the Government by Notification in the official Gazette shall, if he is satisfied that the harvested produce if kept in the thrashing floor till the settlement

of the dispute will perish or be otherwise lost take such action as he thinks expedient in each case to ensure that the harvested produce does not perish or is not otherwise lost till the settlement of the dispute.

(13) Enforcement of Payment of Prescribed Wages:

(1) If any landowner pays less than the prescribed wages or refuses to pay the prescribed wages to any agricultural worker, the agricultural worker or an official of the union of which he is a member may make an application to the Conciliation Officer for a direction under sub-section (2).

(2) On receipt of an application under sub-section (1) the Conciliation Officer shall, after giving the applicant, and the landowner an opportunity of being heard and after such inquiry, if any, as he may consider necessary, direct:

(a) in the case of a claim arising out of the payment of less than the prescribed wages, the payment to the agricultural worker of the amount by which the prescribed wages payable to him exceeds the amount actually paid by the landowner;

(b) in the case of a claim arising out of non-payment of prescribed wages, the payment of the prescribed wages to the agricultural worker.

(3) If as a result of a direction under sub-section (2), any amount of the prescribed wages becomes payable to an agricultural worker; the Conciliation Officer may:

(a) in the case of harvest:

(i) recover in kind or in cash such amount of the prescribed wages at the thrashing floor from out of the harvested paddy; and

(ii) if the harvested paddy or any portion thereof has been removed from the thrashing floor in contravention of the provisions of section 12 recover in kind or in cash the amount of prescribed wages from the land owner concerned and if such recovery is not possible, the Conciliation Officer shall make a report to the Collector specifying the full particulars regarding the amount of cash value of the prescribed wages due to the

agricultural worker concerned and on receipt of such report, the Collector shall proceed to recover the same from the landowner concerned as if it were an arrear of public revenue due on land;

(*b*) in the case of any work other than harvest, recover in kind or in cash the amount of prescribed wages from the land owner concerned and if such recovery is not possible, the Conciliation Officer shall make a report to the Collector specifying the full particulars, regarding the amount or cash value of the prescribed wages due to the agricultural worker concerned and on receipt of such report the Collector shall proceed to recover the same from the landowner concerned as if it were an arrear of land revenue due on land.

Explanation—In this sub-section, "Collector" means the Collector of the District or any other officer appointed by the Government to exercise the powers and perform the functions of a Collector under the Tripura Land Revenue and Land Reforms Act, 1960.

(4) The Conciliation Officer shall have such powers as are necessary to effect the payment of the prescribed wages to the agricultural worker, including the power to enter upon any land on which, or into any building in which, the harvested crop is kept.

(14) Wages for Over-time Work

Where an agricultural worker is required by the land owner to work for more than the number of hours of work fixed or deemed to have been fixed under sub-section (2) of Section 11 he shall be entitled in respect of each hour of such over-time work to wages at the rate of twice his ordinary rate of wages for one hour;

CHAPTER-V

Disputes

(15) Settlement of Agricultural Disputes:

(1) Where an agricultural dispute exists or is apprehended, the Conciliation Officer may hold conciliation proceedings and shall, for the purpose of bringing abut a settlement of the dispute, without delay investigate the same and all matters affecting the merit and the right settlement thereof and may do all such things,

as he thinks fit, for the purpose of inducing the parties to come to a fair and amicable settlement of the dispute.

(2) If a settlement of the dispute or of any of the matters in dispute is arrived at in the course of conciliation proceedings, the Conciliation Officer shall send a report thereof to the such Officer as may be specified by the State Government by Notification in this behalf together with a memorandum of settlement signed by the parties to the dispute.

(3) If no such settlement if arrived at, the Conciliation Officer, shall, as soon as practicable after the close of the investigation send to the Collector of the District through the Officer appointed under sub-clause (2) a full report setting forth the steps taken by him for ascertaining the facts and circumstance relating to the disputes and for bringing about a settlement thereof, together with full statement of such facts and circumstances, and the reason on account of which, in his opinion, a settlement could not be arrived at:

Provided that in a case where the agricultural dispute relates to an agricultural land situated within the local limits of more tan one District, the Conciliation Officer shall send the report to the Collector of the either District with intimation to another.

(4) If on a consideration of the report referred to in sub-section (3), the Collector of the District is satisfied that there is a case of reference to an agricultural Tribunal; he may, by order in writing, refer the agricultural dispute to the said Tribunal for adjudication and where the Collector of the District does not make such a reference, he shall record and communicate to the parties concerned his reasons therefore.

(5) Where an agricultural dispute has been referred to an Agricultural Tribunal under sub-section (4), the Tribunal shall hold its proceedings expeditiously and shall, as soon as practicable after the conclusion of the proceedings, but not later than thirty days from the date of receipt of the reference by the Tribunal, submit its award to the Collector of the District.

(6) The Collector of the District shall, within a period of fifteen days from the date of receipt of the award referred to in sub-section (5), cause the same to be published in his office and in the office of the Agricultural Tribunal in such manner as may be prescribed and shall also forward copies of the award to the parties concerned.

(7) An award referred to in sub-section (5) shall subject to any order of the Government under section 19 become enforceable on the expiry of ten days from the date of its publication in the manner provided in sub-section (6).

(8) Every memorandum of settlement referred to in sub-section (2) and, subject to any order of the Government under section 19 every award of an Agricultural Tribunal shall be final and shall be given effect to by the parties to the agricultural dispute.

(16) Appeal:

(1) Against any order passed by a Conciliation Officer under section 13 an appeal shall lie to the Agricultural Tribunal within a period of thirty days from the date of the order appealed against, and the decision of the Agricultural Tribunal on such appeal shall be final.

(2) The Agricultural Tribunal shall have power to stay the operation of the order of the Conciliation officer pending disposal of the appeal.

(17) Decision in Appeal in Respect of Prescribed Wages to be given Effect to:

(1) Where the amount of prescribed wages paid to an agricultural worker under section 11 or recovered under section 13 for payment to an agricultural worker is less than the amount of prescribed wages payable as a result of the decision in appeal, the balance shall be recovered from the land owner concerned as if it were an arrear of land revenue due on land and paid to the agricultural worker, concerned.

(2) Where the amount of prescribed wages paid to an agricultural worker under section 11 or recovered under section 13 for payment to an agricultural workers is in excess of the amount of prescribed wages payable as a result of the decision in appeal, such excess shall be recovered from the agricultural worker concerned for payment to the land owner concerned and the procedure contained in Section 32 shall apply for such recovery.

(18) Reference of Decision of Disputes by Government:

(1) Notwithstanding anything contained in section 15, where any agricultural dispute exists or is apprehended the Government may, by order in writing and for reasons to be stated therein,

(*a*) refer the dispute to the Agricultural Tribunal constituted for the area in which the dispute exists or is apprehended, for adjudication; or

(*b*) decide the dispute themselves and pass an award.

(2) Where a dispute is referred to an Agricultural Tribunal under clause (a) of sub-section (1), the provisions of sub-sections (5), (6), (7) and 8 of section 15 shall apply as if the reference to the Tribunal were made by the Collector of the District under sub-section (4) of that Section.

(3) The Government shall cause every award passed by them under clause (b) or sub-section (1) to be published in the Official Gazette and in such other manner as may be prescribed.

(4) An award referred to in sub-section (3) shall be final, shall be given effect to by the parties to the agricultural dispute and shall be enforceable on the expiry of five days from the date of its publication in the Official Gazette.

(19) Power of Government in Respect of Awards:

(1) If the Government is of opinion that it is inexpedient on public grounds effecting national economy social justice to give effect to the whole or any part of an award referred to in sub-section (5) of section 15, it may by Notification in the official Gazette declared that the award shall not become enforceable on the expiry of the period mentioned in sub-section (7) of the said section.

(2) Where any declaration has been made in relation to an award under sub-section (1), the Government may within thirty days from the date of publication of the award under sub-section (6) of section 15 made an order rejecting or modifying the award and such order shall be published in the official Gazette.

(3) Where no order has been passed by the Government under sub-section (2), the award shall become enforceable on the expiry of the period of thirty days mentioned in that sub-section.

(4) Where an order has been made by the Government under sub-section (2), the award shall not be enforceable or, as the case may be, the award as modified shall be enforceable on the expiry of a period of five days from the date of publication of such order in the official Gazette.

CHAPTER-VI

Penalties and Procedure

(20) Penalty for Obstructions, etc.

(1) Whoever obstructs any Inspector or Conciliation Officer in the discharge of this duties under this Act or refuses or wilfully neglects to afford any Inspector reasonable facilities for making an inspection, examination or enquiry authorised by or under this Act, shall be punishable with imprisonment for a term which may extend to six months, or with fine which may extend to one thousand rupees, or with both.

(2) Whoever wilfully refuses to produce on the demand of an Inspector any register or other document kept in pursuance of this act or prevents or attempts to prevent or does anything which he has reason to believe is likely to prevent any person from appearing before, or being examined by, an Inspector acting in pursuance of his duties under this Act, shall be punishable with imprisonment for a term which may extend to six months or with fine which may extend to one thousand rupees, or with both.

(21) Penalty for Making False Statements, etc:

Whoever for the purpose of avoiding any payment to be made by him under this act or for enabling any other person to avoid such payment, knowingly makes or causes to be made any false statement or false re-presentation, shall be punishable with imprisonment for a term which may extend to six months or with fine which may extend to one thousand rupees, or with both.

(22) Penalty for Breach of Settlement or Award

Any person who commits a breach of any term of any settlement or award shall be punishable with imprisonment for a term which may extend to one year, or with fine which may extend to one thousand rupees, or with both and where the breach is a continuing one, with a further fine which may extend to one hundred rupees for every day during which the breach continue after conviction for the first such breach, and the Court trying the offence may direct that the whole or any part of the fine realised from him shall be paid by way of compensation to any person who in its opinion has been injured by such breach.

(23) Other Penalties

Whoever contravenes or makes default in complying with any of the provisions of this Act, or of any rule made under this act shall, if no other penalty is elsewhere provided by or under this act for such contravention or non-compliance, be punishable with imprisonment for a term which may extend to six months, or with fine which may extend to one thousand rupees, or with both and, in the case of continuing contravention, with an additional fine which may extend to one hundred rupees for every day during which such contravention continues after conviction for the first such contravention.

(24) Enhanced Penalty After Previous Conviction

If any person who has been convicted of any offence punishable under this Act is again found guilty of an offence involving a contravention of the same provision, he shall be punishable on a subsequent conviction with imprisonment for a term which shall not be less than one month, but which may extend to six months and with fine which shall not be less than five hundred rupees, but which may extend to two thousand rupees:

Provided that for the purpose of this section, no cognizance shall be taken of ay conviction made more than five years before the Commission of the offence which is being punished.

(25) Offences by Companies:

(1) Where an offence under this Act has been committed by a company, every person who at the time the offence was committed was in charge of, and was responsible to the Company for the conduct of the business of Company, as well as the Company, shall be deemed to be guilty of the offence and shall be liable to be proceeded against and punished accordingly:

Provided that nothing, contained in this sub-section shall render any such person liable to any punishment if he proves that the offence was committed without his knowledge or that he exercised all due diligence to prevent the Commission of such offence.

(2) Notwithstanding anything contained in sub-section (1) where an offence under this Act has been committed by a company and it is proved that the offence has been committed with the consent or connivance of or is attributable to any neglect on the

part of, any director, manager, Secretary or other officer shall also be deemed to be guilty of that offence and shall be liable to be proceeded against and punished accordingly.

Explanation—For the purpose of this section—

(a) "company" means any body corporate and includes a firm or other association of individuals; and

(b) "Director", in relation to a firm, means a partner in the firm.

(26) Cognizance of Offences

No court shall take cognizance of offence punishable under this Act, except on complaint made by, or with the previous sanction in writing of, the Government or an officer authorised by the Government in this behalf by notification in the official Gazette, and no Court inferior to that of a Judicial Magistrate of the First Class shall try any offence punishable under this Act.

(27) Limitation of Prosecutions

No Court shall take cognizance of an offence punishable under this Act unless complaint thereof is made within three months from the date on which alleged Commission of the offence comes to the knowledge of the Government or the officer authorised under section 26.

CHAPTER-VII

Miscellaneous

(28) Register of Agricultural Workers:

(1) The executive authority of every local authority shall prepare a register of agricultural workers residing within the jurisdiction of that local authority.

(2) The register shall contain such particulars as may prescribed.

(3) The register shall be maintained by the executive authority in such manner as may be prescribed.

Explanation—For the purpose of this section 'Local authority' in relation to an agricultural worker means a municipality or a Notified Area Authority established under the Bengal Municipality Act, 1932 as adopted in Tripura or a Gaon Panchayat established under the Tripura Panchayats Act, 1983 under the local jurisdiction of which such agricultural worker resides.

(29) Maintenance of Registers and Records by Landowners:

(1) Every landowner shall maintain such registers and records as may be prescribed.

(2) The registers and records referred to in sub-section (1) shall contain such particulars and shall be kept in such place, as may be prescribed.

(30) Bar of Jurisdiction of Civil Courts

No civil court shall entertain any suit or other proceedings to set aside or modify any order or decision passed by any authority or officer under this Act in respect of any of the matters falling within its or his scope.

(31) **Power to take Evidence on Oath, etc**—Any authority or officer exercising powers under this Act shall have the same powers as are vested in a civil court under the Code of Civil procedure, 1908 (Central Act 5 of 1908), when trying a suit in respect of the following matters, namely:

(a) enforcing the attendance of any person and examining him on oath;

(b) requiring the discovery and production of documents;

(c) receiving evidence on affidavit;

(d) issuing commissions for the examination of witnesses; and

(e) such other matters as may be prescribed; and any proceeding, before such authority or officer shall be deemed to be a judicial proceeding within the meaning of sections 193 and 228 and for the purpose of section 196, of the Indian Penal Code (Central Act 45 of 1860).

(32) **Recovery of Money Due from Landowners**—Where any money is due to an agricultural worker from a landowner under settlement referred to in sub-section (2) of Section 15 or an award under sub-section (5) of that section or under clause (b) of sub-section (1) of Section 18 or an award as modified by the Government under sub-section (2) of Section 19 the agricultural worker himself or any other person authorised by him in writing in that behalf or, in the case of the death of the agricultural worker, his assignees or heirs may without prejudice to any other made of recovery make an application to the Collector of the District for

the recovery of the money due to him and if the Collector of the District is satisfied that any money is so due, he shall proceed to recover the same as if it were an arrear of land revenue due on land:

Provided that every such application shall be made within one year from the date on which the money become due to the agricultural worker from the landowner:

Provided further that any such application may be entertained after the expiry of the said period of one year if the collector or of the District is satisfied that the applicant had sufficient cause for not making the application within the said period.

(33) **Effect of Laws and Agreements Inconsistent with this Act:**

(1) The provisions of this Act shall have effect notwithstanding anything inconsistent therewith contained in any other law or in the terms of any award, agreement or contract of service, whether made before or after the commencement of this section;

Provided that where under any such award, agreement contract of service, custom or otherwise, any agricultural worker was enjoying immediately before the commencement of this section benefits in respect of any matter, which are more favourable to him than those to which he would be entitled under this Act, the agricultural worker shall be entitled to the more favourable benefits in respect of that matter notwithstanding that he receives benefits in respect of other matter under this Act.

(2) Nothing contained in this Act shall be construed as precluding any agricultural worker from entering into an agreement with a land owner for granting him rights or privileges in respect of any matter, which are more favourable to him than those to which he would be entitled under this Act.

(3) For the avoidance of doubts, it is hereby declared that nothing contained in sub-section (1) or sub-section (2) shall be deemed to enable a land owner to enter into any agreement in contravention of the provisions of section-7.

(34) **Exemption:**

(1) Nothing contained in this Act other than section—13, 14, 16, 17, clause (b) of sub-section (1) and sub-sections (3) and (4) of

section 18 and sub-section (1) of Section 33 shall apply in relation to a land owner who does not hold more than one hectare in extent of agricultural land.

Explanation—Where the landowner is a member of a family, the extent of land held individually by any member of his family or jointly by some or all of the members of such family shall, for the purposes of this sub-section be deemed to be held by the landowner.

(2) The Government may, by Notification in the Gazette, for reasons to be recorded in writing, exempt any landowner or class of landowners or any agricultural land or class of agricultural lands from all or any of the provisions of this Act other than sections 11, 13, 14, 16 17 clause (b) of sub-section (1) and sub-sections (3) and (4) of section 18 and sub-section (1) of section 33.

(35) Delegation of Powers

The Government may, by notification in the Official Gazette, direct that any power exercisable by them under this Act or the rules made thereunder shall, in relation to such matters and subject to such conditions, if any, as may be specified in the direction, be exercisable also by such officer or authority subordinate to the Government as may be specific in the Notification.

(36) Power to Remove Difficulties

If any difficulty arises in giving effect to the provisions of this Act or any award or settlement under this Act, the Government may, by order, do anything not inconsistent with such provision which appear to them necessary or expedient for the purpose of removing the difficulty.

(37) Protection of Action Taken in Good Faith

No suit, prosecution or other legal proceeding shall lie against the Government or any authority or officer in respect of any thing which is in good faith done oriented to be done in pursuance of this Act, or any rule or order made under this Act.

(38) Power to Make Rules:

(1) The Government may, by Notification in the Gazette, make rules to carry out the purposes of this Act.

(2) In particular, and without prejudice to the generality of the

foregoing power, such rules may provide for—

(*a*) The procedure to be followed by the Conciliation officer and the Agricultural Tribunal.

(*b*) the fees to be paid for applications and appeals under this Act;

(*c*) the powers of the Conciliation Officer necessary for the effective enforcement of the provisions of this Act;

(*d*) the manner of estimating the cash value of the prescribed wages in kind.

(*e*) the procedure to be followed by the Government under sections 18 and 19.

(*f*) any other matter which has to be, or may be, prescribed under the provisions of this Act.

(3) Every rule made under this section and every notification issued under section 36 shall be laid, as soon as may be after it is made or issued, before the Legislative Assembly while it is in session for a total period of fourteen days which may be comprised in one session or in two successive sessions, and if before the expiry of the session in which it is so laid or the session immediately following, the Legislative Assembly makes any modification in the rule or notification or decides that the rule or notification should not be made or issued, the rule or notification shall thereafter have effect only in such modified form or be of no effect, as the case may be; so however that any such modifications or **annulment** shall be without prejudice to the validity of anything previously done under that rule or notification.

By order of the Governor,
A.B. Paul
Deputy Secretary, Law,

Appendix VI

Convention No.141: Convention Concerning Organisations of Rural Workers and Their Role in Economic and Social Development

The General Conference of the International Labour Organisation.

Having been convened at Geneva by the Governing Body of the International Labour Office, and having met in its sixtieth Session on 4 June 1975, and

Recognising that the importance of rural workers in the world makes it urgent to associate them with economic and social development action if their conditions of work and life are to be permanently and effectively improved, and

Noting that in many countries of the world and particularly in developing countries there is massive under-utilisation of land and labour and that this makes it imperative for rural workers to be given every encouragement to develop free and viable organisations capable of protecting and furthering the interests of their members and ensuring their effective contribution to economic and social development, and

Considering that such organisations can and should contribute to the alleviation of the persistent scarcity of food products in various regions of the world, and

Recognising that land reform is in many developing countries an essential factor in the improvement of the conditions of work and life of rural workers and that organisations of such workers should accordingly co-operate and participate actively in the implementation of such reform, and

Recalling the terms of existing international labour Conventions and Recommendations – in particular the Right of Association (Agriculture) Convention, 1921, the Freedom of Association and

Protection of the Right to Organsie Convention, 1948, and the Right to Organise and Collective Bargaining Convention, 1949 – which affirm the right of all workers, including rural workers, to establish free and independent organisations, and the provisions of numerous international labour Conventions and Recommendations applicable to rural workers which call for the participation, inter alia, of workers' organisations in their implementation, and

Noting the joint concern of the United Nations and the specialised agencies, in particular the International Labour Organisation and the Food and Agriculture Organisation of the United Nations, with land reform and rural development, and

Noting that the following standards have been framed in co-operation with the Food and Agriculture Organisation of the United Nations and that, with a view to avoiding duplication, there will be continuing co-operation with that Organisation and with the United Nations in promoting and securing the application of these standards, and

Having decided upon the adoption of certain proposals with regard to organisations of rural workers and their role in economic and social development, which is the fourth item on the agenda of the session, and

Having determined that these proposals shall take the form of an International Convention,

Adopts this twenty-third day of June of the year one thousand nine hundred and seventy-five the following Convention, which may be cited as the Rural Workers' Organisations Convention, 1975:

Article 1

This Convention applies to all types of organisations of rural workers, including organisations not restricted to but representative of rural workers.

Article 1

1. For the purposes of this Convention, the term "Rural Workers" means any person engaged in agriculture, handicrafts or a related occupation in a rural area, whether as a wage earner or, subject to the provisions of paragraph 2 of this Article, as a self-employed person such as a tenant, sharecropper or small owner-occupier.

2. This Convention applies only to those tenants, sharecroppers or small owner-occupiers who derive their main income from agriculture, who work the land themselves, with the help only of their family or with the help of occasional outside labour and who do not-

   (a) Permanently employ workers; or

   (b) Employ a substantial number of seasonal workers; or

   (c) Have any land cultivated by sharecroppers or tenants.

Article 3

1. All categories of rural workers, whether they are wage earners or self-employed, shall have the right to establish and, subject only to the rules of the organisation concerned, to join organisations of their own choosing without previous authorisation.

2. The principles of freedom of association shall be fully respected; rural workers' organisations shall be independent and voluntary in character and shall remain free from all interference, coercion or repression.

3. The acquisition of legal personality by organisations of rural workers shall not be made subject to conditions of such as character as to restrict the application of the provisions of the preceding paragraphs of this Article.

4. In exercising the rights provided for in this Article rural workers and their respective organisations, like other persons or organised collectivities, shall respect the law of the land.

5. The law of the land shall not be such as to impair, nor shall it be so applied as to impair, the guarantees provided for in this Article.

Article 4

It shall be an objective of national policy concerning rural development to facilitate the establishment and growth, on a voluntary basis, of strong and independent organisations of rural workers as an effective means of ensuring the participation of rural workers, without discrimination as defined in the Discrimination

(Employment and Occupation) Convention, 1958, in economic and social development and in the benefits resulting therefrom.

Article 5

1. In order to enable organisations of rural workers to play their role in economic and social development, each Member which ratifies this Convention shall adopt and carry out a policy of active encouragement to these organisations, particularly with a view to eliminating obstacles to their establishment, their growth and the pursuit of their lawful activities, as well as such legislative and administrative discrimination against rural workers' organisations and their members as may exist.
2. Each Member which ratifies this Convention shall ensure that national laws or regulations do not, given the special circumstances of the rural sector, inhibit the establishment and growth of rural workers' organisation.

Article 6

Steps shall be taken to promote the widest possible understanding of the need to further the development of rural workers' organisations and of the contribution they can make to improving employment opportunities and general conditions of work and life in rural areas as well as to increasing the national income and achieving a better distribution thereof.

Appendix VII

PART I

National Rural Employment Guarantee Act, 2005

Passed by the Parliament to provide for one hundred days of guaranteed wage employment in every year to every household whose adult members volunteer to do unskilled manual work.

Entitlement

- A household is entitled for 100 days of work in a year. Within the household entitlement, all adult members of a rural household have the right to demand employment.

Registration of Rural Households for Wage Employment

- A household that wants work under this Act should submit names, age, sex and addresses of its adult members to the local Gram Panchayat for registration.

Job Card to Every Registered Household

- Upon registration, a job Card will be issued by the Gram Panchayat with photographs of adult members of the registered household. It will be valid for five years and will have the registration number of the household.

- A Job Card is a document that gives an applicant an entitlement for employment.

Application for Work

- To get employment the registered adult must submit an application on a plain paper in writing to Gram Panchayat or the Programme Officer (a block level) and get a dated receipt of the application. The application should be submitted for at least 14 days of continuous work.

- Women will get priority to the extent that one-third of persons who are given employment are women who have asked for work.

Allotment for Work

- Within 15 days from submitting the application or from the date when employment is sought, employment should be provided by the Gram Panchayat.
- Gram Panchayat will inform applicants where and when to report for work within 15 days, by means of a letter. Public notice of this will be displayed on the Gram Panchayat's office.
- No contractor will be allowed to work under the scheme.

Payment of Unemployment Allowance

- If the eligible applicant does not get employment within 15 days of demand of work or the date from which he sought work, he shall be provided unemployment allowance if a person does not appear for the work allotted.

Minimum Entitlement of Labourers

- The statutory minimum wage applicable to agricultural workers in the State is to be paid.
- Wages are to be paid not later than a fortnight after the date on which work was done.
- Work will be provided within 5 km of applicants residence. If employment is provided beyond 5 km radius of the applicant's residence then he is entitled to 10% additional wages towards transport and living expenses.
- At work site safe drinking water, shades for children, periods of rest and fist-aid box, shall be provided at every work site by the implementing agency.
- A person may be entrusted with child care responsibilities, if there are more than five children brought along on the site and that person would get paid for the work done like the other workers.
- If a worker gets injured working on the site, free medical treatment will be given by the State Government.

Creation of Double Assets

- The focus of works is on.
- Water conservation and water harvesting.
- Drought proofing, including afforestation and tree plantation.
- Irrigation canals including micro and minor irrigation works.
- Irrigation facilities for land owners by households belonging to SC/ST or to land of beneficiaries of land reforms or that of the beneficiaries under the Indira Awas Yojana.
- Renovation of traditional water bodies, including de-silting of tanks.
- Land development.
- Flood control and protection of works, including drainage in water logged areas.
- Rural connectivity to provide all weather roads.
- Any other work, which may be notified by the Central Government in consultation with State Governments.

Implementation of the Act

- The Gram Sabha will identify works to be taken up. The Panchayats have the principal responsibility for planning, implementing and monitoring.
- All agencies implementing NREGA will be accountable to the public for their work. Social audit and Right to Information will apply to each aspect of implementation.
- Local Vigilance & Monitoring Committee will be set up.

The Act will be notified in 200 districts identified by the Central Government on 2nd February, 2006 in the first phase. Within 5 years it will cover the whole country.

Ministry of Rural Development
Government of India

PART II

Questions & Answers (Q&A) on NREGA

The Parliament has passed the Historical National Rural Employment Guarantee Act (NREGA) that guarantees 100 days of wage employment in a year to every rural household whose adult members are willing to do unskilled manual work. The Act will be notified in the districts identified by the Central Government starting from 2nd February, 2006 in the first phase. Within 5 years it will cover the whole country.

We are starting a series of advertisements to publicise the frequently asked questions and their answers on this momentous legislation of the Government for better understanding and information of the general public.

This is first of the series.

Questions & Answers

- **What does Notification mean?**

  Notification means that the National Rural Employment Guarantee Act will become operative in the notified districts.

- What are the activities to be taken up on that day?

  A Gram Sabha is to be held. People can start applying for registration

- Who can register?

All the adult members of the rural household willing to do unskilled manual work.

- **To whom should they apply for registration?**

  The application has to be made to the Local Gram Panchayat

- **What follows after application for registration is given?**

  The application for registration would be verified by Gram Panchayat for finding out whether the applicant resides in that village and is an adult. If this is authenticated then the Gram Panchayat has to register the applicant.

- **What happens after registration?**

  A job card shall be issued to applicant household by the Gram Panchayat.

- **What happens after a job card is issued?**

  After a job card has been issued the registered household may apply for work.

List of 200 Districts Identified for Implementation of NREGA in First Phase

Andhra Pradesh: Adilabad, Anantpur, Chittoor, Cudappah, Karimnagar, Khammam, Mahbubnagar, Medak, Nalgonda, Nizamabad, Rangareddy, Vizianagaram, Warangal.

Arunachal Pradesh: Upper Subansiri

Assam: Bongaigaon, Dhemaji, Goalpara, Karbi Anglong, Kokrajhar, North Cachar Hills, North Lakhimpur (Laksha),

Bihar: Araria, Aurangabad, Bhojpur, Darbhanga, Gaya, Jamui, Jehanabad, Kaimur(Bhabua), Kathihar, Kishanganj, Lakhisarai, Madhubani, Munger, Muzaffarpur, Nalanda, Nawadah, Patna, Purnia, Rohtas, Samastipur, Sheohar, Supaul, Vaishali.

Chhattisgarh: Bastar, Bilaspur, Dantewada, Shamtari, Jashpur, Kanker, Kawardha, Koriya, Raigarh, Rajnandgaon, Sarguja.

Gujarat: Banskantha, Dangs, Dohad, Narmada, Panchmahals, Sabarkantha.

Haryana: Mohindergarh, Sirsa.

Himachal Pradesh: Chamba, Sirmaur.

Jammu & Kashmir: Doda, Kupwara, Poonch.

Jharkhand: Bokaro, chatra, Dhanbad, Dumka, Garhwa, Giridih, Godda, Gumla, Hazaribagh, Jamtara, Kodarma, Latehar, Lohardagga, Pakaur, Palamu, Ranchi, Sahibganj, Saraikela, Simdega, Pachhim Singhbhum.

Karnataka: Bidar Chitradurga, Davanagere, Culbarga, Raichur.

Kerala: Palakkad, Waynad.

Madhya Pradesh: Balaghat, Barwani, Betul, Chattarpur, Dhar, Dindori, Jhabua, Khandwa (East Nimar), Mandla, Satna, Seoni, Shahdol, Sheopur, Shivpuri, Siddhi, Tikamgarh, Umaria, West Nimar (Khargone).

Maharashtra: Ahmednagar, Amravati, Aurangabad, Bhandara, Chandrapur, Dhule, Gadchiroli, Gondya, Hingoli, Nanded, Nandurbar, Yawatmal,.

Manipur: Tamenlong

Meghalaya: South Garo Hills, West Garo Hills

Mizoram: Lawngtlai, Saiha.

Nagaland: Mon

Orissa: Bolangir, Boudh, Debagarh, Dhenkanal, Gajapati, Ganjam, Jharsuguda, Kalahandi, Keonjhar, Koraput, Malkangiri, Mayurbhanj, Nabarangpur, Nuapada, Phulbani, Rayagada, Sambalpur, Sonepur, Sundargarh.

Punjab: Hoshiarpur

Rajasthan: Banswara, Dungarpur, Jhalawar, Karauli, Sirohi, Udaipur, Sonepur, Sundargarh.

Punjab: Hoshiarpur.

Rajasthan: Banswara, Dungarpur, Jhalawar, Karauli, Sirohi, Udaipur.

Sikkim: North Sikkim

Tripura: Dhalai

Tamil Nadu: Dinidigual, Nagapattinam, Sivagangai, South Arcot/Cuddalore, Tiruvannamalai, Villupuram.

Uttranchal: Chamoli, Champawat, Tehri Garhwal.

Uttar Pradesh: Azamgarh, Banda, Barabanki, Chandauli, Chitrakoot, Fatehpur, Gorakhpur, Hamirpur, Hardoi, Jalaun, Jaunpur, Kaushambi, Kushinagar, Lakhimpur Kheri, Lalitpur, Mahoba, Mirzapur, Pratapgarh, Raebareli, Sitapur, Sonebhadra, Unnao.

West Bengal: South 24 Parganas, Bankura, Birhbhum, Jalpaiguri, Malda, Murshidabad, Purulia, Dakshin Dinajpur, Midnapur West, Uttar Dinajpur

PART III

Questions & Answers (Q&A) on NREGA (Part-II)

The Parliament has passed the Historical National Rural Employment Guarantee Act (NREGA) that guarantees 100 days of wage employment in a year to every rural household whose adult members are willing to do unskilled manual work.

The Act will be notified in the districts identified by the Central Government starting from 2nd February, 2006 in the first phase. Within 5 years it will cover the whole country.

This is the second part of the question and answer series on NREGA

- **Who can apply for employment under the Act?**

  All adult members of a rural household who have a Job Card. Ever if a person is already employed/ engaged in work, he/she has right to demand employment as unskilled manual worker under this Act.

  Women will get priority and 1/3rd beneficiaries under the Programme are to be women.

- **Can individual application for work be submitted?**

  Yes. Registration of employment seekers is done household-wise. But within a registered households' entitlement for 100 days of employment in a year the individual members of the household can also apply for work.

- How can one apply for work?

  To get employment the registered adult holding Job Card should ask for it through an application on a plain paper in writing to the Gram Panchayat or Programme Officer (at block level) and ask for a dated receipt of application.

- **How many days of the year can one get this employment?**

  A household is entitled for 100 days of work in a financial year and that can be divided among adult members of the household.

  The work duration shall ordinarily be at least 14 days continuously with not more than 6 days a week.

- When can one get employment?

  Within 15 days of submitting the application or from the day work is demanded, employment will be provided to the applicant.

- Who will allot employment?

  Gram Panchayat or the Programme Officer whoever has been requested.

- How will one know that one has been given employment?

  Applicants are to be told where and when to report for work within 15 days, by a letter sent by sent by the Gram Panchayat/Programme Officer. There will also be a public notice displayed on the notice board of the Gram Panchayat and at the office of the Programme Officer at the Block Level, providing information on the place, date and names of those provided employment.

- What has the applicant to do once the employment letter has been received?

  Report for work with Job Card on the date specified at the site where work has been allotted.

- What happens if he/she does not report for work?

  If the person does not report for work within fifteen days of being notified by the Gram Panchayat or Programme Officer, he or she would nor be entitled for unemployment allowance.

- Can he/she re-apply for work?

  Yes.

PART IV

Questions & Answers (Q&A) on NREGA (Part-II)

The Parliament has passed the Historical National Rural Employment Guarantee Act (NREGA) that guarantees 100 days of wage employment in a year to every rural household whose adult members are willing to do unskilled manual work.

The Act will be notified in the districts identified by the Central Government starting from 2nd February, 2006 in the first phase. Within 5 years it will cover the whole country.

This is the third part of the question and answer series on NREGA

- **If a person applies for work under the Act where has the work to be provided?**

  Within 5 km of applicant's residence. If employment is provided beyond 5km radius of the applicant's residence then he/she is entitled for 10% additional wages towards transport and living expenses. If some persons are directed for work beyond 5 kilometre, than persons older in age and women shall be given preference to work on worksites near the village.

- **What are the wages a worker will get?**

  The statutory minimum wage applicable to agricultural workers in the State.

- **What will be the mode of payment-daily wages or piece rates?**

  Both are permitted under the Act. If wages are paid on a piece-rate basis, the schedule of rates has to be such that a person working for seven hours would normally earn the minimum wage.

- **When will wages be paid?**

  Wages are to be paid every week, or in any case "not later than a fortnight after the date on which such work was done". A proportion of the wages in cash may be paid on a daily basis.

- What happens if employment is not given to the eligible applicant?

  If the eligible applicant does not get employment with 15 days of demand of work or the date from which he sought work (date of submitting application), he shall be provided unemployment allowance as per laid down term and conditions.

  Allowance rate: The rate of unemployment allowance will be 25% of the wage rate for the first 30 days and 50% of the wage rate after that during the financial year subject to the household entitlements of days of employment.

Bibliography

—(2002) *Annual Report: 2001—20002*. Ministry of Rural Development.

—(2002) *Economic Survey*, New Delhi.

All India Congress Committee (1951) *Report of the congress Agrarian Reform Committee*. New Delhi.

Appu, P.S. (1996) *Land Reforms in India: A Survey of Policy, Legislation and Implementation* : N. Delhi, Vikas Publishing House Pvt. Ltd.

Bardhan, Pranab K (1984), *The Political Economy of Development in India*, Basil Blackwell, Oxford, 1984.

Battacharya, V.R. (1982) *New Face of rural India - March of New 2- Point Programme*, New Delhi, Metropolitan.

Berstecher, Dieter (1985) *Education and Rural Development: Issues for Planning and Research*, International Institute for Educational Planning UNESCO, Paris.

Brahmananda P.R. Narayan, D. L. and Kalappa (1987), *Dimension of Rural Development in India*, Himalaya Publishing House, Bombay.

Burkey, Stan (1993) *People First - A Guide to Self-Reliant Participatory Rural Development*, London, Zed Books Ltd.

CENDIT (Centre for Development of Instructional Technology) (1995), *Indian Social and Economic Development: An Index to the Literature*, Sage Publications, New Delhi, Thousand Oaks and London.

Chauhan, P.S. (1997) DWCRA: *An Evaluation Study of Dist. Jodhpur Rajasthan*, NOIDA, V.V. Giri National Labour Institute (Mimeo).

Choudhary, Dr. D. Paul, (1978), *New Partnership in Rural Development*, M.N. Publishers, New Delhi.

Choudhary, R.C. & Rajakutty, S. (Eds.) (1998) *Fifty Years of Rural Development in India: Retrospect and Prospect*. Hyderabad, National Institute of Rural Development.

Desai, A.R. (1979) *Rural India in Transition*, Popular Prakashan, Bombay.

Desai, A.R. (1984) *India's Path of Development - A Marxist Approach*. Bombay, Popular Prakashan.

El. ghonemy, M. Riad (1990) *The Political Economy of Rural Poverty: The case for Land Reform*. London, Routledge.

Gaur, Keshav Dev, (ed.) (1992), *Dynamics of Rural Development in India*, Mittal Publications, New Delhi.

Gehlawat, J.K. Kant, K (1987) *Strategies for Rural Development*, Arnold Publishers, New Delhi.

Giriappa, S. (1993) *Rural Development in Action: A Case Study of Coastal Areas*, Daya Publishing House, Delhi.

Giriappa, S. (1993), *The Prospects of Rural Development*, Daya Publishing House, Delhi.

Government of India (1990) *National Seminar on Agricultural Labour: Proceedings and Conclusions*. New Delhi, Ministry of Labour.

Govt. of India (1991) *Report of the National commission on Rural Labour*. Vol. I, New Delhi, Ministry of Labour.

Hashim, S.R. (1998) "Poverty Alleviation Programmes in India: An Overview". In R.C. Choudhary & S. Rajakutty (eds.), *Fifty Years of Rural Development in India; Retrospect and Prospect*. Hyderabad, National Institute of Rural Development.

Hebbar, Kusumakara C. (1991) *Integrated Rural Development Programme (IRDP): Retrospect and Prospect*. Deep and Deep Publications, New Delhi.

Huizer, G. (1984) 'Harmony vs. Conflict', In Wignaraja, P. (ed.) (1984). Reversing Anti-Rural Development.

ILO (1987) *Rural Employment creation in Asia and Pacific: Papers and Proceedings*.

Jain, C.M. Cangan, T. (1993) *Forth Years of Rural Development in India*. Indian Institute of Rural Management & Print well, Jaipur.

Joshi, P.C. (1981) "*Fieldwork Experience: Relived and Reconsidered: The Agrarian Society of Uttar Pradesh. The Journal of Peasant Studies*. Vol. 8, No. 4, pp 455-487.

Jumani, Usha (1991) *Dealing with Poverty: Self-employment for Poor Rural Women*, Sage, New Delhi, Newbury Park and London.

Long, Norman (1977) *An Introduction to the Sociology of Rural Development*, Tavistock Publications, London, 1977.

Maheshwari, S. (1995) *Rural Development in India - A Public Policy Approach*. New Delhi, Sage Publications.

Mandal, Gobinda C. (1992) *Rural Development: Retrospect and Prospect*, Concept Publishing Company, New Delhi.

Mehta, Uday (1975) *Agrarian Strategy in India*. Vora & Company Publishers Pvt. Ltd.

Mencher, Joan P. (1983) Agricultural Labourers in Peasants societies: The case of South Asia in Joan P. Mencher (ed.) *Social Anthropology of Peasantry*. Somaya Publication Pvt. Ltd. Bombay, 1983.

Ministry of Rural Development (MRD) (1999) *Annual Report 1998-99*. New Delhi, Government of India.

Ministry of Rural Areas and Employment (1999) *Annual Report 1998-99*. Depts. of Rural Employment and Poverty Alleviation, Rural Development & Wastelands Development, Government of India.

Ministry of Agriculture (1989) *Jawahar Rozgar Yojana: Manual*. Dept. of Rural Development, New Delhi, Govt. of India.

Misra, B.B. (1983) *District Administration and Rural Development*. Delhi, Oxford University Press.

Mishra, S.N. (1989), *New Horizons in Rural Development Administration* Mittal Publications, Delhi.

Mishra, S.N. (1992), *Participative Management and Rural Development* Mittal Publications, New Delhi.

Mukherjee, Neela (1993) *Participatory Rural Appraisal: Methodology and Applications*. Concept Publishing Company, New Delhi.

Naidu, K. Munirathna (ed.), (1992), "*Rural Development and Planning Perspectives*", Proceedings of a National Seminar on Grass Roots Level Planning and Rural Development in India, Reliance Publishing House, New Delhi.

NSSO (1992) *Some Aspects of Household Ownership Holdings Report 1*. NSS Forty-eighth Round. Dept. of Statistics, Ministry of Planning and Programme Institute, Government of India.

Oakley, Peter, et. al. (1991), *Projects with People: The Practice of Participation in Rural Development*. ILO, Geneva.

Pawar, S.N., Patil, R.B. (eds.) (1994) *Problems and Prospects of Development in Rural India*, Mittal Publications, New Delhi.

Planning Commission (1973) *Report of the Task Force on Agrarian Relations*. Government of India, New Delhi.

Planning Commission (1956) *Fortieth Report of the Estimates Committees*, Part II, New Delhi, Lok Sabha Secretariat. G.O.I.

Purushotham, P. (1998), TRYSEM: A Critical Review. In Choudhary, R.C. & Rajakutty, S., *Fifty Years of Rural Development in India: Retrospect and Prospect*. Hyderabad, NIRD.

Raj, K.N. and Michael Tharakan (1980) "Agrarian Reform in Kerala and Its Impact on Rural Economy—A Preliminary Assessment" in Ajit K. Ghose (ed.) *Agrarian Reform in contemporary Developing countries*. Croom Helm, London, 1980.

Rehamn, M.M. (1990) *Pattern of Land Relations and its impact on Agricultural Development of West Bengal - with Special Reference to Agricultural Labour Movements.* Unpublished Ph.D. Thesis. New Delhi, Jamia Millia Islamia.

Registrar General (1997) *Census of India-Availability of Infrastructural Facilities in Rural Areas of India: An Analysis of Village Directory data.* New Delhi, India.

Rehman, M.M. & Poonam S. Chauhan (1997) *Employment Assurance Scheme - An Evaluation Scheme.* NOIDA, V.V. Giri National Labour Institute (mimeo).

Rehman, M.M. and Poonam S. Chauhan (2002) *Handbook of Development Programmes and Schemes for Rural Development.* Noida, V.V. Giri National Labour Institute.

Saradamoni, K. (1980) *Emergence of a Slave Caste: Pulayas of Kerala.* New Delhi, People's Publishing House.

Sarup A. & Brahme, S. (1990) *Planning for the Millions.* New Delhi, wiley Eastern Limited.

Sen, L.K. (1972) *Integrated Area Planning: Concepts and Methods.* New Delhi, Training Division, Department of personnel, Cabinet Secretariat.

Sharma, B.D. (1889) *The Web of Poverty.* Shillong, North-Eastern Hill University.

Singh, A.K. (1973) "Integrated Area Development: Concepts and Issues", Indian Journal of Agricultural Economics, 28(4), (Oct.-Dec.).

Singh, R.P. (1998) "Poverty Alleviation Strategy in India: An Overview". In Choudhary, R.C. & Rajakutty, S. (eds.) *Fifty Years of Rural Development in India,* Hyderabad, NIRD.

Singh, Mohinder, Sharma, R.N., (eds.) (1978), *Rural Development: A Select Bibliography.* Uppal Publishing House, New Delhi.

Singh, Mohinder (1998), *Rural Development Administration and Anti-Poverty Programmes.* Deep & Deep Publications, New Delhi.

Shah, Ghanshyam, Chaturvedi, H.R. (1983), *Gandhian Approach to Rural Development.* Ajanta Publications, Delhi.

Sharma, Anita, (1994), *Rural Employment Programme in India.* Mohit Publications, New Delhi.

Society of Social Economists, Tamil Nadu (1987), *Readings in Integrated Rural Development,* Oxford & IBH Publishing Co. Pvt. Ltd., New Delhi.

Srivastava, Uma Kant, George, P.S. (1977), *Rural Development in Action: The Experience of a Voluntary Agency.* Somaiya Publications Pvt. Ltd. Bombay & Delhi.

Thimmaiah, G. (ed.) (1979), *Studies in Rural Development*, Caugh Publications, Allahabad.

Tiwari, Jai Kant (1994) *Rural Transformation in India.* Reliance Publishing House, New Delhi.

Tiwari, Jai Kant (1994) *Rural Transformation in India.* Reliance Publishing House, New Delhi.

'Achievements of I.R.D. Programme', *Kurkshetra,* Vol. XXX, No. 14, Apr. 1982, pp. 11-12.

Alexander, K.C. Verma, G.L. Jayakumar, E.C. and A.V. Yadappanavar, *Employment and Income Generation Through IRDP, NREP and DRM in Madhya Pradesh Journal of Rural Development,* Vol. 4, No. 5, pp. 614-629, Sep. 1985.

Borayan, M.P., *Need for Rural Development Education, Kurukshetra,* Vol. XXX, No. 7, Jan, 1982, pp. 10-11.

Chaturvedi, H.R., *Public Participation in Rural Development: Myth and Reality, Journal of Social and Economic Studies.* Vol. 2, No. 4, pp. 323-341, Oct.-Dec., 1985.

Dreze, Jean, Poverty in India and the IRDP Delusion, *Economic and Political Weekly,* Vol. XXV, No. 39, Sep. 1990, pp. A-95-A-104.

George, P.T., Ramachandraiah, C. Rao, DVLNV Prasada. and E.C. Jayakumar, *Employment and Income Generation Through IRDP, NREP and DRM in Karnataka, Journal of Rural Development*, Vol. 4, No. 5, Sep. 1985, pp. 661-705.

George, P.T. Ramachandraiah, G. Srivastava, K.B. and A.C. Jena, *Employment and Income Generation Through IRDP, NREP and DRM in Uttar Pradesh, Journal of Rural Development,* Vol. 4, No. 5, pp. 629-669, Sep. 1985.

Grewel, R.S., Nandal, D.S. and D.D. Gupta, *Impact of Rural Development Programme on Rural Women in Bhiwani District of Haryana, Indian Journal of Agricultural Economics.* Vol. XL, No. 3, pp. 259-262, Jul.-Sep., 1985.

Joshi, Naveen Chandra, *Rural Development Through Banks, Kurukshetra,* Vol. XXX, No. 7, Jan, 1982, pp. 7-9.

Jain, S.C., *How Voluntary Agencies can Help Rural Development, Kurukshetra,* Vol. XXX, No. 3, Nov. 1981, pp. 14-17.

Joshi, Naveen Chandra, *Creating Viability could be the Main Aim, Kurukshetra,* Vol. XXXII, No. 4, 1984, pp. 28-31.

Krishnamurthi, V., *Voluntary Action in rural Development: A Survey, Kurukshetra,* Vol. XXXIV, No. 1, pp. 33-36, Oct. 1985.

Krishnamurthi, V., *Voluntary Agencies and Rural Development, Kurukshetra,* Vol., XXX, No. 18, June 1982, pp. 4-7.

Kumar, Naresh, How Banks Help in Rural Development, Kurukshetra, Vol. XXX, No. 17, June, 1982, pp. 12-16.

Mathur, J.M.L., *How I.R.D.P. is Changing the Rural Scene, Kurukshetra,* Vol. XXX, No. 7, Jan, 1982, pp. 12-13.

Mathur, Man Singh, *Sir Chhotu Ram: The Pioneer Peasant Leader, Kurukshetra,* Vol. XXXII, No. 4, 1984, pp. 36-38

Mandal, Kalyan K., *Village Level Workers and Rural Development: A Case Study, Yojana,* Vol. 39, No. 8, June 1995, pp. 44-45.

Mukherjee, Dr. Neela, *I.R.D.P.:* Experience be the Guide, Yojana, Vol. 39, No. 14, Dec. 1995, pp. 33-35.

Mehta, Balraj, *"Rural Development: The Critical Snag. Kurukshetra,* Vol. XXXII, No. 4, Jan. 1984, pp. 11-14.

Pande, P.N. Rural Development: Education is an Important Input, Kurukshetra, Vol. XXX, No. 17, June 1982, pp. 9-11.

Prakash, Brahm, Raza Moonis, Rural Development: Issues to Ponder, Kurukshetra (Spl. Vol. on Rural Development), Vol. XXXII, No. 4, Jan. 1984, pp. 4-10.

'Project Canbank Village': A Bank Sets a Standard, Kurukshetra, Vol. XXIX, No. 16, May, 1981, pp. 26-28.

Patel, A.R., *Rural Development: Planning and Implementation, Kurukshetra.* Vol. XXX, No. 7, 1983, pp. 4-6.

Pramhansa, V.R.K., *How Mass Media can Help in Rural Development, Kurukshetra,* Vol. XXXII, No. 4, 1984, pp. 32-35.

Patel, A.R., *Rural Development: Experience is the Best Teacher, Kurukshetra,* Vol. XXXII, No. 4, Jan. 1984, pp. 19-24.

I.A. Padmanabha Rao, and J. Gouripathi, *An Integrated Approach to Rural Reconstruction, Kurukshetra,* Vol. XXX, No. 7, Jan. 1982, pp. 14-16.

Ray, Debal K. Singha, Pleasant Movements, Grass Roots Mobilisation and Empowerment of Rural Women, *Economic and Political Review,* Vol. XXX, No. 37, Sep. 1995, pp. 2306-2311.

Ramchandran, Sushma, *Rural Development Programmes: A Reappraisal, Kurukshetra,* Vol. XXXII, No. 4, Jan. 1984, pp. 25-27.

Reddy, J. Ramdas *Structural Changes and Removal of Poverty in Rural India, Kurukshetra,* Vol. XXXIV, No. 2, Nov. 1985, pp. 29-30,33.

"Report of the Committee on Industry and Rural Development", The Associated Chambers of Committee & Industry of India.

Siwal, B.R., *Population Education in Rural Development, Kurukshetra,* Vol. XXX, No. 14, April, 1982, pp. 13-15.

Satpathy, K.M. *IRDP: Some Lessons, Kurukshetra,* Vol. XXXII, No. 4, 1984, pp. 39-42.

Siwal, Beg Raj, *Organising Rural Poor, Kurukshetra,* Vol. XXXIX, No. 19, July 1-15, 1981, pp. 4-5.

Shankar, Kripa, *"On Voluntary Organisations". Economic and Political Weekly,* Vol. XXXII, No. 1 & 2, Jan. 4-11, 1997, p. 60.

Saith, Ashwani, *'Development Strategies and the Rural Poor', The Journal of Peasant Studies,* Vol. 17, No. 12, pp. 171-244, 1990.

Thapliyal, B.K. *Integrated Rural Development Planning in India: Planning Methodologies in Practice and an Alternative, Framework, Journal of Rural Development,* Vol. 2, No. 4, July 1983, pp. 444-467.

Tripathi, D., *"It's not a One Shoot Affair, Please 1 "Kurukshetra,* Vol. XXXII, No. 4, Jan. 1984, pp. 15-18.

Tewari, Amitabh, *Role of Banks in Rural Development, Kurukshetra,* Vol. XXX, No. 14, Ap. 1982, pp. 7-10.

UNDP (2001) *Empowering People: A Guide to Participation.* New York.

U.N. *Social Services in Rural Development,* United Nations, New York, 1979.

Zachariah, Job, *Rural Development: Malappuram Model, Yojana,* Vol. 39, No. 8, Jan. 1995, p. 43.

INDEX